European Development Cooperation and the Poor

European Development Cooperation and the Poor

Aidan Cox
Evaluation Adviser
UNDP
New York

John Healey
Senior Research Associate
Overseas Development Institute
London

with

Paul Hoebink
Senior Lecturer
Third World Centre
Catholic University
Nijmegen

and

Timo Voipio
Research Fellow
IDS – Helsinki

 **odi**

in association with
OVERSEAS DEVELOPMENT INSTITUTE

First published in Great Britain 2000 by
MACMILLAN PRESS LTD
Houndmills, Basingstoke, Hampshire RG21 6XS and London
Companies and representatives throughout the world

A catalogue record for this book is available from the British Library.

ISBN 0–333–74476–4 hardcover
ISBN 0–333–74477–2 paperback

First published in the United States of America 2000 by
ST. MARTIN'S PRESS, INC.,
Scholarly and Reference Division,
175 Fifth Avenue, New York, N.Y. 10010

ISBN 0–312–23054–0

Library of Congress Cataloging-in-Publication Data
Cox, Aidan.
European development cooperation and the poor / Aidan Cox, John Healey ; with
Paul Hoebink and Timo Voipio.
p.   cm.
Includes bibliographical references and index.
ISBN 0–312–23054–0
1. Economic assistance, European—Case studies. 2. Poverty—Developing
countries—Case studies. 3. Economic development projects—Case studies. I.
Healey, J. M. (John Michael) II. Title.

HC60 .C667   2000
338.91'094—dc21
00–023939

HC
60
.C667
2000

This book is printed on paper suitable for recycling and made from fully managed and sustained
forest sources.

10   9   8   7   6   5   4   3   2   1
09   08   07   06   05   04   03   02   01   00

Printed and bound in Great Britain by
Antony Rowe Ltd, Chippenham, Wiltshire

Contents

List of Tables, Figures and Boxes

Acronyms

ALA	Asia and Latin America
APC	Africa, Pacific and Caribbean
BMZ (Germany)	Federal Ministry for Economic Cooperation
CCM (Tanzania)	Chama Cha Mapuduzi (Party of Revolution)
CSP	Country Strategy Paper
DAC/OECD	Development Assistance Committee, Organization for Economic Cooperation and Development
Danida	Danish International Development Agency
DFID (UK)	Department for International Development
DGIS (Netherlands)	Directorate General for International Development
DPEP (India)	District Primary Education Programme
DPSPE	District Based Support to Primary Education
EC	European Commission
ESAP	Economic Structural Adjustment Programme
Finnida (Finland)	Department of International Development Cooperation
GARDP (Nepal)	Gulmi Arghakhanchi Rural Development Project
GTZ (Germany)	Deutsche Gessellschaft für Technische Zusammenarbeit
HIT	Heifer in Trust Scheme
HSD	Human and Social Development
IEC	Information, Education and Communication
IRDP	Integrated Rural Development Programme
JFMP	Joint Forest Management and Planning
KfW	Kreditanstalt für Wiederaufbau
LRP (Zimbabwe)	Land Resettlement Programme
MMD (Zambia)	Movement for Multiparty Democracy
NGO	Non-Governmental Organization
PAAP (Zimbabwe)	Poverty Alleviation Action Programme
PR	Poverty Reduction
PRI (India)	Panchayati Raj Institution

PRIDE (Tanzania)	Promotion of Rural Initiative and Development Enterprise
PUSH	Project Urban Self Help
RIPS	Rural Integrated Programme Support
SAF/ESAF	Structural Adjustment Facility/Extended SAF
SIDA (Sweden)	Swedish International Development Cooperation Agency
SPA	Special Programme of Assistance for Africa
SSA	Sub-Saharan Africa
TSDDP (Tanzania)	Tango Smallholder's Dairy Development Project
UNDP	United Nations Development Programme
UNIP (Zambia)	United Nations Independence Party
VARENA (Burkina Faso)	Project de valorisation des resources naturelles par l'autopromotion
ZANU (PF)	Zimbabwe African National Union

Preface

This book begins with the challenge posed by poverty in the Third World. Its main purpose, however, is to assess what ten European development cooperation agencies have been trying to do about poverty in the 1990s.

The effectiveness of these external agencies in reducing poverty depends crucially on the poverty context in the countries where they operate, and especially the degree of commitment of the domestic authorities to their poorest people and their capacity to implement policies and measures to help them. It also depends on the commitment of the European agencies, the effectiveness of their management systems and how they interrelate with their partners.

The book therefore begins with a brief account of the context of poverty in seven poor countries and the opportunities and constraints on the role of external agencies in promoting reduction in the degree of poverty. It then has the following sequence. First, it sets out and compares the explicit goals and aims of the European agencies, the trends in their commitment to poverty reduction in the 1990s and the present degree of consensus on these issues. Next, it examines the role that the agencies can play in relation to these aims and their general record in practice. It then explores strategies to address the problems of poor people in the agencies' country programmes, drawing on field studies in seven poor countries where several European agencies operate: Bolivia, Burkina Faso, India, Nepal, Tanzania, Zambia and Zimbabwe. This encompasses the poverty orientation of their spending portfolios and the record of their dialogue with their partners on poverty issues. To obtain a picture of effectiveness and impact on the poor of the agencies' specific interventions, 90 poverty-oriented projects and programmes in these seven countries were reviewed. Conclusions are drawn about the effectiveness of these interventions in relation to the participation of the poor in their identification, design and implementation, their degree of gender sensitivity, their targeting on poor people and, of course, their impact and likely sustainability. Lessons of good and bad practice are extracted from individual case studies.

In the last few years new thinking has emerged on how the agencies might be more effective in pursuit of the poverty reduction goal, including ideas of partnership, wider more integrated approaches and a sectoral rather than a project focus on the poor. These ideas are reviewed, although it is too soon to provide much evidence on how well they work. The study ends with a critical review of the management systems of these external agencies in achieving their poverty reduction goals. A range of suggestions are made for possible improved organizational and management effectiveness in relation to poverty reduction activities.

The book is based on the findings of a collaborative European research programme carried out between 1996 and 1998. The ten European development cooperation agencies studied were those of Denmark, the European Commission, Finland, France, Germany, Italy, the Netherlands, Spain, Sweden and the United Kingdom. The study was coordinated by the Overseas Development Institute (ODI) and involved the following other Institutes and individual researchers from these Institutes.

- Asociación de Investigation y Especialización sobre Temas Ibero Americanos (AIETI), Madrid; Christian Freres
- Centre for Development Research (CDR), Copenhagen; Steen Folke, Lars Udsholt and Neil Webster
- Centro Studii Politica Internazionale (CeSPI), Rome; José Luis Rhi-Sausi and Marco Zupi
- Deutsches Institut für Entwicklungspolitik/German Development Institute (GDI), Berlin; Hans Gsaenger and Eva Weidnitzer
- Développement des Investigations sur l'Ajustment à Long terme (DIAL), Paris; Lionel de Boisdeffre
- European Centre for Development Policy Management (ECDPM), Maastricht; Jean Bossuyt, Antonique Koning, Christiane Loquai and Kathleen Van Hove
- Institute of Development Studies (IDS), Helsinki; Timo Voipio
- Nordic Africa Institute (NAI), Uppsala; Jerker Carlsson
- Overseas Development Institute (ODI), London; Aidan Cox, John Healey and Tony Killick
- Third World Centre, Catholic University of Nijmegen; Paul Hoebink and Lau Schulpen

The authors would like to acknowledge the contribution that each of the authors of the individual donor and country case studies made to the information and insights on which this synthesis is based, as well as their personal assistance in the preparation of this synthesis document: Jean Bossuyt, Jerker Carlsson, Lionel de Boisdeffre, Steen Folke, Christian Freres, Hans Gsaenger, Tony Killick, Antonique Koning, Christiane Loquai, José Luis Rhi-Sausi, Lau Schulpen, Lars Udsholt, Kathleen Van Hove, Timo Voipio, Neil Webster, Eva Weidnitzer, and Marco Zupi.

The ODI wishes to acknowledge a grant from the UK Department for International Development (DFID) and the personal encouragement of Dr Charles Clift for the contribution which ODI made to the whole project. DFID supports policies, programmes and projects to promote international development and the funds provided for this study form part of that objective. The views and opinions expressed in the study are, however, those of the authors alone. Other Institutes funded their own contributions, often with the support of the relevant development agency. The authors wish to acknowledge the cooperation and assistance of the ten development cooperation agencies and their field offices, especially the time which officials devoted to assisting researchers with the case studies, and their generosity in providing documentation.

Thanks are due to Caroline Dobbing, Alison Popp, Chemaine Hettiaratchy and Alana Coyle at ODI for patiently editing and formatting successive drafts and also to Margaret Cornell for her usual thorough editing of the draft text.

Foreword

The complexities of foreign aid

Can external aid help to reduce poverty and if so, under which conditions? This has been the main question in international development assistance since its start, some fifty years ago. The other main question has been whether external aid fosters the sustainability of a nation. There is a relation between these two main themes in the debate on development aid: people's poverty and the self-reliance of nations. The sustainability of a group or a nation requires a fair distribution within that society, a reasonable degree of equity and equality, as well as the efficient operation of its economic, social and political processes.

Although these are good objectives, they are difficult to implement. Equity yes, but who shall decide how much, when and for whom? The distribution of power in any society is unequal. Change and reform are decided by the more powerful people. They have a vested interest in the status quo. They will tend to postpone change that will deprive them of their power. In developing countries the attitude of the ruling elite normally tends to be 'more equality, okay, but let us first try to become more efficient, to increase our productivity and to grow more. We should postpone redistribution of income and assets until there is more to be shared for us all.' In such a situation there are three options. All of them have been tried.

The first option is a revolution, a violent change in the power relations. A new start, hopefully, but often no more than a change of guards. Often during the process of revolution itself or shortly thereafter, the new power relations turned out to be as unequal as before. The new rulers had come to like power and postponed the realization of freedoms, the redistribution of assets and the reduction of poverty. After a change of regime, aid has sometimes been used to support the new rulers if they were considered acceptable.

A second option is democratic chage, better governance, a gradual shift in the distribution of land, assets, income and access to services through improved, enlightened leadership. Enlightened leaders understand that such a change is in the interest not only of the poor, but of society as a whole and also of themselves. They can stay in power, unchallenged and earn international respect. This model has been followed in quite a few countries. It has failed as often as it has worked. This model has sometimes failed because the leaders did not deliver on reform, where the institutional capability of the state was inadequate to meet the expectations of its citizens. Often in such a situation foreign assistance has been provided to enhance this capacity and to strengthen national institutions. This is a good example of foreign assistance serving both purposes at the same time: decreasing poverty and sustaining national self-reliance.

A third option is for external aid to combat poverty directly within a nation where the distribution of power and the structure of governance remains unchanged. This has been tried sometimes in the expectation that foreign aid would be a catalyst domestically. Mingled with this has been the hope that the example set by foreign assistance could raise expectations and enhance the awareness of the poor people concerned who then would press their leaders to follow suit. Whether such hopes and expectations of aid agencies were realistic and the extent to which they have been fulfilled and under which conditions, is a major question posed by the authors of this book.

From the very beginning of international development cooperation, aid agencies and 'partners in development' have wrestled with the question how to kill two birds with one stone: the poverty of people and the weakness of a nation. The latter aim has been perceived in many different ways, depending on whether the focus was on the economy, the society or the state. Weak nations, soft states, vulnerable economies, fragile societies of poor and less poor people, loose structures of different peoples or ethnic groups were to be sustained from outside in such a way that, in particular, the poor people within these societies would benefit. That this would require much more than only economic aid was quickly understood. The idea that the benefits of such aid would trickle-down from the macro level to the grassroots is not widely accepted by aid agencies now. The dualistic structure of economies, cultural stratification within societies and the politics of development tend to prevent this. This book argues that an effective aid strategy requires a proper identification of the poor and the choice of an appropriate set of policies and measures to reach and support the poor.

Donors have tried different ways to achieve these two objectives: assistance to community development in the fifties; aid to fill trade and investment gaps in the sixties; aid to provide for basic human needs in the seventies; structural adjustment assistance in the eighties; humanitarian assistance in combination with support for rehabilitation of countries after the civil wars of the nineties; aid for sustainable human development at present; and aid to foster democratic governance at the turn of this century.

Donor agency efforts to promote poverty reduction or national self-reliance have been hampered or complicated by a range of other donor country interests. These include maintaining the status quo in international relations, extension of the donor country's sphere of influence, exporting a specific ideology or culture, preserving political stability, and strengthening export markets or protecting against competing imports. Perhaps the importance of these other non-development interests has diminished somewhat after the end of the Cold War. However, there were other impediments particularly for poverty interventions, including lack of knowledge about the societies concerned and slowness in learning lessons from their experience of aid giving and that of their partners.

There now seems to be a broad consensus amongst aid agencies themselves and increasing convergence in their practices. Differences between them are often due less to diverging philosophies than the various constraints they meet. The authors of this book make this quite clear on the basis of a thorough survey of the aid strategies of a number of Western-European countries. It is unlikely that there will be ever full consensus and convergence. This may be due to causes beyond the control of aid agencies. But efforts to further strengthen consensus, coordination and coherence are far from futile.

In this book the authors focus in particular on the poverty reduction aim and the impact of external aid on poverty. The other theme – self-reliance – is only addressed indirectly, for instance, when they refer to the dialogue between donors and recipients. In describing the relation between aid and poverty reduction the authors follow a systematic approach. They pose all the necessary questions, refrain from answers where these cannot yet be given and suggest possible directions. Not only do they provide directions for further study which is always useful, but they focus in particular on concrete actions: the 'do's' and 'don'ts' of aid, the limitations of conditionality, the limits of external intervention in domestic processes, good and bad examples of donor management, the trade-off between quick top-down results and gradual but sustainable bottom-up approaches. In short, the need to be ambitious and modest at the same time.

I have been active in the field of international development cooperation in different capacities for about thirty-five years during half a century when aid agencies and other development policy makers have sought to learn lessons from their own and others' experience. I have learned a lot from this book. Much of its findings look familiar, some are debatable, quite a few give rise to embarrassment or even alarm. All findings are challenging and stimulating. Policy makers who are sincere in expressing and interest in combating people's poverty with the help of aid or otherwise have an obligation to seriously study the real impact of their policies. Well-meant but inadequate development aid policies may produce results which not only fall short of expectations but are even the opposite to those intended. Learning and applying lessons from the past, such as the ones presented in this book, will help to avoid perverse consequences of development aid and contribute to its most basic purpose: less poverty and more human development in sustainable societies.

Jan Pronk
Former Minister for Development
The Netherlands

1
The Context of Poverty

This is a study of the aspirations, roles, actions and effectiveness of European development agencies in trying to improve the lot of the poor. Yet inevitably the main determinants of the possibilities and chances of succeeding rest with the specific partner country – the nature of its poverty, its culture, its politics and government attitudes, policies and capacities. It is appropriate therefore to begin with a brief review of the poverty situation in the seven poor or relatively poor countries which form the focus of this study. Although these seven countries are not necessarily representative of the poverty context in the developing world as a whole, they do cover three continents: India and Nepal in Asia, Burkina Faso, Tanzania, Zambia and Zimbabwe in Africa, and Bolivia in Latin America. The types of problems and opportunities posed are reasonably typical of many of the other country contexts in which the European agencies work.

At the core of poverty is material deprivation, low income and consumption levels leading to poor food and nutritional status, inadequate clothing and housing and sub-standard access to health and schooling. Vulnerability and the resultant insecurity are further characteristics. Poverty also has important non-material aspects, including dependence arising from unequal relationships and social exclusion. The poor are also somewhat heterogeneous. The study as a whole has used a multidimensional conceptualization of poverty, which complements analyses based on income and consumption with assessments of livelihood, including vulnerability, access to resources, levels of knowledge and rights. A brief analytical review of the nature and dimensions of poverty prepared by Tony Killick is set out in Annex 1.

To set the scene for the aims and operations of the external agencies, four major aspects of the conditions in these countries are briefly explored.

- the nature of their poverty and hence the basic challenge posed to reduce poverty levels in the next 20 years;
- current attitudes towards the poor and the policies for poverty reduction of the government authorities;
- politics and the poor;
- decentralization processes and the poor.

Poverty situation

Table 1.1 provides statistical indicators of some of the multiple dimensions of poverty in the seven countries under review here. It shows that the case study countries, apart from Bolivia, have very low rankings in terms of human development, with all falling in the bottom 65 countries out of 175, and Burkina Faso (at 172), Nepal (at 154), Tanzania (at 149), Zambia (at 143) within the bottom 25. The very poorest in per capita income terms measured in purchasing power parity were Tanzania, Burkina Faso and Zambia, followed by Nepal, India, Zimbabwe and Bolivia.

Access to resources, such as health care, education, clean drinking water and sanitation, was inadequate or non-existent for significant sections of the population. The health, water and sanitation, and nutrition section of Table 1.1 shows Burkina Faso and Zambia to have particularly poor indicators. Malnutrition is most severe in Nepal, where it affects a staggering 70 per cent of all children under five, and also in India, where over half of all children are affected, falling to 16 per cent in Zimbabwe. Access to education services is a further dimension of poverty. Education standards, assessed in terms of literacy, are particularly low in Burkina Faso and Nepal, where 81 and 73 per cent, respectively, of the population are illiterate. In every case women and girls are particularly discriminated against, with about 90 per cent of women being illiterate in Burkina Faso and Nepal and 60 per cent in India.

The proportion of people below the specified absolute (income) poverty line is high (over 40 per cent) in most of these countries, and only somewhat lower in India (35 per cent), and Zimbabwe

(25 per cent), although it should be remembered that the line cho-sen varies across countries. In all cases on average, poverty is most prevalent and severe in the rural areas, despite some rise in urban poverty. In the past five to ten years poverty actually deepened in four of the case study countries – Burkina Faso, Nepal, Zambia and Zimbabwe – while official figures show some improvements in India and Tanzania and to a limited extent, Bolivia. For India, figures show a fall from 55 per cent poor in 1973–74, to 39 per cent in 1987–88, and 35 per cent in 1993–94.

The relationship between inequality and poverty comes out clearly in distribution of income figures, which show that the poor-est 10 per cent enjoy, at most, 3.7 per cent of income/consumption (in India) falling to less than 2 per cent in Zambia and Zimbabwe (see Table 1.1 under income poverty indicators). The income and consumption of the poorest 20 per cent ranges from 8.5 per cent (in India) to less than 4 per cent in Zambia. Hence the pattern of income distribution (and presumably growth) is distinctly anti-poor, and is particularly biased against the poor in the African cases.

The degree of concentration of poverty across different areas or groups varies widely between the seven countries, with important policy implications for donor agencies and governments, particu-larly in relation to targeting mechanisms. While in Burkina Faso and Zambia poverty is fairly widespread, recent evidence from Tanzania shows considerable regional differences in welfare levels which outweigh intra-regional inequalities. Similarly, for Zimbabwe, although the inequalities between white and black are particularly stark, large differences exist among black Zimbabweans. Much of this relates to land distribution, and results in the particularly concentrated nature of poverty relative to other African states. Substantial inequalities also exist in Nepal, not only between the Hills and the Terai (plains), but also between the urban areas (including the Kathmandu Valley) and the rural and more remote areas where land holding is highly biased in favour of the better-off. Data disaggregated by district reveal that these inequalities translate into widely varying social indicators, such as life expectancy and literacy rates. In Bolivia there are wide variations between regions, and between indigenous and non-indigenous groups, particularly in urban areas (von Gleich, 1997). In India, there is substantial regional (inter-State) variation in both income *per capita* and human

Table 1.1 Indicators of poverty in seven countries

	Bolivia	Burkina Faso	India	Nepal	Tanzania	Zambia	Zimbabwe
General							
GNP per capita, (PPP/US$) 1995	2540	780	1400	1170	640	930	2030
Consumption per capita growth (annual %) 1980–90/1990–95	–1.4/0.7	0/1.7	3.1/2.6	4.0/7.4		–0.4/–	–2.5/3.7
Population growth (annual %)	2	3	2	3	3	3	2
Income/Consumption poverty indicators							
% living below poverty line (head count) very poor/poor	36/71	42/44.5	–/35	49/–	–/51.1	70/84	7/25
% of poor who live in rural areas	c60	c50		95	85	70	96
Trends in poverty over last five to ten years	Slight fall	Increase	Decrease	Increase	Decrease	Increase	Increase
Share of income/consumption of lowest 10%/20%	2.3/5.6	–	3.7/8.5	3.2/7.6	2.9/6.9	1.5/3.9	1.8/4.8
Other poverty indicators							
Human Development Index (HDI): rank (out of 175)	113	172	138	154	149	143	129
Health, Water and Sanitation, and Nutrition							
Health services (% of population with access) 1990–95	67	–	85	–	42	11	85

Life expectancy at birth, female (years)	62	47	63	56	52	46	58
Life expectancy at birth, male (years)	59	45	62	57	50	45	56
Life expectancy at birth, total (years)	60	49	62	55	51	46	57
Infant mortality rate (per 000) 1990–95	75	101	n/a	92	85	110	25
Safe water (% of population with access) 1990–96	67	78	63	63	38	47	77
Sanitation (% of population with access) 1990–96	65	18	29	18	86	42	66
Malnutrition prevalence (% of children under five) 1989–95	13	43	53	70	28	27	16
Education							
Primary school enrollment rate/% of female pupils	86/–	37/39	105/43	107/39	68/49	104/–	119/48
Illiteracy rate, adult female (% of females 15+)	24	91	62	86	43	29	20
Illiteracy rate, adult male (% of males 15+)	10	71	35	59	21	14	10
Illiteracy rate, adult total (% of people 15+)	17	81	48	73	32	22	15
Aid Dependency							
Aid (% of central government expenditures)	42	80	5	76	–	294	–
Aid (% of Gross Domestic Investment)	72	106	3	50	92	282	39
Aid (% of imports of goods and services)	35	84	3	34	48	43	20

Sources: UNDP, 1997; World Bank, 1997; Hanmer *et al.*, 1997; Von Gleich, 1996; Wangwe, 1997; Voipio and Hoebink, 1999.
Notes: For Bolivia and Burkina Faso, aid is indicated as a percentage of public investment. For some countries national sources were used and drawn from country studies (Table 2.1).

development indicators, although variation within States may also be considerable.

Table 1.1 shows that poverty, in one form or another, is a serious challenge for all seven countries. Its predominantly rural character is one indication of where an anti-poverty strategy ought to focus. Equally, relative performance against different poverty indicators provides a further clue. Differences in the degree to which poverty is concentrated are a further factor. Thus the strategy is likely to be different in countries where poverty is generally diffused, for example Burkina Faso, as opposed to those countries where it tends to be more concentrated and related to land distribution (such as Zimbabwe). The extent to which the strategy includes targeting mechanisms, for instance, should also vary depending on the extent to which there are significant regional/district differences in the level of welfare, such as exist in India and Tanzania. It clearly is not enough for European donors to have a standard strategy; they should examine each country situation carefully and tailor their strategy to the particular context.

Attitudes and policies of the authorities towards the poor and poverty reduction

A key factor determining prospects for poverty reduction is the attitude of the government authorities towards the poor and their degree of commitment to pro-poor policies. Commitment can of course be assessed in terms of the ideology or formal strategy of the government, but it is better judged in terms of the implementation record as opposed to the rhetoric. Currently, governments dependent on aid are tending to produce formal strategies to suit the requirements of the donors on poverty reduction. Since these can be cosmetic and deceptive in terms of real commitment, it is essential to look not simply at currently emerging strategies, but at what the same governments have actually done in the past in relation to pledges on poverty and equity.

Since independence, the *government of Tanzania* has been characterized by socialist rhetoric in support of a more equal distribution of income and an improvement in social indicators. Poverty reduction has been a formal policy objective since the Declaration of Arusha in 1967. However, during the course of the 1970s the economy lost its capacity to deliver on the social objectives. Adjustment measures taken in response to the crisis of the early 1980s eventually stimulated improved growth between 1986 and 1996, which stood at 4 to 5 per cent per annum. As a result, income poverty declined during the 1980s, although this trend may have been reversed after 1993. However, most of the employment generated has been in the informal sector, and the benefits from growth have been uneven, with the very poor being bypassed and 51 per cent of the population remaining below the poverty line.

The government's limited attention to small-scale agriculture and basic social services raises some questions about its commitment to the poor. The budgetary cuts appear to have fallen most heavily on those sub-sectors which are potentially the most favourable to the poor. Not only has education spending decreased as a share of government expenditure, but more importantly the cuts have fallen more on the basic services rather than on support for tertiary education. The distribution of health service expenditure has not been so unfavourable to the poor but the quality of services has remained a major problem because of inefficient public management and weak incentives systems. User charges have yet to be effectively implemented but there appear to be no special arrangements to protect the access of the poor. There is little evidence that regional policy favours the poorer regions. The matching grant system for basic education and health policies introduced with support from the World Bank is not a progressive one. Public subsidies for water are highly skewed in favour of the better-off in the urban areas. In fiscal terms, too, the system has not been progressive, with reduced tax rates and excessive personal allowances and benefits for upper income groups. Overall, therefore, the record clearly does not reflect a particularly pro-poor stance on public expenditure policy. Instead, scarce government resources have tended to be skewed disproportionately toward the richest quintile of the population living in the towns, who capture the most valuable subsidies.

The government has faced serious constraints, including heavy debt service (representing about one-third of total budget expenditure), which have undoubtedly hampered the adequate funding of essential social infrastructure and services. Questions have been raised as to whether basic service expenditures have actually been cut after local, as well as central, expenditures are taken into account. In addition, there has been a substantial growth in non-government provision of hospitals, health centres and dispensaries, and infant mortality rates have been shown to have fallen (see Wangwe, 1997).

There has been little recognition, within government, of the role of gender relations in determining the nature and extent of poverty, and the way it is experienced at macro, meso and intra-household levels. There have been few laws to protect or promote women's rights in the last 20 years. Discriminatory treatment under marriage and inheritance laws in the courts, and in law enforcement generally, remains a serious impediment to poverty reduction. One reflection of the gendered nature of poverty is the 43 per cent female illiteracy rate, compared to 21 per cent for men.

In 1998 the government produced a National Poverty Eradication Strategy which commits it to halving absolute poverty by 2010. This includes a range of highly relevant anti-poverty measures. The strategy is based on higher and accelerating rates of economic growth (4 per cent per annum rising to 10 per cent), although without exploring more pessimistic scenarios. Since 1995 there has been a small poverty eradication division in the Vice President's Office which, with the assistance of UNDP, has produced this strategy and has developed locally specific poverty and welfare monitoring indicators for significant parts of what is a large country. The most comprehensive income-generation programme for the poor (the National Income Generation Programme) uses targeting mechanisms and currently operates in four pilot regions, with the intention of being scaled up with non-governmental organization (NGO) and private sector backing. The requirements for a more poverty-focused orientation of policy include efforts to spread public resources less thinly and to concentrate on 'core' projects in social and economic infrastructure and to leave much more to the private sector (Voipio and Hoebink, 1999).

In *Burkina Faso* there is no coherent strategy for addressing the problems of poverty and little political commitment to this objective. But the government does want Burkina to be a pilot country in implementing the commitment of the Social Summit in Copenhagen to the 20:20 principle for budgetary allocations to activities concerned with poverty (see Chapter 2, note 1). There is no central direction given to line Ministries to ensure their policies take adequate account of the needs of the poor and no poverty unit centrally or in the line Ministries, to provide direction.

Certain specific policies have been broadly pro-poor in the sense that the government has emphasized reforms designed to increase productivity and production in the agricultural sector, and there has been a shift in the internal terms of trade in favour of agriculture. Special measures to provide ploughs and mills for villages have been inadequate, however, covering only one in eight villages. The six domestic banks have allocated little credit for productive activities despite a surplus of deposits since the 1994 devaluation, preferring to lend to state and international institutions and to make safe private sector investments. In the social areas there has been some increase in the provision of primary schooling, including provision in marginal areas, and some subsidization of fees for the schooling of poorer people. (For a fuller account see Sawadogo, 1997.)

In the third African country, *Zambia*, the democratically elected MMD Government seems to manifest less concern with social equity issues than its predecessor UNIP, although poverty reduction features as a national goal in policy documents. In the last 8 years, the authorities have not pursued economic policies favourable to broad-based growth, nor have they shown much interest in the poor in general. There have been no moves to improve formal recognition of women's rights and women continue to be treated under law as their husbands' property.

Over a long period of time, economic policy has been biased against agriculture and rural development, with inappropriate pricing and marketing policies and discrimination against non-maize crops. Infrastructure support for the farming community has been weak and has favoured farmers closer to the urban areas. Inadequate extension services have given preference to the larger-scale commercial farmers. Despite long-standing social aims like universal access to basic education and health services, there has been an unwillingness and/or lack of capacity to reorient budget allocations or to implement budget intentions in this direction in the 1990s. Primary education was neglected under UNIP in the 1980s, and in the 1990s, despite the drastic fall in the level and share of the education budget, priority has nevertheless been given to secondary and tertiary rather than primary and vocational education. By 1993, the expenditure per pupil in primary education had fallen to US$15 compared with US$2460 per university student. One reason for this is that primary school enrolment has continued to rise while the budget allocation (20 per cent of the total education budget) has fallen. In health, the budget has also fallen in recent years and 80 per cent of it is apparently spent on central and teaching hospitals (Hanmer *et al.*, 1997). There have been special poverty alleviation programmes but in 1993 they accounted for only Kwacha 1 bn out of a total budget of Kwacha 233 bn, and only 25 per cent of the 1 bn was actually spent. Some of this neglect of equitable concerns stems from political lack of interest, but weak management, especially at the central level, is also responsible, with the result that levels of assistance allocated are not adhered to and guidelines for beneficiaries are ignored. The Social Action Programme, for example, failed to discharge its responsibilities, with an unimpressive record of targeting poor groups (for a fuller account see Saasa *et al.*, 1998).

Zimbabwe is on average the least poor of the African countries in our sample, but one which contains highly concentrated areas of poverty. In the 1980s the government attempted to address poverty through increased social expenditures, and initially increased expenditures in agriculture but with limited land reforms. Policies to encourage capital-intensive growth failed to generate the hoped-for increases in formal sector employment, and the welfare approach became fiscally unsustainable. The momentum towards decreasing inequalities has dissipated during the 1990s, and overall there has been no coherent policy or public investment commitment to support small-scale agriculture and rural development for the poor. Government efforts to shift resources in favour of smallholders have largely been focused on farmers in the high potential areas. The government has followed a cautious and conservative land policy offering little scope for redistribution, although in November 1998 it reaffirmed proposals for the confiscation of white-owned farms. Poverty-oriented planning is currently effected largely at the level of specific local project and programme initiatives, but there is no linkage between this micro level and the national level.

Social service provision remains skewed against the poor. Cuts in the education budget have tended to fall disproportionately on primary education, which is most likely to benefit the children from poor families. The cuts in health spending also fell disproportionately on preventive health services and family planning, which are the services most relevant to poor people. The provisions to ease the social effects of structural adjustment in the 1990s have been neither a priority nor effective, and no great effort was put into designing the Economic Structural Adjustment Programme (ESAP) programme in order to minimize its adverse effects on the poor.

The overall ambiguity is reflected in the government's Poverty Alleviation Action Programme (PAAP), whose progress has been inhibited by interdepartmental rivalries and whose secretariat has been starved of resources. In sum, currently poverty reduction does not rank high in the government's priorities at national level and there is no grand strategy or general policy. However, the government is not hostile to poverty reduction overall, and there are government departments which are both sympathetic to, and active in, pursuing the PR objective (for a fuller account of Zimbabwe see Killick *et al.*, 1998).

In the two South Asian countries in our sample, poverty reduction has been a political objective for decades. In *Nepal*, the latest Ninth Plan (1997–2001) has poverty reduction as the overriding goal with many pro-poor features. However, in the past, despite a series of national plans with poverty-alleviating objectives, the record of implementation reveals a low level of commitment to improving the lot of the poor on the part of the political and policy-making elite. The Sixth and Seventh Plans (1980–90) aimed to enhance the supply of basic goods and services but lacked effective measures to increase the income of the poor and had little impact. The Eighth Plan's objective was to reduce poverty from 49 per cent in 1992 to 42 per cent in 1997, but instead poverty has worsened.

Poverty-reduction strategies were not effectively implemented due to a lack of poverty mapping, resulting in a failure to identify poor families and underdeveloped areas or to create many employment-generating schemes for them. More specifically, various aspects of Nepalese policy have not been particularly pro-poor. In agriculture there has been little delivery of extension and other support services to small farmers and most of the research and extension conducted has been relevant mainly to larger farmers with irrigation or those planting cash crops. The fertilizer subsidy has benefited only a few peri-urban farmers and traders. Credit programmes for farmers have been developed over the last 20 years and have extended networks but without significant benefit to small or marginal farmers or poor women, mainly because of their limited coverage, high transaction costs and poor targeting. There has been no political commitment to reform a biased land distribution with feudal, absentee landlords. Informal tenancy is still prevalent.

Insufficient priority has been given to social expenditures in spite of high illiteracy and child mortality, lack of access to safe water and so forth. Health has taken only a static 3 per cent of the public budget, excluding official donor and NGO programmes, and a third of this is deployed on urban-based curative facilities with little priority for preventive and primary health care. Despite targets for access, expenditure on safe drinking water has been falling. Education's share of the budget is larger, but there has been inadequate allocation to primary and secondary education and to adult literacy. The poor have benefited little from the distribution of subsidized food, since only 25 per cent goes to the remote areas, and even this is not targeted on poor families. The government's Food for Work Programme, in contrast, is self-targeted and has been reasonably effective in creating rural off-season employment and infrastructure. There has been inadequate attention to the protection of workers or of children and vulnerable groups. Fiscally, the high proportion of indirect taxation results in a largely regressive system in terms of poverty impact (for a fuller account of Nepal see Gsaenger and Voipio, 1999).

In *India*, economic growth during the 1960s and 1970s was not fast enough to deliver trickle-down benefits to the poor on any scale. Since the 1980s, growth has been faster and there has been some fall in poverty levels. For almost four decades, achieving basic minimum living standards has been a recurrent refrain in Indian plans, with the focus being on absolute poverty since 1964. Subsequently, there has been an enormous growth in the scale and coverage of special poverty alleviation programmes, which by the early 1990s absorbed some 2.2 per cent of GDP.

The six main programmes cover food subsidies, rural employment, nutrition, small-scale credit (Integrated Rural Development Programme), child and maternal health, and urban employment. The main features of these programmes, which are largely funded by the central government, are their top-down management and lack of adequate targeting of the poor. Central and State governments have not supported genuine decentralization to district and local levels, resulting in poor information flows, a failure to target the poor and large leakages of benefits to the non-poor. The administration of the schemes has tended to be understaffed and of low quality. The allocation of poverty programme outlays between and within States is not systematically related to indicators of poverty, unemployment or deficiency in basic amenities. Frequently the non-poor gain access to substantial benefits via political patronage or corruption, and access by women to the schemes usually falls short of targets. Although some attempts have been made to improve targeting through more effective monitoring of beneficiaries and self-selection, the schemes remain seriously flawed and insufficiently accountable (World Bank, 1995: Annex V).

In *Bolivia*, past growth rates, although accelerating more recently to 4 per cent per annum, have not been sufficient to permit a significant reduction in poverty. Since 1986, however, governments have committed themselves to ambitious and comprehensive programmes of reform in which poverty reduction has been a central objective. Strategies have not assumed trickle-down but have clearly focused on those groups (rural, indigenous, women and children) which most need attention. With the government of President de Lozada in 1993 came a new integrated programme with social equity as a major objective, and a new ministry to drive it. Although it encompasses a broad range of elements relevant to poverty reduction, efforts have been made to retain a coordinated approach. In agriculture, land reform legislation has been passed relating to the problems of the *latifundios* and *minifundios,* with new implementing institutions replacing the earlier corrupt and ineffective ones. The aim is to regularize land titles and execute settlement programmes. In addition, attempts are being made to channel formal credit to the poor in a way that has not happened in the past.

In the social sector, the picture is less clear. Following the innovative but rather ineffective Emergency Social Fund (1986), the design of the Social Investment Fund (1990) reflects the lessons learned, resulting in improved targeting and project selection. Over 50 per cent of the funds have been targeted to the poorest 25 per cent of the population. A universal contributory pension scheme has been introduced. There are programmes for women and children, nutrition, and family planning, though coverage has been limited in some cases. There are plans to undertake reform in education and improve the efficiency of basic services. A common theme has been the decentralization of financial responsibility with the objective of promoting greater participation at the local level (see below), which is intended to make the provision of health, education and sanitation services more responsive to local needs in municipalities and rural areas.

While it is too early to judge the performance of many of these recent reforms, which may well take some time to take root, questions can be raised about the record of social sector measures to help the poorest areas and groups. Thus, although education spending rose between 1986 and 1994, the allocation to primary and secondary education fell. Moreover, departmental and municipal per capita spending on health, education and sanitation was quite regressive, and tended, with one exception, to favour the better-off regions. The poor receive only slightly more than their population share of access to public health care services. Illiteracy rates remain high, especially in rural areas and particularly among females and indigenous groups.

While there are promising initiatives and attitudes to the poor in Bolivia, the prospects for effective implementation remain uncertain at this stage. The main constraint is insufficient institutional management capacity to implement the ambitious programmes (see von Gleich, 1997).

Politics and the poor

While countries in Asia have developed national poverty alleviation strategies for many decades, in Africa poverty reduction has only recently become an explicit policy objective. However, in both cases poverty reduction enjoys growing prominence in the terminology used in official declarations and policy documents, partly as a response to donor concerns, even with authorities which have shown little real concern for the poor. It is perhaps not surprising, therefore, that the implementation record does not necessarily reflect a real pro-poor reorientation of government priorities or actions. In most of the countries studied here, specific policies for agriculture, rural development, the social sectors and safety net programmes frequently reveal a lack of focus and effectiveness in meeting the needs of the poorer sections of the population. The opportunities for change are therefore considerable but there are major constraints on change which arise from the political situation and culture.

The nature of domestic political systems and processes influences the responsiveness of governments to the needs of all members of society including the poor. Clearly, the depth and extent of political organization within civil society, including the degree to which the voice or voices of the poor are articulated, can influence governments to respond better to their needs.

Political changes have taken place in *Tanzania* since 1992 with multi-party elections and the important emergence of a separation of powers between the ruling party, the central executive and the legislative assembly. This has not generated an effective political opposition since the former single party (the CCM) is still dominant. However, a free press has emerged as the *de facto* strongest counterweight to the ruling party. With the reversal of the party's past record of suppressing or coopting autonomous civic organizations, new forms of participatory and associational life have been developing. These assist the poorer sections of society such as ethnic and region-based welfare societies, but independent organizations have made demands on the state, to ease licensing restrictions on the poor, for example, and end the militia's harassment of vendors (Tripp, 1992). At the same time the position of women is changing only slowly and in many parts of the country customary law prevents women from inheriting assets.

In *Burkina Faso* the political situation is not promising for the poor. There is a weak electoral system, characterized by a dominant party and a splintered opposition, in which votes are bought for electoral promises of public expenditure. It is far from clear whether this favours the poor or poor regions. Although there are some laws to protect women, and some civil human rights movements have developed, there continues to be widespread gender discrimination (de Boisdeffre, 1998a).

In *Zambia*, in line with general recent experience, the advent of multi-party democracy has not so far given the poor greater leverage. For example, the early years of the democratically elected MMD suggest that the new government has moved away from balanced regional and district budget allocations towards a system built on political favouritism. Nonetheless, civic society demonstrates some vitality, and the churches in particular wield an increasing influence on public policy through vigorous campaigning concentrating on the rights of the poor. The NGO voice has also become more powerful, especially since playing an important role in the national drought relief programme (Cromwell, 1995: 198, 164).

In *Zimbabwe* there has been an authoritarian centralized style of government since independence, which has provided little scope for autonomous civil organizations to flourish, and in which consultation with civil society is minimal. Patronage has been more important than poverty reduction in domestic politics. The ruling party (ZANU(PF)) has used drought relief to poor regions (often funded by external donors) to reinforce its dominance there. Poverty reduction projects tend to be concentrated in the party's strongholds with funds being channelled via local ZANU structures. Redistributive policies, especially on land, are seen by many to be central to poverty reduction in Zimbabwe, potentially bringing benefits to large numbers of the electorate, but a number of powerful factors are working against this.

The first is the highly visible economic power of the whites relative to the largely rural poor, who are weakly organized and lack political clout. This is reinforced by the growing marginalization of the trade unions. The policies of the major black farmers' organization, the Zimbabwe Farmers' Union, have tended to be dominated by the demands of the elite, and marginalized communities have exerted pressure only by more direct methods such as 'squatting' and 'poaching'. Second, the opposition parties tend to be urban-based and unfocused on rural issues and, in any case, have restricted influence. Third, since the umbrella NGO organization demonstrated its ability to exert influence on policy matters such as land reform the government has sought and obtained powers to control or close NGOs, thus undermining an important counterweight for the poor (Killick *et al.*, 1998; Raftopoulos and Jazdowska, 1997).

In *Nepal*, despite the restoration of multi-party democracy, participation by the electorate remains limited and government has become neither more accountable nor transparent. A firmly hierarchical and authoritarian political culture remains in place, with little apparent concern for the needs of poor, low-caste or ethnic groups (Gsaenger and Voipio, 1999).

In *India* the significant growth and diversity of special poverty alleviation programmes since 1970 reflect their appeal to every political party. This reflects the compulsions of one form of electoral politics in which parties have vied with each other to initiate new schemes designed to woo different regions and groups of poor people. In general, it has happened without the poor exerting conscious organized pressure. However, although the political system may superficially appear responsive to the needs of the poor, political patronage has pervaded these schemes to such a degree that their effectiveness as instruments of poverty reduction has been drastically reduced (Vaidyanathan, 1996).

In *Bolivia* more democratic systems with free elections are now reasonably established, though the opposition parties are weak and political leaders and parliamentarians rank low in public opinion. Judicial reform is still in its early stages and has not yet given confidence to poor people. There has been increased social conflict as a result of economic adjustment processes since the 1980s. Nevertheless, there is a growing awareness and consensus across most groups in society on the need to give greater priority to improving the lot of the poor and disadvantaged (von Gleich, 1997).

Decentralization and the poor

It is possible to see administrative and political decentralization of central government responsibilities and resources to lower level bodies as a means of ensuring greater participation by local people in decision-making, increased focus on the needs of poor and vulnerable people, as well as better, more targeted delivery of social services, for example. While effective decentralization may be a necessary condition for more effective poverty reducing actions, it is not always sufficient. Local elites are not necessarily more progressive or pro-poor than national ones. Many NGOs in which the poor and near poor participate, are dominated by better-off members whose interests may differ, although equally there have been important examples of effective local organization, including actions by poor cultivators usually focused on pressing practical needs (Nelson, 1992: 237).

Most of the seven countries have passed decentralization legislation in the 1980s or 1990s. In *Tanzania*, the district councils are primarily responsible for education, health, local roads and the rural water supply. However, most of their expenditure is financed from central government grants (largely with aid funds), and in practice top-down planning has predominated over participatory decision-making processes. Currently local government reform and the sectoral reforms of education and health policies are geared to reviving the democratic and participatory nature of decision-making at the district level. Responsibilities for implementation have been removed from regional administrations (satellites of the centre) to the district councils. Local inhabitants will increasingly be expected to contribute in matching central government grants, with a view to enhancing ownership. Mechanisms aimed at ensuring the geographical equality of such systems are currently being tested in several districts.

In *Zambia*, since 1993 the government has attempted to decentralize responsibilities for the delivery of health services and poverty reducing activities, partly in response to the lack of experienced managers at the centre. But, at least in the short to medium term, this merely transfers the same problem downwards, since local level institutions are also weak and face inadequate resources and limited transfers from an underfunded centre. However, there has been a rapid growth of NGOs whose role in delivery services to local (including poor) communities is now recognized and valued by the government, which has accepted in principle the channelling of external agency funds directly to NGOs.

Decentralization decrees in *Zimbabwe* have provided since 1984 for the establishment of elected representation at village, ward, district and provincial levels and for their interaction in planning the use of resources. Local power structures are seen as the basis of a community development programme for poverty alleviation. Yet these processes have proved problematic. The central government has dominated and has not ensured financial decentralization. At the local level the ruling party has continued to play a major role. Traditional leaders retain substantial influence and poor planning skills are the norm. Moreover,

> local leaders, both male and female, are among the wealthier members of the communities and thus tend to represent vested interests with direct personal concerns about how additional resources enter their community. This situation has often created a barrier or distortionary impact on pro-poor oriented activities.

In such cases participation and involvement of local communities
often turns out to mean co-option of local elites and leadership.
(quoted by Raftopoulos and Jazdowska, 1997: 28)

The Rural District Councils (RDCs) in Zimbabwe have a good repu-
tation for getting things done, but their economic base is weak,
their link with the national planning system is unclear and few have
developed clear strategies for their operations. Killick *et al.* (1998)
conclude that the current emphasis on RDCs does not imply a
change from a top-down planning system nor does it necessarily
lead to a better outcome for poverty reduction.

In *Burkina Faso*, the recently launched national decentralization
and its accompanying National Decentralization Commission have
had a specific and explicit focus on poverty reduction. Since 1995
some 33 municipalities have been endowed with an elected council
and a measure of autonomy, but these have yet to be fully empowered or to benefit from appropriate transfers of government funds
(de Boisdeffre, 1998a). However, there was evidence from four urban
municipalities that some anti-poverty actions had been undertaken
and some extra primary schools established in the poor quarters of
Ougadougou (Sawadogo, 1997).

In *Nepal*, decentralization legislation since 1982 has had many
potential pro-poor features, but it has yet to have major poverty
reduction effects because participation of the poor, and women in
particular, in local bodies is still lacking. However, the central government's lump-sum subsidies to all Village Councils, introduced in
1994, have in theory empowered the village communities considerably, though in most cases spending decisions at the village council
level have been dominated by the local (caste) elites, excluding the
disadvantaged lower castes, ethnic minorities and women. Many
donors have tried to use Nepalese NGOs as an alternative parallel
channel to reach the poorer segments of the population, but many
of the NGOs are being 'hijacked' by the well-off (Gsaenger and
Voipio, 1999).

In *India*, local Panchayat Raj institutions have existed for a long
time but the State governments have been reluctant to devolve powers and resources to them. Impetus towards decentralization has
been strengthened recently with an amendment to the Constitution
providing for a three-tier system of local government based on

mandatory elections every five years. This requires States to devolve specific powers and resources to these bodies. There is also an explicit requirement for a substantial proportion of elected positions to be reserved for scheduled castes, tribes and women. There is a concern that the dominant landowning elites will control power in the highly stratified and unequal socio-economic structure of many Indian villages. The possibility of a realignment of the power structure to favour the disadvantaged will be helped by the growing political consciousness of the lower castes, by commercialization which is loosening traditional social structures, and by NGOs playing a greater role in making people aware of their entitlements and motivating and organizing local committees. It will also require State bureaucracies to change from a controlling to a supportive role especially in providing expertise locally, and for the local bodies to accept responsibility for mobilizing some resources themselves (Vaidyanathan, 1996: World Bank, 1995).

In *Bolivia*, the Popular Participation Law (1994) and the Law for Decentralization of Administration (1995) have potentially important implications for poverty reduction. These reforms explicitly aim to improve income distribution, to increase the role of citizens, and to give municipalities power and resources to determine their own local strategies within a national framework. As a result, 75 per cent of the national budget is now managed locally and departmentally (compared with 25 per cent before). Municipal involvement is 20 per cent (compared with 1 per cent before). This process still has a short history and the participatory approach is not yet sufficiently internalized among the population or the officials who are supposed to implement it. It remains to be seen how far it will improve the distributional consequences of the development process and improve conditions for the poor (see Freres *et al.*, 2000).

Conclusion

This brief review of seven poor countries reveals a wide range of opportunities for external agencies who seek to pursue poverty reduction objectives. These include the need for:

- more effective economic policies to promote employment-creating growth;

- a shift of resources and services into rural areas;
- a reorientation of public social services and an improvement in their quality at basic levels;
- the creation of mechanisms to assist poorer regions and districts;
- better targeting of credit and other measures to help the poor;
- a redistribution of land ownership and use;
- strengthened institutional capacities at local levels.

Further progress in reducing heavy debt-service payments would, also contribute, provided the budgetary funds released are likely to be used in a pro-poor way.

Most of these countries have moved towards some degree of greater political freedom and pluralism which is potentially helpful. Yet, in terms of political processes and cultures, formidable obstacles remain to the redistribution of public subsidies, and even more to the redistribution of assets like land, and the reduction of discrimination against (poor) women.

Joan Nelson (1992: 233), a long-time analyst of the politics of poverty, has written as follows:

> most governments have little incentive to protect or promote the interests of the very poor. The problem is not simply the weakness of the poor and indifference of elites. Working and popular classes themselves are fairly poor, often demand more government attention to their needs and predictably resist government attempts to re-target subsidies and social programmes such as education and health to better serve the truly needy. The key question then becomes the conditions under which governments are nonetheless likely to adopt pro-poor measures.

Nelson (1992: 237) offers no easy formulas but discusses the role of domestic political and international pressures in favour of the poor.

> Competitive democratic elections are no guarantee of influence for the poor. A great deal of historical evidence supports the generalisation that at early stages of development, the extension of electoral and other channels for popular participation empowers urban and rural middle strata and skews government policies in their favour. As participation spreads among the poor at later stages, the balance may be partly redressed, but middle class and

upper level working class groups usually retain advantages in organisation, information, contacts and financial resources. However, more specific institutional features can enhance the influence of poorer groups in democratic contexts...

Domestically, political alliances with more influential groups can provide the poor with some benefits through broader-based programmes, though the poor remain subordinate partners and broader programmes are less sustainable by governments with severe budgetary constraints.

From the perspective of external donor agencies, Nelson has argued that those 'distributive' measures like provision of relief and targeted social programmes, which obviously involve *additional* direct funding from external sources, are likely to be more politically acceptable than 'redistribution' of *existing* public expenditure towards poor people. While this view may have some validity, the external aid agencies often fund a substantial proportion of the domestic budget (see Table 1.1), and the distinction between additional external funding and existing expenditures becomes blurred and may not make a reallocation in the poor's favour more politically palatable. Most aid is ultimately fungible, and thus no real distinction exists between domestic and external funding. In addition, increasing donor enthusiasm for sector-wide approaches implies that donor finances feed into an integrated reform process funded out of a common donor-government pot.

What is clear, however, is that a powerful potential role remains for external agencies as an 'external lobby' on behalf of the poor within these countries. This is potentially because, apart from the government of India, these countries are highly aid-dependent (see Table 1.1). The manner in which this advocacy role is pursued raises important questions concerning the nature of partnership and dialogue. Other questions include the extent to which it is appropriate to use pro-poor conditionality or selectivity in the provision of external funds, and how far support should be channelled directly to non-state domestic bodies, potentially bypassing the politics of the public administration system. These issues, and others, are taken up in later chapters.

2
Poverty Reduction Goals and Strategies of the European Development Cooperation Agencies

In this chapter we pose several major questions. What are the poverty reduction goals of the European development agencies in the countries with which they have relations? How have their strategies changed? Have there been changes in donor commitment to poverty goals, in their conceptualization of poverty, or in the degree of consensus they share on the operational aims to pursue greater poverty reduction? How feasible are these aims? Chapter 3 then examines in more detail the various roles that donor agencies can play in promoting poverty reduction. Subsequent chapters consider how effective donor-supported interventions have actually been, and what lessons can be learned.

Goals and strategies

Most European aid agencies assert their concern with poverty and poverty reduction (PR) in one way or another. While some have done so over quite a long period, others have shown greater concern only in the 1990s. Table 2.1 shows points of both commonality and difference in the actual PR goals and strategies of the ten European donors.

First, it is possible to classify the European donors according to whether they have an overarching PR goal, whether PR is one among other high priority objectives, or whether it does not feature explicitly at all. Overarching PR goals are a feature of a group of donors including Denmark, Finland, Sweden, the Netherlands and the UK (since 1995, reinforced in 1997). Some bilateral donors, such as Germany and Italy, have a poverty reducing objective which is

Table 2.1   PR strategies of European donors

Denmark	From the mid-1970s basic commitment to PR as the overall basis for the aid programme. Until 1994 an absence of strategy and policy papers laying out the implications of the general commitment to PR. During the 1970s and 1980s tension between PR and tied aid programme objectives. More strategic approach only introduced in 1994 and strategy paper on PR in 1995. Strong focus on least developed and low-income countries in bilateral aid.
European Union	Council Resolutions (1993 and 1996) define strategic goals in terms of PR and people-oriented development. While PR is seen as central to all interventions, there is no clear prioritization between PR and other goals. Poverty conceptualization is open-ended but seen largely as a relative concept and a multi-dimensional problem. Target groups are identified broadly as deprived and discriminated against sections of population (including old, landless, uneducated and others). Aid for ALA region is formally concentrated on poor countries. Aid within the Lomé IV agreement – largely to Africa – is not *de facto* allocated by level of *per capita* income. The priority to PR within the successor to Lomé IV is proposed but is still unclear. Increased support envisaged for partners with policy commitment to Council Resolution guidelines.
Finland	PR is one among three priority goals. Reconfirmation of commitment to allocate the majority of aid to the poorest countries, especially in SSA. Lack of recipient government commitment to PR is regarded as a justification to freeze or terminate the aid relationship.
France	No overarching poverty goal but the campaign against poverty is one of six goals. No formal priority for allocation to poor countries. Poverty seen as symptom of underdevelopment. No concept of a poor group or a distinctive poverty strategy.
Germany	No overarching goal but emphasis on improved economic and social situation of poor people with PR as a priority. Development commitment of recipient government (not PR explicitly) is one of five criteria for aid allocation. BMZ does not accept a trickle-down theory of PR. Recognizes concept of absolute poverty and poor/disadvantaged groups. Criteria for poor not entirely clear. Participation and self-help are central to PR.
Italy	No overarching poverty goal, but PR interventions since 1985 reflect especially a humanitarian response to emergencies. The fight against poverty is one of a number of aims in the new 1995 guidelines for development cooperation.

(Table 2.1 continued)

	Particular focus on 'special situations' (conflict, emergencies, refugees and rehabilitation, etc.) and special programmes with PR implications. Explicit high allocation to least developed and poor countries.
Netherlands	Sustainable PR is a central goal, with focus on the poorest countries and poor people within them. The needs of the poorest women and their 'autonomy' are given a central position. The identification of poor groups is based on sex, time and place; the landless in Asia, small peasants in Africa and the urban unemployed in Latin America. There is a strong emphasis on poor women and on children.
Spain	No overarching poverty goal but PR is *an* objective. Formal priority for poor countries but not effectively implemented. No PR conceptualisation.
Sweden	The primary goal is to improve the quality of life of poor people. Poor and disadvantaged groups seen to need special attention: mainly female-headed households, mothers and children, poor areas, marginalized ethnic groups, the disabled. Priority in aid allocation for poor countries and those with a commitment to PR.
United Kingdom	The White Paper in 1997 puts poverty elimination as the top priority of the aid programme, and seeks consistency with poverty elimination in UK government's approach to trade, agriculture, investment, the environment, and political and financial sustainability. The share of bilateral aid to the least developed and low-income countries has fallen by 20 per cent in the past decade, but is set to rise. Strong commitment to International Poverty Goals.

one among others. The European Commission is formally governed by the 'campaign against poverty' mandate enshrined in the Maastricht Treaty and the Council Resolutions of 1993 on the fight against poverty and of 1996 on Human and Social Development (HSD), but there is no overarching commitment to PR. France and Spain have not given explicit priority to PR.

   An overarching PR goal represents the strongest and most comprehensive commitment by a donor, since in principle all their activities should be oriented and justified in terms of the ultimate goal. However, there remains a risk of generality in which every activity can be interpreted as 'poverty reducing' without adequate justification. On the other hand, donors who have a specific PR goal, among a number of others, rarely reveal the true priority that they give to it so that they can be judged on their performance.

Donors vary considerably in their explicit commitment to a policy of giving *priority to poor countries* as well as in their actual allocations to them. Thus, in the case of France with no explicit commitment to poor countries and Spain with a formal commitment, the proportion of gross disbursements of aid to low-income countries was low, at 52.1 and 40.4 per cent respectively in 1995–96 (see Table 2.2). Denmark, Finland, Sweden and the UK give low-income countries explicit priority and the actual allocation to them exceeded 71 per cent in all cases. In between lie Germany, the Netherlands, and the European Community, with an explicit commitment and actual disbursements of around 60 per cent. However, these figures must be treated with care, since they conceal part of the picture. Although widely quoted, they refer only to Official Development Assistance (ODA), and therefore exclude aid disbursements to so-called Part II countries, mainly Central and Eastern European countries and the former Soviet republics. In reality, aid to these countries is usually considered to form part of each donor's aid budget and is managed by officials within the same ministry. Therefore, the decision to allocate increasing resources to Part II countries during the 1990s has often occurred at the cost of falling shares of the total aid budget to the poorest

Table 2.2 Shares of bilateral official development aid (ODA) to least developed and low-income countries 1995–96 (%)

Denmark	78.4
European Community	59.7
Finland	71.1
France	52.1
Germany	58.4
Italy	61.8
Netherlands	64.3
Spain	40.4
Sweden	71.5
UK	74.3
DAC Average	52.7

Source: DAC, *Development Cooperation*, 1998. Paris: OECD.

countries. Taking the UK as an example, the share of *total* UK bilateral aid to least developed and low-income countries in 1996–97 was only 63.1 per cent, compared with 74.3 per cent when only ODA is considered. The shares for several other European donors would also fall, especially Germany which provides huge grants under both heads.

Nevertheless, those agencies like Spain in particular, France and DG VIII in the European Commission which give low (*de facto*) priority to poor people also tend to give lower priority to the allocation of aid to poor countries. Denmark, Finland, Sweden and the UK (since 1997) give quite high priority to both. Germany, the Netherlands and Italy give higher priority to one than the other.

Trends and conceptualization

Is there a trend towards greater donor commitment to PR goals?

The level of commitment is not easy to judge. Rhetoric is plentiful but hardly a good test. EU donors generally are not particularly accountable for their PR performance. Few have benchmarks for judging how far they are achieving their PR goals and how far performance has improved over time. Systematic statistical information or records of their PR or social spending on basic services, whether intentions or outcomes, are very patchy. They are partially developed for the Netherlands Directorate General for International Development (DGIS), the UK's Department for International Development (DFID), Germany's Federal Ministry for Economic Cooperation and Development (BMZ), Sweden's International Development Cooperation Agency (Sida) and Finland's Department of International Development Cooperation (Finnida), but none achieve World Bank standards in providing systematic and quantitative as well as qualitative assessments of their performance against their poverty objective. Donors like Spain, Italy and France provide little or no indication of their spending intentions or outcomes in relation to PR aims.

Nevertheless, our overall judgement is that there is a higher level of formal commitment to PR objectives in 1998 than in 1990 for the majority of EU donors. This is based on the following evidence:

- Since the early 1990s, the Netherlands and Germany have had clear and well formulated strategies for poverty reduction and have made efforts to implement them. Sida and the Danish International Development Agency (Danida) with long-standing poverty goals, have undertaken major internal reviews and made moves toward more effective operationalization. Some donors have recently announced stronger strategic goals on PR, most notably DFID (UK) in its 1997 White Paper. Italy and Belgium have shown signs of a greater commitment in the 1990s. European Council Resolutions, since 1993, concerning the 'struggle against poverty' (*la lutte contre la pauvreté*) should in principle influence the Commission's activities, although operational moves to implement them have been limited within the Commission. However, there is little or no apparent change in the French and Spanish positions.

• All European donors have now adopted the international poverty reduction goals which are enshrined in the OECD/DAC document *Shaping the 21st Century: the Contribution of Development Cooperation*. These commit donors to work in partnership with developing countries to achieve a reduction by one half in the proportion of people living in extreme poverty by 2015. Sub-goals include the elimination of gender disparity in primary and secondary education by 2005, access through primary health care to reproductive services as soon as possible, and a two-thirds reduction in the mortality of under-fives. In practice, however, commitment to the international goals varies among the donors, with some thoroughly integrating the goals into their policies and strategies and others going little further than expressing their support.

• There now exists a group of donors – Germany, the Netherlands, the Nordic States and the UK – who seem 'like-minded' in their commitment to greater operationalization of their PR objectives.

Donor conceptualization of poverty and the poor

How do these aid agencies perceive the nature of poverty and identify the 'poor'? Most of the European agencies now perceive poverty as a multi-dimensional concept. Poverty is no longer viewed as simply a lack of monetary income or consumption or assets, important as these are. The poor are now recognized as having a wider range of disadvantages (most explicitly by Denmark, the European Union, Finland, the Netherlands, Sweden and the UK). These are seen to involve vulnerability and insecurity of livelihood, isolation and lack of self-esteem, physical weaknesses (stemming from malnutrition, sickness, old age, disablement), powerlessness and social exclusion, including discrimination by society particularly against women, low-caste groups and ethnic minorities. Some of these insights have been garnered from the perceptions of the poor themselves, whose opinions have been sought only in recent years.

The agencies which are aware of these wider dimensions of poverty have tried to develop approaches that seek to address some of them. For specific interventions at community level, donors have sought more participatory, awareness-creating, institution-strengthening approaches. They have encompassed attempts to improve physical conditions through better access to basic education, literacy, basic health and nutrition, drinking water and sanitation. Approaches to the empowerment of the poor and the reduction of discrimination and exclusion are being developed more slowly through, for example, support for organizations which help make the poor and women more aware of their rights and access to them, and more indirectly via initiatives for the decentralization of government responsibilities and resources to local levels. The actual effectiveness of implementation of these intentions is examined in Chapters 5 and 6.

How are the poor defined or identified? Those agencies with fairly strong poverty-focused strategies are nevertheless not particularly precise in their 'mission' statements about who are 'the poor' whom they wish to assist. For Germany, the poor are defined in absolute terms, while the UK is ambiguous, sometimes using an absolute measure and sometimes emphasizing the relative nature of poverty, with a general focus on rural populations and female-headed households. For Sweden, the poor are defined as the poorest groups in society, including female-headed households, households in poor areas, marginalized ethnic groups and the disabled. For Denmark, the focus is seen in terms of women and girls, the rural population, small-holders and small enterprises (not always poor farmers and poor entrepreneurs) and marginalized groups. Finland defines its primary target group as women and children, ethnic minorities and the disabled. The Netherlands places a strong emphasis on poor women, the landless in Asia, small peasants in Africa and the urban unemployed in Latin America. The European Commission tends towards a relative concept of poverty, with a broad concept of deprived people (unemployed, uneducated or old) as well as those who are marginalized and discriminated against.

The Italian and French positions have been somewhat different. Italy has mainly perceived the problem (in terms of its actions) as the vulnerability of displaced populations, refugees and migrants 'in special situations' rather than chronic poverty more generally. For the French there is no concept of an identifiable economic or social group termed the poor. Nor do they see poverty as a particular phenomenon to be addressed by a specific strategy or measures. Poverty is perceived as congruent with underdevelopment. However, they have recognized certain vulnerable groups in urban areas (the young, sick, immigrants, single women) for special action. Spain lacks any explicit concept of the poor.

The essential point would seem to be evidence of an understanding of the various dimensions of poverty, which can then be applied within the context of a poverty assessment at the country level, to develop appropriate PR strategies. Understanding the various dimensions of poverty assists not only in the identification of who and where the poor are, but also in developing measures which tackle the interrelated causes of poverty (see Annex 2 for fuller discussion).

Aims of the European Agencies: consensus and feasibility

Is there a consensus?

Agencies seek to achieve their strategic PR goals through their operational aims. The explicitness and clarity of these aims are important for guidance to task managers, field-level consultants and country partners, and consensus among donors is important if they are to be pursued effectively. What are these aims and how far is there a consensus on them?

Pro-poor economic aims

It is useful to start with the position of the World Bank (initially spelt out in 1990 in the *World Development Report*) since it has been a benchmark for the thinking of most donors during the 1990s. The Bank considers sustained growth to be a necessary condition for PR, and its latest research suggests that this has been the most important factor in reducing poverty. However, it states that the benefits which trickle down to the poor from economic growth are insufficient unless the distribution of the benefits from growth are tilted in the poor's favour, especially in terms of employment opportunities.

The Bank's 1990 *World Development Report* postulated a 'three-pronged' pro-poor operational strategy. The first priority is to aim for a pattern of growth in which the poor participate, particularly by taking advantage of opportunities for improved livelihoods. Achievement of this objective is seen to depend mainly on support for macroeconomic and market reform policies to eliminate the bias against the demand for unskilled labour, and to remove discrimination in markets against poor small-scale producers (especially women) and improve incentives for them.

The second priority is to aim to create assets for poor people in order to improve their productivity, especially by investing in their human development. The routes are to be through improving the access of the poor to public services for human capital development especially at primary level, including reorientation of public expenditure and decentralization of public services in recipient countries. Third, the Bank suggests that safety nets should be provided for those who cannot take advantage of these policies, for example, the aged or disabled in particular and those who are temporarily affected adversely by shocks.

Most 'Northern' development agencies appear to take the same position as the World Bank; Denmark, Finland, Germany, Sweden, the Netherlands and the UK similarly do not accept a purely trickle-down view of poverty reduction. They all see the need for a wide range of structural reforms to create an environment more favourable to opportunities for poor people. They tend to favour 'broad-based' growth. Sweden, Denmark and Finland favour 'socially balanced growth' or social equalization (citizen-based entitlements to social security). The European Union sees the need for growth that generates employment and for a redistribution of resources. However, the conception of pro-poor economic growth policies is not particularly precise for any of these donors.

France has tended to view economic growth as the most efficient means to reduce poverty, a view that seems to assume that the benefits will automatically trickle down to the poor. More recently there may have been some slight shift in its position since it now

recognizes that, for sub-Saharan Africa, there is a need to skew policies and management to favour more equitable access of the poor to
basic infrastructure services although there is no concept of targeting the poor (de Boisdeffre, 1997; Secretariat d'Etat, 1997). Spain
and Italy do not appear to have developed clear pro-poor operational aims.

Nevertheless virtually all these donors see the need to prioritize
the rural sector where they observe that most of the poor are concentrated. They want to improve the productive assets and productivity of small farmers (and sometimes more explicitly poor farmers)
mainly through better access to credit, capital and knowledge.
However, not much prominence is given to adaptive research in
agriculture, which may be the key to employment creation and
improved livelihoods of the rural poor in many regions. Some
exceptions are the UK and Sida.

Basic needs and social services for poor

There is now general support for the idea of focusing on the basic
needs of the poor through primary health care and education, preventive health, drinking water and sanitation, particularly by
Denmark, Finland, the Netherlands, Germany, the UK and France
(mainly with respect to basic education). Some, such as Sida, Danida,
the Netherlands and the UK explicitly favour efforts to reorient public expenditure. The EC has focused mainly on Human and Social
Development (HSD), but more recently in a Council Resolution
(European Commission, 1994a) it is proposing a more pro-poor
focus through a greater concentration on the quality of basic and
non-formal education and training, as well as some shift away from
the tertiary education sectors favoured by the Lomé Convention sig-
natories towards more primary levels especially for girls. The 1994
Council Resolution on Health (European Commission, 1994b: 6) targets the most disadvantaged population groups and shows a clear
shift away from curative sources, favouring basic and first referral
systems which are seen as most relevant for poorer sections of the
population (Loquai *et al.*, 1998: 22). Germany, the Netherlands and
Denmark have adopted the 20:20 principle which provides a more
pro-poor orientation in the content of the social expenditure target,
as noted earlier. Finland, Sweden and the UK took a more reserved
position on the 20:20 principle.[1]

Participatory approaches and empowerment

Domestic and local ownership is seen as a vital requirement for effective change. Priority is increasingly given by the European agencies, at least in their rhetoric, to the need for institution building and for genuine participation by the poor. Thus, Danida focuses on local authorities and Sida and the UK on the electoral processes that improve the participation of the poor and particularly of women. The Netherlands, Denmark and Finland support popular participation and decentralization so that the poor are included. Germany emphasizes the promotion of poor self-help groups on a long-term basis. The UK has also placed increased emphasis on 'stakeholder' approaches to its interventions. France, with less focus on poverty, nevertheless pursues a decentralization approach (*'coopération de proximité'*) which has potential for PR. The implementation of this and other measures often leaves much to be desired, however, as will be indicated below.

Gender sensitivity

Virtually all donors say that they aim to reduce gender discrimination *per se*, but some now recognize that effective strategies to reduce poverty will usually require an understanding of gender relations. Donors may seek to influence the structure of power relations or of income or asset distribution at the level of local communities, or even within the household. Donor objectives include an emphasis on better access of women to education and maternal and child health as well as to technology, knowledge and credit. It is not always clear whether this is access specifically for poor women. Among donors, Sweden, Denmark and Finland seem to be the most active advocates of a focus on gender.

Safety nets

The World Bank's strategy is sometimes termed a 'two-and-a-half-legged strategy' since relatively less emphasis has been given to safety net programmes. The definition of what safety nets might constitute has itself been vague, though it often centres on self-selecting employment-generation schemes. There are strong ideological and political differences between the various European donors' perceptions on social security. The concept of a 'safety net' belongs to the school of thought which promotes strictly targeted and means-tested social security provided by the government for the most vulnerable people only, with private services and social security arrangements for the better-off, who can afford them. The Nordic governments favour broader-based social security and social service arrangements, where the main aim is to ensure quality services for all. France, Germany, the Netherlands and the EC tend to view (formal sector) employment as the primary instrument and source of entitlement for social security. These differences of views reflect the donor governments domestic social policy traditions.

Fiscal and asset redistribution

There are some agencies – those of Denmark, Finland, France, Germany, Sweden and, to some extent, the UK – which explicitly favour redistributive fiscal policies. Most favour higher user charges for those tertiary services, such as higher education, which largely benefit the rich. It is also accepted in principle that the poor should not be required to pay user charges for basic services. A redistribution of public expenditures in a more pro-poor direction is generally supported. However, a range of agencies do not explicitly mention the landless and there would seem to be little enthusiasm among them to tackle land rights and redistribution of land. (Sida is one exception to this.)

Governance and poverty reduction

During the 1990s virtually all the European donors started to emphasize the importance of good governance, by which they tended to mean respect for human rights and the rule of law and some sort of electoral, preferably democratic and pluralist, system. More recently, governance has been viewed by several agencies, particularly Sida, Finnida, DFID, Danida and the EC, as being a component in any strategy for poverty reduction. First, the emphasis on human rights is seen as highly relevant to equality in rights for the poor – regardless of sex, ethnicity, status or language. Second, more pluralist governance is seen as likely to give a greater voice to the poor, while more efficient and accountable governance is seen as more likely to be responsive to these needs.

It remains rather less clear how donors can support this objective in practical terms and deliver real benefits to the poor. One mechanism is by supporting the decentralization of government powers to

local but accountable authorities and communities. Danida specifically favours support for popular organizations rooted in the rural
population, while the EC favours strengthening socio-economic
associations and their partnership and dialogue at central and local
levels. Nonetheless, this remains an area where further research
would help to clarify the options open to external agencies and
their likely impact on the poor.

Debt relief

Debt relief can assist by releasing potential extra public resources for
allocation to pro-poor uses, though it does not, of course, ensure
that this happens. Problems of indebtedness in the poor countries
currently arise not so much from past bilateral aid but from 'pre-
ferred creditors' like the IMF and from officially guaranteed private
credit. Policy therefore rests with Ministries of Finance and Central
Banks in the creditor countries. Nevertheless, coherence in policy
towards developing countries suggests that aid agencies should play
some role in changing national policy. No doubt they have done so,
though outside pressures from NGOs played a major role in the
Cologne Summit initiative in June 1999 to provide significantly
greater debt reduction for the Highly Indebted Poor Countries
(HIPCs). This second phase of the HIPC scheme links the provision
of relief for countries to a poverty reduction framework and
increased social spending.[2]

How feasible are these aims for reducing poverty?[3]

Despite the generally high degree of consensus, some questions can
be raised about the appropriateness of this basket of donor aims and
strategies. The broad-based approach to growth is assumed to generate demand for the goods and services produced by unskilled labour
which the poor possess in abundance. However, without complementary skills, capital and land which the poor often do not posses,
there is not likely to be much productive employment. Of course,
the focus on primary health care and education is seen to contribute
to the skills of the poor and to reduce the population growth rate at
least in the long run. Yet it seems inadequate to rely on growth promotion and enhancing human capital through improved education
and health in a context where the population growth rate is high
and the prospects for growth low. This is precisely the context

facing many sub-Saharan African countries for the foreseeable future and also some poor countries outside of Africa.

Under these conditions, such a strategy is unlikely to be pro-poor, in the sense that it is unlikely to result in rapid poverty reduction, certainly insufficiently rapid to meet the international goals on PR. What is lacking is enough attention to the redistribution of productive assets in order to achieve poverty reduction within a reasonable time scale. The bulk of the poor live in the rural areas, yet redistribution of credit towards the rural poor, in particular, appears to be hardly addressed by aid agencies. Instead, they appear to focus on the small farmers who may or may not be poor, and in general they say little or nothing about the landless or virtually landless or their scope for access to funds.

An equally important weakness is the lack of attention by most donors to the question of land distribution, land rights and rights for water resources for draining, irrigation, fishing, and the concomitant reform. To bias slow growth with a growing population towards the poorest rural sections would seem to require their having much greater access to land (and credit) whether by transfer or by migration, in order to increase their productivity. Such a change in the ownership of or rights to land use is particularly important for women, and represents an important route out of poverty for families. Scope for the creation of livelihoods for the poor in more skilled industrial and service activities, even with better basic education, seems to be a highly optimistic expectation of many donors. Finally, donor-supported governance reforms promoting greater pluralism, democracy and decentralization lack specificity on the precise processes which will allow greater effective participation by the poor and vulnerable. Indeed, they take little account of past evidence that such systems are a necessary but rarely a sufficient condition for the empowerment of the poor.

A similar assessment has been made recently by Professor Rehman Sobhan of the new UK White Paper on Poverty Elimination (DFID, 1997), but it is pertinent to the position of all the European development agencies. He points out that unless donors themselves have rethought their old policy design for what is appropriate to the issues of poverty, they are not going to have a powerful enough agenda to carry credibility with clients. In this regard the White Paper has serious problems in addressing the fundamental issues of

poverty. There is no recognition of the essence of a policy of inclusion or the need to create structural change within the community
to make stakeholders out of the poor in the development process.
There is really no redistributive agenda which brings in issues of
controlling productive assets like land, water courses, corporate
wealth. There is no major attention to the issues of the political
empowerment of the poor so that they can in fact emerge as democratic actors in the political process.[4]

Summary

Although all the European agencies have adopted the international
targets to reduce poverty by 2015, not all of them share a common
strategy on poverty and the poor. Currently there are a group for
whom PR is an overarching goal – Denmark, the Netherlands,
Sweden and the UK (since 1997). It is one priority among others for
Finland, Germany, Italy and Spain, although neither of the last two
has an explicit elaborated strategy. For France there is no concept of
an identifiable group termed the poor for whom a special strategy is
seen to be required. The European Union is governed by Council
resolutions which define strategic poverty alleviation and people-
oriented development goals, but both DGI and DGVIII have been
rather slow in developing systematic operational strategies.

Those agencies where poverty concerns represent an overarching
goal indicate, in principle, the strongest and most comprehensive
commitment since all their activities should be oriented and justified in terms of it. Those agencies which give high priority to poor
people also tend to allocate the bulk of their funds to poor countries. Spain, France and the European Commission (DGVIII) tend to
give lower priority to both.

Virtually all the European agencies see poverty as a multi-dimensional concept. It is no longer viewed as simply a lack of monetary
income or consumption, important as these are. The poor tend to be
defined and identified in rather general terms. There are also differences. For Germany, the poor are defined in absolute terms; the
European Commission tends towards a relative concept of poverty,
while the UK is ambiguous between these. Only two agencies – the
UK's DFID and Danida – focus on the rural population. Most agencies focus on the marginalized and discriminated-against groups

(often ethnic), and women and female-headed households (though not all agencies specify poor women). Denmark and the Netherlands focus on small-holders and small enterprises (not always necessarily poor farmers or poor entrepreneurs), and the latter on the landless in Asia. Finland and the European Commission give importance to the disabled. Italy has tended to focus on those groups which need help arising from 'special situations' (conflict, emergencies, refugees and migrants and their rehabilitation). These formal positions of the agencies may not necessarily indicate the focus of their actual operations.

There has been a distinct increase in the commitment of a group of agencies – Denmark, Sweden, Germany, the UK and the Netherlands – to poverty objectives during the 1990s with greater attention to more effective operationalization. These now form a distinct group of like-minded agencies on poverty issues. Finland and Italy have shifted their positions a little, the European Union is very slowly articulating its own position and operational guidelines, but France and Spain have not obviously shifted their positions.

For the 'like-minded' group of agencies at least, there is a considerable consensus on economic and social aims to achieve their goals. Economic growth, though vital, is not seen as sufficient to achieve adequate reduction in the degree of poverty, especially in slow growing areas like sub-Saharan Africa. They share the notion of economic policies for 'broad-based' or pro-poor growth to provide opportunities for the poor, especially through greater employment. Their approach includes measures to improve the access of the poor to credit and knowledge to boost their productivity as well as improved basic infrastructure for rural development. Priority is given to the provision of more and better quality basic social services – especially primary education and health, drinking water and sanitation – to offer easier access for the poor. Some focus on the need to re-orient public expenditure in this direction in their partner countries.

Questions remain about the feasibility of some of these aims such as doubts about the creation of significant employment for the unskilled poor and inadequate attention to the redistribution of assets (especially land and land-use rights) for some country situations at least. In their approaches to interventions, the agencies have increasingly recognized that the keys to an effective PR strategy within partner countries are a strategy and specific programmes that are 'owned' locally and not imposed from outside. In their specific project interventions since the early 1990s most agencies favour approaches that allow more participation of local communities (including potential poor beneficiaries) in both their ongoing projects and new ones.

More fundamentally, the agencies now see political reform – multi-party electoralism, pluralism, better central administration and decentralization – as essential for more effective PR. However, they are not usually explicit about how the political and governance reforms espoused will promote greater responsiveness to the needs of the poor, or will counter gender discrimination and increase the participation of the poor in decision-making.

We turn in the next chapter to the question of the role that these agencies themselves can play in achieving these objectives and the modes of intervention open to them.

3

Role and Modes of Intervention of the Development Cooperation Agencies for Poverty Reduction

Potential role of aid agencies in poverty reduction

Chapter 2 reviewed the poverty reduction goals and aims of the European development agencies, but what are their own roles in helping to achieve them? This chapter considers the nature of these roles and the modes of intervention that can be used, and poses some choices which donors need to make between the options available to them. It then looks at the limited published evidence on the fulfillment of these roles.

Within any specific country there are at least five types of role that bilateral aid agencies can play in trying to make a difference to the welfare of really poor people.[1] First, external funds, skills and influence can support *faster general economic growth* in a country and hence some 'trickle-down' benefits for the poorest groups. This includes efforts to ensure the stabilization and adjustment of economies to stem decline and restore growth.

Second, external agencies can help create a more pro-poor domestic *policy environment* which improves opportunities for poor and marginalized people to obtain better livelihoods and increased access to resources, knowledge and rights. These enabling measures help to improve the extent to which the poor share in the fruits of any economic growth, increasing the rate or extent of trickle-down benefits. They encompass changes in the regulatory systems and credit allocation procedures which make it easier and cheaper for the poor to get access to resources. They encompass efforts to reorient public expenditure so that the incidence of subsidies, user charges and taxes is less regressive (for example, shifts from tertiary to primary health and education services and improvement in the management and quality of basic social services). They can also encompass changes in land ownership and rights to usage.

Third, external agencies can help *improve domestic institutions*, most obviously the political, legal, judicial and administrative systems (from central to local level). The political system can be reformed to be made more accountable and responsive to the needs of poor people, while changes in law and practice can reduce the degree of exclusion and discrimination against vulnerable groups, such as women or indigenous groups.

Fourth, external agencies can use their resources and skills to make *specific poverty-focused interventions*. These can be targeted to benefit directly and exclusively the poor and marginalized groups of people that have been identified. More widely targeted programmes can be designed to provide them with a disproportionate share of the benefits. These interventions, in principle, can help improve the approaches and the management and standards of initiatives at the local community level. A similar process can be undertaken with sector-wide approaches, at the level of central ministries and regional authorities, to help strengthen the focus and administrative capabilities, whose design and implementation may or may not reflect an awareness of the particular needs of poor groups.

Fifth, and relatedly, external agencies can play a role as *innovators in PR schemes*. With their greater resources and ability to take risks they can support pilot ventures to establish, in principle, types of approaches and activities which, if successful, can be 'scaled up' and 'replicated' more widely by the domestic authorities.

These roles are largely complementary rather than mutually exclusive, and to some extent they overlap. The external agencies have some important choices to make, however, in the instruments or modes of intervention which they deploy to play these roles. The strong evidence that much aid is fungible must condition the realism and choice of these instruments.

Modes of intervention: some important choices

Partners: conditionality/dialogue

The most fundamental decision concerns which partners to work with and how to approach the overall provision of external assistance for reaching poor people better. If potential partners do not share these goals, or not fully or consistently, then it is possible to apply conditions to the financial support which relate to the partners' performance in carrying out the policy change. Although conditions have frequently been applied in relation to structural adjustment policy changes, there is currently little enthusiasm among the agencies for applying conditions to pro-poor policy change. Indeed, the European agencies (with some exceptions) have become very disillusioned with the effectiveness of conditionality in any area of policy. Domestic ownership is seen as a much more promising way forward on PR goals. The choice is easy if partners can be found who share the same poverty reduction goals as the agencies. The most difficult choice arises if the partners' goals and policies are not pro-poor and their economic management for growth is also very weak. The first option here is for intensive, informed and regular 'dialogue' on these poverty issues by the external agencies – both bilaterally and collectively. This is a process of research and negotiation to achieve a consensus on domestic strategies and policies which all the agencies can support. Where this does not prove effective, the final option becomes the difficult one of not 'selecting' the partner for external support.

Balance of interventions: growth-promoting versus poverty-reducing

The second choice for donors within their country strategies for poverty reduction is what priority to attach to interventions which primarily assist general development or economic growth (such as infrastructure and productive investments) on the one hand, and those interventions for which the linkages to PR are more direct or immediate. For the former, benefits may accrue to the poor in the longer term through trickle-down effects, but the linkages are indirect and often depend upon additional parallel or subsequent actions being taken. The balance between these will vary among partner countries depending on the extent of private external support, but it will require a collective judgement by donors since most are too small to make a sensible judgement solely on their own contribution. Some donors who seek to 'mainstream' poverty concerns are tempted to see links to PR which may not exist. Some basically growth-promoting measures can potentially include clear linkages to impact on poverty. DFID's support for the power sector in Orissa is justified on the grounds of the expected growth-inducing effect of a reliable power supply *and* because of the potential for reducing the huge level of subsidies, thus freeing resources for allocation to basic health and education. But there need to be good grounds or plausible mechanisms for belief that the government of Orissa will indeed redirect any savings into the social sector. DFID has not sought to tie its assistance to such a budgetary reorientation. The key point is that it is more important for agencies to decide the balance of their strategy between growth-promoting interventions *per se* and those with clear and obvious PR characteristics, rather than seek some unrealistic or implausible link to PR through the former.

There is a range of interventions which can clearly be linked to benefits for a target group of poor or vulnerable people – the poverty-oriented interventions. Within these, a further choice of options is recognized by most agencies. These can be interventions or actions which are 'focused predominantly on the needs of poor people' (DFID wording) or 'directly targeted on poor people and where the majority of the benefits are intended to accrue to them' (BMZ wording). This approach requires a careful identification of the target group and tends to be at the local or community level. In principle it requires the participation of the poor in the design and implementation of the project to ensure that the benefits are focused on them. The European agencies, nevertheless, do not share precisely the same interpretation of what constitutes an action or intervention 'focused' on the poor. Thus the EC, for example, relies upon identifying poor groups. The UK also recognizes the value of targeting benefits to particular socio-economic groups which serve as proxies for the poor. However, it also attempts to target the poor through interventions in poor regions, by supporting advocacy groups and community-based organizations and by strengthening poor people's human rights. Denmark has a particular accent on facilitating the participation of poor groups in society. A sub-choice in this category is the extent to which the official agency should use NGOs – Northern and Southern – to execute the interventions. Most have done so, but the extent has varied greatly.

On the other hand, there are 'broad-based' actions which are 'inclusive' of the poor (Sida and DFID) but are not narrowly or exclusively focused on them. Other donors (for example, BMZ) term these 'indirect poverty' actions, and they often encompass sectoral interventions in basic education or health, extension services or basic infrastructure like water and feeder roads. There needs to be a plausible link, whether implicit or explicit, between the activity and PR, which leaves considerable room for interpretation. Strictly, to qualify as indirect PR measures, they should be expected to provide substantial benefits to the poor as well as to the better-off, such that the proportion of the benefits to the poor would exceed their representation in the population at large. Primary education programmes in poor regions and districts would qualify, particularly if they sought to target girls, since they should disproportionately increase access by poor and excluded children.

The agencies have a choice between *ad hoc* project interventions and wider programme sector-based interventions involving budgetary support plus technical assistance and dialogue on the wider administrative and policy framework. In the past they have largely pursued the *ad hoc* project option, but opinion is recently changing in favour of a sectoral approach to PR interventions which would fall into the 'indirect' category (some of these issues of choice are pursued more systematically in Chapter 7).

Some choices of mode: 'Poverty bangs per buck'

Ideally it is necessary to establish the PR effectiveness or impact of different modes of intervention in relation to their likely cost. Whether:

a) intensive agency dialogue with partners on pro-poor policy and the institutional environment is likely to be more effective than conditionality applied or no dialogue at all;
b) the same volume of resources invested in growth-producing investments is likely to benefit the poor indirectly *via* trickledown more than the same funds focused directly or indirectly on them;
c) funds deployed sectorally can be more effective in reaching the poor than through a range of smaller *ad hoc* projects;
d) interventions are more effective if narrowly targeted on the poor or more cost-effective when indirectly targeted;
e) and to what extent it is better for agencies to sub-contract poverty projects to Northern or Southern NGOs, or undertake them with their own field staff or contracted consultants (expatriate or local).

These require judgements to be made concerning trade-offs between the scale of impact (numbers benefited), the degree of benefit obtained, and the timescale in which the benefit is delivered. They also require estimates not only of the resources required to benefit poor people but also the administrative, incentive and transaction costs involved (including skills) in delivery.

The balance of evidence on (a) is that conditionality does not work although it has not been applied much to pro-poor policies. The case for dialogue, instead of no dialogue, is self-evident, although the demands on skills and time will be considerable. Unfortunately, evidence on the relative 'bangs per buck' of different modes of intervention is very limited. Indeed little is known about the PR impact of *any* interventions. There is no evidence on (b). For (c) there is limited evidence on the effectiveness of donor project interventions but virtually none on sectoral approaches. Neither is there evidence on (d), the relative benefits of direct versus indirect targeting. Although there is more evidence on (e), few attempts have been made to compare NGO effectiveness with that of official aid donors. This lack of evidence inhibits any conclusions on the comparative effectiveness of these options. Some light, however, is thrown on part of choice (b) and especially on (d) in Chapters 5 to 7 below.

What is the record of donors in playing these roles?

Currently available information and insight from donors is scarce on the extent to which they play these roles and even more on their effectiveness. Something is known about the modes of intervention that different donors have or have not used and these are summarised in Table 3.1. They cover the use of country strategies, use of budgetary or programme aid funds, specific project interventions and the use of NGOs.

As regards the first role, the availability of European resource flows has undoubtedly made recovery or *economic growth* possible. However, all the evidence indicates that external aid flows assist the growth rate most effectively where the policy environment is appropriate. Growth is important for poverty reduction especially because distribution tends to be stable over time. A recent estimate (Bruno *et al.*, 1998) indicates that a 1 per cent growth in *per capita* income reduces poverty by 2 per cent (for example, the proportion of people living

Table 3.1 Modes of intervention of European agencies

Country level approaches	Programme aid/budgetary funds	Projects	NGOs
Denmark Recent focus on country strategies and increased emphasis on a constructive dialogue on strategies to reduce poverty.	Limited tradition for use of block grants in bilateral assistance although increasing trend during last two years. New focus on sector programming in place of projects.	Projects within social infrastructure (primarily health, water supply and sanitation) loom large within the Danida portfolio. However, only a little information is available on the share of basic services. Tradition of targeting individual projects to vulnerable groups and poor regions. However, little explicit concern for different dimensions of poverty. The role of targeting in the envisaged sector support programmes is being debated.	Channels a larger share of bilateral aid to NGOs than any other European donor, currently standing at 17 per cent.
EC For ACP, National Indicative Programmes Guidelines require dialogue with partners to determine a framework, commitments, priorities and conditions for implementing PR, including	Favours budgetary support with dialogue on reform of social policies. However, only recent focus on more basic social expenditures (for example, education and health) which	Screening for PR objectives in (larger) ACP projects but inhibited by time constraints. Procedures have encouraged participation for poor in design, but not identification so far.	Cofinancing with NGOs.

identification of poor groups. However, slow so far. For ALA guidelines, strategies and dialogue less developed.		ALA projects not yet effectively screened for PR objectives. Currently favours shift from grass-roots projects to emphasis on pro-poor sector interventions.	are more accessible to poor.
Finland New emphasis on bilateral dialogue on governance and human rights issues as key to PR. Choice of partners influenced by their records on PR.	Counterpart funds of mixed export credits have often been used for pro-poor social sector purposes. Commitment to the single-country strategy and donor coordination and joint financing of sector reform/development programmes in pro-poor sectors (education, health, agriculture, etc.). Development of the fiscal management systems of poor country governments on central and local levels is a precondition for financing.	New project design, monitoring and evaluation guidelines more sensitive to PR than the old guidelines. Plus user-friendly operational tools (checking lists, standard formats for contracts) which take into account PR. Disillusion with project mode and investment for poor.	4–6 per cent of Finnish ODA has been channelled through NGOs.
France No country strategy on PR for French aid agencies.	Budgetary aid not directed at PR. Structural adjustment finance not linked to PR conditions/objectives	No special mechanisms or procedures for orienting projects for PR.	Limited funding of NGOs.

(*Table 3.1 continued*)

Country level approaches	Programme aid/budgetary funds	Projects	NGOs
		However, there are some projects to aid micro enterprises and households via credit and savings systems. Social Development Funds (since 1994) targeted on groups disadvantaged by by devaluation and so on.	
Germany Country strategy and programming are important instruments. Dialogue not particularly prominent and no clear-cut pro-poor economic reforms identified.	German programme aid supports World Bank economic reforms but wants these to be pro-poor from beginning. Little German sectoral aid.	Self-help targeted projects. Main focus on project approach aimed at people below the official poverty line; special emphasis on women. Initiative must already exist, participation must be ensured and target group must make contribution of its own and make broad and sustainable impact. Classification of PR projects requires 50 per cent of beneficiaries to be poor. Cost/affordability not a criterion for services.	Increasing support of NGOs and use in management.
Italy Recent steps towards country instead of sector focus.		No evidence of Italian project procedures for	NGOs receive substantial support in Latin America

	PR orientation. Some major PR programmes, for example, Italian Aid Fund (FAI) programme for alleviation of hunger, poverty and infant mortality in LLDCs. Usually programmes are financed or co-financed with design and implementation by UNDP and World Bank.		but NGO support generally declining.
Netherlands Some country strategy but also major thematic (non-country) strategies, for example, urban poverty.	Little used except in India (for agricultural credits and informal education for women).	Most recent approaches more people-centred and flexible. Key features: participation and ownership; poor people to formulate and execute their own projects. Choice of projects is less important in countries which give high priority to distribution of welfare.	Increased direct funding of NGOs and through co-financing organizations in countries.
Spain Country approaches being developed but no poverty orientation explicit yet.	Rarely used and no public expenditure reform conditions.	No mechanisms for PR objectives in project cycle. Weak methods and no viability studies. Limited participation of beneficiaries in project cycle especially in early stages. Some projects are likely to benefit poor areas.	NGOs seen as most effective mechanisms for PR. Aid co-financing of NGOs based on criteria including PR.

(*Table 3.1 continued*)

Country level approaches	Programme aid/budgetary funds	Projects	NGOs
Sweden Strong focus on country strategy and dialogue on PR. Choice of partners will depend on will and capacity to implement policy against poverty. Seeks partnerships and open dialogue with civil society.	Aim to shift to programme aid based on domestic PR priorities but to continue with specific local participatory projects.	All project proposals must define their target and participant groups and indicate their impact on the poor. Some doubts about efficiency of project mode. Aims to make them more poor-participatory.	Where recipient government is not committed to PR, SIDA favours non-official aid channelled directly to the poor. NGOs receive 11 per cent of SIDA budget.
United Kingdom Country strategy for PR important especially where 'partnership' to be agreed. UK has reviewed the poverty content of its country strategy papers and recognized the need for substantial improvement.	Some past sector aid linked to reform but not PR-focused. New strategy favours sector-wide approaches in 'partnership' countries (for example, health).	Continued role for project interventions. Participatory approach emphasized, with community involvement. 'Process' not blueprint approach.	UK NGOs play major role (15 per cent of bilateral aid). Increased emphasis given to direct assistance to 'southern' NGOs.

below a certain level). Thus, poverty levels have fallen in some Asian countries with reasonably satisfactory growth rates (for example, India) but not generally in the African countries with poor growth performance (for example, Burkina, Zambia and Zimbabwe).

There is evidence that policy reforms have led to faster growth in various countries, though not systematically. Structural adjustment does not generally seem to have been damaging to the poor. Bourguignon and Morrisson (1992: 51) conclude that '*all* adjustment policies are, according to our simulations, more efficient (less fall in economic activity) and more equitable (smaller increases in poverty) than not adjusting'. A study by Sahn (1996: 21) of ten African countries also concludes that 'removing distortions in markets and altering relative prices ... generally improve income distribution and raise the income of the poor, albeit marginally, even in the absence of large supply responses'.

The contribution of the European agencies to the vital improvement of policy management was rather limited in the 1980s because (with the exception of the UK) they were slow to become aware of the need for this. They became more effective in terms of the provision of structural adjustment assistance and concern with improved domestic economic policies during the 1990s, especially in sub-Saharan Africa (Cox *et al.*, 1997: Chapter 6).

Second, what role have the European agencies played in generating a more *pro-poor policy environment*? The most direct role is through dialogue with partners on their attitudes, policies and expenditures in relation to poor people. Dialogue processes are not very transparent to the outside observer. It is known that budgetary (and programme) aid has not been used by European agencies for pro-poor policy reform or support, apart from the EC and perhaps the UK (see Table 2.1). Conditionality has rarely been used for pro-poor reforms such as public expenditure reorientation or land reform. There is increasing disillusion with the conditionality mode on the part of both independent observers (see Killick, 1998) and development cooperation agencies themselves. Hence there is little current enthusiasm to attach aid conditions related to specific pro-poor policy changes.

The agencies have for some time set themselves the aim of achieving a redistribution of public expenditure towards basic social services to which the poor are likely to gain greater access and of providing more resources for this purpose themselves. Yet the available evidence does not confirm that the allocation of public expenditure (subsidies) in a number of countries, favours basic services, nor did it appear to have shifted in that direction by the mid-1990s. Thus a recent IMF review (IMF, 1997: 19) of 23 countries with SAF/ESAF programmes over the period 1986–95 stated:

> a substantial re-allocation of expenditures in favour of higher education and curative health care did take place and the distribution of benefits at the end of the programme still disproportionately favoured the higher income groups. ... In the education sector the percentage of benefits accruing to the poorest quintile of the population averaged 13 per cent for eight SAF/ESAF countries compared with 32 per cent for the richest quintile. The benefit incidence could be improved [for the poor] by increasing the share of educational expenditures for primary education and imposing user charges for tertiary education in combination with a system of financial aid for poorer students.

A similar picture applies to health expenditure. While these outcomes reflect the outcomes of decisions made domestically within the countries themselves, they do suggest either that the external agencies (and not just the European ones) had not played an influential role or, if they had, that it had not been very effective. Moreover, the ten European agencies examined appear to have played an insignificant role in terms of their *own* spending commitments for basic health and education. DAC/OECD figures on donor commitments as a proportion of bilateral commitments on basic health on average (arithmetic mean) constituted only 2.4 per cent in 1991–92 and 2.8 per cent by 1996, although Denmark, the UK and Spain raised their contributions in 1996. For basic education it was only 1.3 per cent on average in 1991–92, although it had risen to 5 per cent in 1996 mainly due to a sharp rise in UK bilateral commitments (to 15 per cent). Of course, there are fungibility questions here, even if they had done more.

Some donors – the Netherlands, Germany and Denmark – indicated in 1996 that they would select countries on which to concentrate their aid on the basis of constructive dialogue with the recipient on policies and strategies to reach the poor. Sida's 1996 guidance makes selection for aid dependent on a country's capacity to implement an anti-poverty policy against poverty and its willingness to conduct an open dialogue with civil society. Germany, the Netherlands and Finland have for some time made their country allocation of resources depend, *inter alia,* on an explicit commitment to PR policies by poor country governments. More recently, both Sida and DFID (UK) have announced their intentions to enter a deeper, long-term partnership and provide more aid, and more flexible aid, to those governments of low-income countries which are committed to international targets for the elimination of poverty through pro-poor growth and appropriate policies. These existing and new approaches can be seen as a form of pressure for more domestic pro-poor policies, though it is difficult in principle to test their actual impact on allocation or their effectiveness in changing the policy environment, or premature to try to do so. Because of the inconclusive picture emerging on the European donors, this study looked at seven countries to see how far they have played a role in terms of dialogue on poverty-related issues and policies with their partners. The results of this assessment are set out in Chapter 4.

Third, some agencies made efforts to improve *domestic institutional* performance, for example through civil service reform, and some have been evaluated. However, it is seldom clear exactly how the poor have benefitted from this, although more efficient and accountable administrations must offer some benefits of this kind potentially. Where institutional reform has been conducted within the context of a sector programme, it has sometimes sought to improve the delivery of services to the poor. For example, DFID has recently been negotiating a sector reform programme in the health sector with the government of Orissa in India, the major objective of which is to improve institutional capacity in a way which brings concrete benefits for the poor.

Fourth, systematic and comprehensive information on the role of the agencies in *specific poverty-focused* interventions is generally not published, with the exception of the Netherlands and the UK and more recently others such as Finnida. The European Commission has sought to introduce a coding system, but so far has failed to implement it. No agencies publish the pattern of their operations for individual recipient countries. Surprisingly, no statistical records exist on the proportion of poverty-oriented interventions for Germany,

Sweden, the Netherlands or Denmark, although new monitoring systems are being developed in Denmark. There are no records for Spain, France or Italy, although the PR share is undoubtedly limited for these donors.

Nonetheless, the information available makes it possible to form a picture for a few agencies. The overall impression is that the European agencies' role is a fairly modest one measured simply by the share of specific poverty-focused interventions in their bilateral aid portfolios. The share for the Netherlands in 1994–95 was 19 per cent, while for the UK projects with a direct poverty focus accounted for only 11 per cent of expenditure which could be classified over the 1995–96 to 1996–97 period (up from 7 per cent three years earlier but set to rise considerably). Germany provides technical cooperation for self-help projects which tend to have a PR focus. The share of expenditure on this mode has risen from 8 per cent in 1991 to 19 per cent in 1995. An independent study for Italy estimates that poverty-focused expenditures were about 11 per cent of total grant aid in the 1980s but fell to 7 per cent by 1995 (Rhi-Sausi and Zupi, 1997). It is unlikely that the proportions will be significant for the EC, France or Spain.

Most donors have been predominantly project-oriented in their mode of intervention, but the balance between *directly targeted* and more *widely targeted* projects is not clear from donor records, except arguably for the Netherlands and the UK. Support to NGOs, as a channel for reaching poor people, has grown significantly, though it varies widely across donors. It accounts for a small proportion of French and EC funds, whereas the proportion for Denmark and the UK is 17 and 15 per cent respectively. Some donors contract NGOs to help implement their own projects, while others (for example, Finnida and EC) rely more on consultants. Currently there is some disillusion with *ad hoc* projects as a mode for effective PR, most obviously within Danida, Finnida and the European Commission. They have announced a switch from the *ad hoc* project to the sector programme approach, although it is unclear how far the sector approach will have a PR orientation. Chapters 5 and 6 set out the evidence on 90 specific European poverty-oriented interventions in the seven countries and their apparent effectiveness.

Fifth, a number of donors see support for innovative approaches to PR as a way of obtaining a 'multiplier' effect from aid funds, particularly in some countries outside of sub-Saharan Africa where aid budgets tend to be smaller relative to domestic resources. Donors are in a position to take the risks posed by innovative approaches which often cannot be afforded by governments/bureaucrats either financially, politically or in terms of career security. Innovation is, however, likely to fail and prove unsustainable unless it resonates with some people within government, and thus does not conflict with promoting ownership. There are examples of donors helping to accelerate change or slightly tilting the balance in favour of change, but little systematic evidence exists as to the extent to which donor approaches to PR have been innovative and successfully so. Some evidence is explored in Chapter 6, drawing on the seven country case studies.

Summary

The European external agencies have played a role in terms of supporting growth and policies for adjustment to achieve general economic recovery/growth, though the extent to which this has trickled down to reduce poverty levels has depended on the level of growth rates and the initial distribution conditions. The agencies' role in dialogue to achieve a more pro-poor policy environment in partner countries is not apparent nor have most of them used budgetary support for pro-poor objectives. They have contributed little of their own funds for basic social expenditures which tend to benefit poor people disproportionately, nor do they appear to have influenced a reorientation of domestic public expenditures within these countries in this direction. While they have been involved in a range of specific poverty-focused interventions mainly via *ad hoc* projects, these in aggregate have constituted a rather modest proportion of their bilateral portfolios, even for the more committed. Some agencies have used NGOs on a large scale to reach poor people, while others have not significantly followed this course. There has been some institutional support for improved administration and some innovative interventions, but evidence on precise benefits to the poor is unclear. Given the patchy picture available from the European aid agencies themselves about their role and modes of intervention, this study has carried out field studies of their operations and effectiveness in seven poor countries (Burkina Faso,

Bolivia, Nepal, India, Tanzania, Zimbabwe and Zambia). This focuses mainly on their country strategies and dialogue and their specific poverty-focused interventions, but does not cover the role and effectiveness of NGOs. The evidence from these country studies is set out in Chapters 4 to 6 and some new thinking is reviewed in Chapter 7.

4
The Approach to Poverty Reduction in the Country Programmes

What donors actually do: starting questions

This chapter does not start with a 'model' of how the agencies ought to go about their country operations if they are serious about poverty reduction. However, five questions are posed about their recent country operations which are considered to bear significantly on effectiveness and indeed which reflect the actual formal policies of some agencies.

- Do the European agencies have a clear conception of who the poor are? Do they identify and target the poor by geographical area or socio-economic group?
- Are their operational strategies or specific interventions designed on the basis of participatory processes, involving a wide or narrower domestic community in decisions?
- Do they engage in dialogue with their partners on how to reach poor people most effectively through policies and measures?
- What is the nature of their portfolios of interventions to achieve their poverty goals and what modes or instruments have they chosen to implement them effectively?
- Do they try to ensure that local governments and communities 'own' their poverty initiatives?

To test actual practices and some answers to these questions the activities of the main European agencies operating within them were examined in seven countries (Bolivia, Burkina Faso, India, Nepal, Tanzania, Zambia and Zimbabwe). Those donors without serious poverty objectives obviously did not offer much evidence. We have concentrated here on the EC, Denmark, Finland, France, the Netherlands, Sweden, Germany and the UK (see Table 4.1).

Country programming and strategies: PR orientation

We begin with the questions about how the European development agencies incorporated PR objectives into their country strategies.

To pursue a poverty-focused country programme makes a prior assumption that the agencies will have a predominantly country programming approach with regularly formulated country strategies which guide their actions and for which the programme managers are accountable and motivated. In fact, some bilateral agencies, for example France and Spain, have not used explicit country strategies and programming as instruments and hence do not incorporate PR priorities and directions. While the Netherlands has largely switched from country programming towards thematic programming (rural development, urban poverty, education and so on) most European aid agencies, namely, in Sweden, the UK, the EC (more for DGVIII than for DGI), Denmark, Finland and Germany unambiguously, use the country strategy and programming instrument. Italy, since the 1992 reorganization, has shifted to management by geographical areas.

Table 4.1 EU donor country strategies and dialogue

Bolivia (Denmark, EC, Germany, Netherlands, Spain, Sweden)
Denmark, Germany, the Netherlands and Sweden have a reasonably clear PR strategy. They focus on the poorest regions and sometimes on indigenous groups. The EC and Spain have no PR strategy, although the EC implemented integrated rural development projects in poor areas and more recently has initiated a large food security programme which is considered promising. Only Germany and Denmark pursue fairly deep and regular dialogue covering policies.

Burkina Faso (Belgium, Denmark, France, Germany, Netherlands)
Both Germany and the Netherlands conducted studies of poverty context, identified poor groups and formulated a PR strategy. This was largely an internal exercise for Germany, but the Netherlands made additional efforts to support Burkinabe policies on PR. There was little dialogue at national level (both presented rather than discussed their own strategies), but considerable dialogue at project level, and for the Dutch, at sector level. On the other hand, France, the largest donor, had no PR strategy or dialogue and virtually no targeting of the poor. The EC performed no poverty analysis,

(Table 4.1 continued)

had no poverty objective or target groups, nor any dialogue on these issues. Belgium was similar but is now formulating a PR strategy.

India (EC, Denmark, Germany, Netherlands, Sweden, UK)
The PR objective is weakened by the need to take care of business interests (for example, Denmark and Sweden). Nature and causes of poverty are rarely analysed (though some sector reports by Danida, some state analyses by Netherlands, and UK has embarked on some analysis). Country strategies were not consultative and were entirely top-down and donor-driven. These may become participatory for Sida, Danida (post-review) and the UK. Strategies did not appear very operational. The link between the donors' PR objective and their current and planned specific interventions was weak.

It was rare for poverty to be discussed in depth as a generic issue in any dialogue channels. However, Germany has been most effective in bilateral dialogue with the Indian authorities in gaining their acceptance of the principle of self-help in its PR interventions. Donors see themselves generally as having little leverage, given the relative paucity of their resources in the all-India context of poverty, although opportunities may have been missed. Nevertheless, dialogue is opening up, especially at a State level where donors have more clout. European donors, led by the UNDP, also began discussions on social development at the last Consultative Group meeting. Sectoral approaches are increasingly prominent, partly reflecting dissatisfaction with the impact of projects, but were not necessarily linked to PR. Conditionality was often applied with respect to decentralization of power to local government (particularly the Panchayat Raj) and at project level. Indian partner institutions were encouraged to adopt a participatory approach aimed at demand creation.

Nepal (EC, Denmark, France, Germany, UK)
Donors conduct little poverty analysis. Only GTZ and the Nordic donors had a relatively comprehensive PR strategy. EC, France and the UK lacked a poverty focus and there was no donor coordination or consensus on PR. No poverty-related conditions were applied to aid. The government of Nepal lacked both commitment and a clear strategy on poverty reduction. Any dialogue at national policy level lacked focus on PR, though far more useful dialogue took place at sectoral level, especially for GTZ and Danida who sought to understand local perspectives. There was limited targeting of poor groups, especially indigenous ethnic and low-caste groups and targeting was discouraged until recently by government.

Tanzania (Danida, Finland, France, Italy, Spain, UK)
Some bilateral agencies, for example, in France, Spain and Italy, scarcely claim to have PR objectives, focusing instead on image, diplomacy and commercial interests, but the rest promoted PR. Danida had the clearest PR strategy. Donors differ in their targeting strategy: some favour very specific

(Table 4.1 continued)

---

target group identification, for example, the Dutch, Finns, Germans, and the UK, but others considered targeting a waste of time since 'all the people are poor'. The Nordics take part in fairly active dialogue with the authorities on the causes of poverty and best approaches for joint action. The agenda on PR is set by dialogue between the World Bank/UNDP and the government.

Zambia (Denmark, EC, Finland, Germany, Netherlands, Sweden, UK)
The process of donor country strategy preparation was largely internal and non-consultative. Although all donors saw PR as a major (or their major) objective, there was little analysis of the poverty context, apart from efforts by Denmark and Sweden. Donors did not identify poor target groups, and were unclear on what they meant by poverty, although most (Denmark, Finland, Netherlands and Sweden) considered women as a specific target group. Five donors considered support for the economic reform process as a top priority. Next most emphasized were social sectors, with particular attention to urban poor, rural development (smallholders and forestry) and women. The main mode of intervention was projects, though three donors (UK, Sweden and Denmark particularly strongly) focused on sector approaches. Any dialogue was at the sectoral level for Denmark, Finland and Netherlands.

Zimbabwe (Denmark, EC, Germany, Netherlands, Sweden, UK)
Germany and the Netherlands lacked commitment to PR. The four donors with more serious PR intentions (Denmark, EC, Sweden and the UK) had not undertaken any systematic analysis of the poverty context, except for a special assessment of the problems of women. The UK and EC did not specify a PR strategy and Sweden was not precise. Poor target groups were not identified, except by Denmark. Donor country strategies were usually discussed with government officials, though they tended to be top-down processes. Only Sweden undertook wider consultation and sought consensus building. For all four, there was limited coherence between PR goals and chosen interventions.

Sources: de Boisdeffre, 1998a; Loquai and Van Hove, 1997; Freres and Rhi-Sausi, 1999; Cox *et al.*, 2000; Gsaenger and Voipio, 1999; Voipio and Hoebink, 1999; Saasa *et al.*, 1998; Killick *et al.*, 1998.

The experience from the seven country studies, which is summarized in Table 4.1, leads to the following general points:

- Few European agencies had done much work on the domestic poverty situation and only a few had drawn up a clearly formulated poverty-oriented country strategy with precise identification of poor groups.
- Country strategies were almost always drawn up by the donors in a 'top-down' way, with little consultation within the recipient country. However, since the fieldwork for this study was carried

out in 1997 some agencies (for example, DFID, Sida) have committed themselves to consult civil society organizations in drawing up their country strategies.

- Agencies indicated little clear prioritization between the PR objective and other development objectives and (often conflicting) commercial objectives.
- Strategies were sometimes too vague to provide operational guidance and they provide no benchmarks for judgement about the quality of implementation.

There were some exceptions to the generally weak procedures. Thus, the Netherlands in Burkina Faso had a PR strategy which identified poor groups clearly. Germany had made efforts at targeting in Burkina Faso and in Nepal, Sida and Finnida to some extent in Tanzania, and the Nordic donors and the Netherlands in Bolivia. In Zimbabwe, Sweden set something of a model by taking local consultations seriously in its country analysis and policy formulation. It consulted extensively within the partner country not only with the central and line Ministries but also with NGOs and a range of independent expert people outside government. These wider discussions covered issues central to PR like decentralization, the land issue and small-scale enterprise.

In addition, some donors are in transition in their operations and may be improving their focus. Thus, the European Commission (DGVIII) has recently circulated guidance on how to incorporate PR objectives into national programming (for the Lomé Convention countries). The UK in its 1997 White Paper points to measures to sharpen up its focus on the poor in its country programmes and to open up the process to wider consultation. In Zimbabwe, where donor efforts were rather weak in this field, some donors, for example, Danida and DFID, were making changes to improve matters.

Dialogue on PR – bilateral and collective

In relation to dialogue on PR issues, the main points to emerge from the seven country studies (Table 4.1) are the following:

- Bilateral dialogue on PR with the recipient is generally weak and variable.
- Dialogue at the national/macro policy level on poverty-related strategies and policies appears negligible at official level. (Some

exceptions were Sweden in Zimbabwe, the Nordic donors in Tanzania, Germany in Bolivia and the Netherlands in Burkina Faso.) However, it is possible that some dialogue has taken place at a high political level between Ministers from the donor and the partner countries, which it was not possible for this study to observe.

- There is very limited cooperation and coordination between European agencies themselves on these issues or even exchange of information and lessons of experience. Some exceptions include the Netherlands, the Nordic donors, and UNDP in Tanzania, and the UK and the EC in India.
- There were some cases of regular dialogue with the partners on issues relevant to poverty at the meso/sectoral level, for example, Germany and Denmark in India and Nepal, Germany and the Netherlands in Burkina Faso. Sometimes donors differ substantially in their perspectives on poverty-oriented policies.
- There are examples of donors adopting a position on social policies as a counterweight to the more economic perspective seen to be taken by the World Bank in Consultative Groups, for example, on Nepal and Bolivia.
- Where national commitment to PR has not been strong, donors have sought pro-poor alliances at the intermediate level of government, for example, in line Ministries.
- Conditionality is rarely a feature of poverty-focused strategies. However, in India some donors have made decentralization a condition of aid (for example, for the Panchayat Raj). This is a policy change that can potentially be helpful to PR activity but does not often guarantee it.
- While commitment to 'local ownership' is an ideal for several donors, few have 'bought into' locally initiated PR schemes in the seven case studies (exceptions include EC and UK, among others, involvement in the domestically owned District Primary Education programme in India, and GTZ and Danida 'buying into' national NGO PR schemes in Nepal).

Poverty dialogue: opportunities for and constraints on donors

The weakness in bilateral dialogue, and the lack of collective dialogue on poverty issues except sometimes at sectoral level, seems to undermine any expectation that European donors can have significant influence on the course of PR in partner countries. Clearly there are considerable opportunities for more fruitful and effective dialogue. Nevertheless, these do pose difficulties and dilemmas for aid agencies. The following sub-sections reflect on some of these.

Dialogue at the national/macro level on poverty orientation

There are opportunities for such dialogue at the national or macro level. Although this is perhaps the most difficult level, especially for bilateral donors, it should not be shirked. The key requirements for pursuing dialogue at national level seem to be the following:

- The development agencies need to do much more 'homework' and develop a precise and well-elaborated idea of what constitutes a pro-poor strategy for each partner country in which they have a significant stake.[1] This might be done collectively, but in any case, they need to form a consensus view in order to have a collective discussion with the partner government. This is clearly more important where the partner has no real PR strategy.

- To help the partner to formulate a possible strategy ideally requires strengthening its technocratic capacity, which donors do not seem to have done systematically. Where the partner has a PR strategy it is still desirable for the donors also to have a clear independent idea, otherwise it is difficult for them to judge whether they should be supporting the local strategy or seeking to influence a change in its character in order to support it. This is particularly important if the partners read the signs and produce a rather cosmetic response to demands for a poverty strategy in order to maintain aid flows.

- The ultimate objective must be agreement or consensus on a 'single strategy' for the country. This has for some time been the recommendation of the SPA Working Group and has the support of a number of European agencies, for example, Finnida and DFID. It has to be a collective consensus-seeking process and cannot proceed sensibly on a unilateral basis.

- There needs to be an institution, institutions or institutional mechanisms on which such dialogue or exchange of views can focus nationally (and of course involving high-level political involvement if it is to be worthwhile).

The opportunities and dilemmas can be illustrated from four country cases: Zimbabwe, Nepal, India and Bolivia.

In *Zimbabwe*, there is a government that scores strongly on 'ownership' and on governance capacity, yet poverty reduction does not rank high in the priorities of the current political regime. While the Office of the President might be the most obvious focus for national dialogue, it has, not surprisingly, been resistant to ideas of reform. The Ministry of Finance is an alternative option but it claims that it lacks the expertise. To focus on relevant line Ministries – such as the Ministry of Public Service, Labour and Social Welfare or the Ministry of Health – risks focusing on specific programmes rather than overarching strategies and is likely to hinder integrated and comprehensive solutions, spanning several ministries. If there were a Planning Ministry or a Cabinet Committee focused on poverty or a central poverty unit, this could be a dialogue focus for external agencies. However, a lack of political will means that such institutions do not exist. An independent wider forum for debate on poverty has recently been created in Zimbabwe, but, although useful as a way of bringing civic as well as government opinion to bear on these issues, it is too far removed from the seat of power for donors to be able to use it to press for policy reorientation effectively. So far donors have not pressed for change and are seen by local opinion as unwilling to rock the political boat. Yet, given Zimbabwe's actual aid dependence (aid was estimated at 39 per cent of investment in 1994 compared with 34 per cent in the rest of sub-Saharan Africa), donors are, in principle, in a position to take up a much more active stance to press for more to be done for the poor and to seek an institutional focus for this within the Zimbabwe government machine (Killick *et al.*, 1998).

In *Nepal*, the external agencies face a situation where there has been a whole series of rapidly changing governments that have been 'aid-dependent' in attitude. The agencies talk of recipient country 'ownership' of policies and wait for the government of Nepal to set out its perspective and strategy. So far the government has not invited the donor community to talk about poverty issues. Aid dependence has resulted in an unwillingness on the part of Nepalese governments to take charge and 'own' policies, which, ironically, is seen as risking donor displeasure. They do not have a clear vision of a PR strategy and indeed they may not particularly want one.

For example, the government has not been enthusiastic in the past for development agencies to focus attention on the low caste and ethnic groups that constitute much of the poor. Policy analysis is hampered by the institutional weaknesses of policy centres such as the National Planning Commission, the Ministry of Finance, and the planning cells of line ministries. There are matching weaknesses on the part of the external agencies and a remarkable lack of coordination among them, partly stemming from inter-agency rivalry. There has been little willingness to meet to exchange experiences, and no indication of a willingness to prepare a 'single country strategy' jointly with the government (Gsaenger and Voipio, 1999: Chapter 15).

In *Tanzania* the 1990s have seen two parallel, partly mutually supportive but also partly competing, processes of PR agenda setting. The bilateral European development agencies have played only a marginal role in both processes. One involved the World Bank in sponsoring an ambitious round of commissioned research and national PR workshops, resulting in a set of high quality analytical papers, but rather weak national ownership. The second was led by UNDP, which drew on its broader links with the Tanzanian political framework, establishing a Poverty Eradication Unit within the Vice President's office, charged with drafting a National Poverty Eradication Strategy. The Unit initiated a slow but widely participatory process where the characteristics and causes of Tanzanian poverty were identified by several hundreds of participants in PR workshops in various parts of the country. The slow process has finally resulted in the National Poverty Eradication Strategy, which was approved by the Cabinet in 1998. Several bilateral donors have participated in and supported this process as well, including the Netherlands and Finland. The Poverty Eradication Unit and UNDP have started a new round of regional consultations to try to develop a series of poverty indicators appropriate to the various areas of Tanzania.

There is clearly scope for European donors to have a greater role and influence, for example in reorienting public expenditure in a pro-poor direction. Chapter 3 indicated how regressive social expenditures were in most of the study countries. All of them except India are highly aid-dependent, with development cooperation financing a high proportion of government budgets. Even in India, the development agencies should find it possible to play a more constructive role by agreeing a common approach at State level. The agencies should focus on shifting patterns of spending towards primary education and away from tertiary levels, towards poor districts, towards primary and preventive health, towards less subsidization of the better-off in water services and towards better targeting of domestic PR measures, and so on. This requires them to form a consensus in their approach and to play a role as an 'external lobby' in a local context which lacks sufficiently organized and powerful indigenous interests and pressures on behalf of poor people and their interests.

Dialogue at sectoral level

There is more scope for dialogue on poverty issues and public policy change at the sectoral/meso level. Development agency financing may be quite significant for particular sectors, thus giving agencies better access to decision-makers. Government resources are often so stretched that bureaucrats have little time available for strategic planning. They may also be unable to afford the rates demanded even by national experts. In this context agency technical cooperation may be well received and influential. Finally, governments are not monoliths, and particular sectoral ministries may well present a PR commitment that is lacking at the national level or may contain individual senior officials who are highly committed to the poor.

There are some positive examples of such dialogue taking place, with bilateral agencies such as Danida, Sida and the Netherlands taking the lead. Ironically, although the European Commission's aid programme has the largest resources available for sector-wide approaches, it lacks the technical expertise to allow it to play the lead role in sectoral dialogue. India provides a good example, however, of the Commission and, in this case, the UK demonstrating the vision to cooperate on health-sector reform, whereby the UK's greater technical expertise in health backed up the Commission's Euros. Those donors such as the Netherlands and the UK, with a staff allocation pattern which places sector experts permanently in the field, find that this provides them with an asset which gives them disproportionate influence in national-level sectoral reform processes, such as education sectoral reform in Tanzania.

Opportunities and constraints can be illustrated from the India and Bolivia case studies. India is an interesting case. Most donors consider that India's lack of aid dependence makes it hard for them to exert influence through policy dialogue at the central level. Recently, however, the Government of India has become more open to donors conducting dialogue directly with State governments, where donor resources in individual sectors carry more weight. Some donors are beginning to engage in pro-poor dialogue with State governments in health, education and agriculture. Developing stronger State-level partnerships may result in higher levels of trust and commitment and in donors improving their understanding of the political processes determining budgetary allocations. The fact that UK assistance over 15 years to the primary education sector in Andhra Pradesh was accompanied by a fall in the State budgetary allocation to primary education underlines the importance of effective dialogue and partnership.

In Tanzania, the Netherlands and Finland have made major impressions on shifting the policies and attitudes of district and regional-level authorities in a more participatory and pro-poor direction through their support for integrated rural development programmes. In Bolivia, the government has shown its commitment to PR through various broad and more targeted programmes. The depth of the dialogue with European donors has depended on the degree of their commitment and it has been shallower for Spain and the EC, for example, than for Germany and the Netherlands. The latter have pursued dialogue on sectoral programmes like education, with the help of some advisers in planning and development-related Ministries.[2] There is growing scope for dialogue between external agencies and decentralized administrations. These include regional departments (Prefectures) and also municipalities which have competencies over various social sector policies at local level, such as health centres and schools, as well as through bodies like the Social Investment Fund (IFS). Sectoral dialogue with these bodies has the potential to bring donors closer to local and regional realities.

Ownership

Some dilemmas

Most of the European agencies now subscribe to the view that policies and programmes for poverty reduction must be 'owned' by the domestic authorities and the people themselves if they are to be effective. In effect, an external agency should then formally choose a 'hands-off' approach rather than a 'hands-on' approach to the

country. The dilemmas and the facts of the situation are well illustrated by the following review of the situation in Tanzania (Voipio
and Hoebink, 1999: 73–74).

A *'hands-off'* approach is possible if the donors trust the capacity
of either the Tanzanian government, the NGOs or the market to
allocate the aid resources so that the poorer segments of the population will also benefit. The 'Tanzania-in-the-driver's-seat' approach,
advocated most strongly by Sweden and Norway, focuses its energies
on an intensive dialogue with, and capacity-building process within,
the central government of Tanzania, hoping that a better organized,
more competent and more accountable *government* will in future be
able to allocate the aid resources more effectively and more equitably to the benefit of poor Tanzanians than any parallel donor
machinery could ever do. Modified versions of the neo-liberal narra-
tive accept that the government too has a role to play and that the
donors need therefore to help the government to analyse and to
change its policies in order to shift the distribution of benefits
towards the poorer segments of the population.

In reality, none of the donors has as yet trusted the capacity (or
will) of the Tanzanian government, the NGOs or the market enough
to dare to adopt a pure 'hands-off' approach. Different versions of
these approaches have been much more common. In all 'hands-on'
approaches the donor considers itself more 'pro-poor' than the government or the market, and therefore takes on itself part at least of
the responsibility to allocate the aid resources so that the poorer
Tanzanians receive an equal (or disproportionately larger) share of
the benefits. A fairly strong distrust of the capacity and will of the
central government of Tanzania to cater for the needs of the poor is
an essential characteristic in the (implicit) thinking of those donors
who prefer to support participatory projects and programmes in the
isolated rural areas of the country. The poor people there are
believed to know their needs and development opportunities better
than the bureaucrats in the central government. On the other hand,
the strongest advocates of participatory approaches have ended up
realizing that the replication and scaling up of the participatory
processes can neither be expected to be administered in the longer
run by the (prohibitively costly) expatriate facilitators nor be left to
be directed by the market forces of demand and supply alone, but
that there is an important role to be played by the (local and

central) government authorities. Therefore, without exception, all the participatory interventions supported by donors in Tanzania have ended up focusing a substantial proportion of their efforts on improving the attitudes and capacities of the Tanzanian civil servants to enable them to play their role in supporting the 'bottom-up' initiatives of the poor members of their communities.

Buying into local anti-poverty schemes

On the same 'ownership' criteria, donors should seek to 'buy into' anti-poverty schemes which have been devised locally by national and local governments. However, in the seven countries examined, there has been an apparent reluctance among donors to finance poverty-focused programmes designed by governments, one example being the 'cold shoulder' they showed to the Zimbabwean Government's Poverty Alleviation Action Programme (PAAP) (see Killick *et al.*, 1998). In this case, and in others too, donors have sometimes argued that 'home-grown' schemes are seriously flawed, but they might respond by providing technical support to strengthen such programmes rather than simply rejecting them. However, there are a few examples of donors buying into local schemes, such as donor financing of the nationally owned District Primary Education Programme in India (Cox *et al.*, 1999). Sometimes the different approaches of donors to working closely with government reflect their different conclusions or ideological positions, as illustrated by the differing tactics of Germany and Denmark in Nepal. Germany has clearly become frustrated with the weak capacity and what it perceives as anti-poor attitudes of the government of Nepal, and has opted to work through poverty-oriented national NGOs instead. Danida, on the other hand, appears to believe that sustainable PR cannot be achieved without building capacity and accountability within the state machinery. It has therefore insisted on supporting capacity-building measures within central and local government.

Specific interventions: patterns of the European development agencies

Sample country PR portfolios

What is the pattern of an external agency's country portfolios from the point of view of their poverty intentions and effects? Donor interventions can be classified according to how directly focused they are on benefiting poor groups: directly, indirectly or other (see p. 81 for a detailed definition).

It was possible to assess the balance of interventions for a number of the major donors in Zimbabwe, Zambia and India (see Table 4.2). *Zambia* reveals that development agencies have given a very low priority to interventions with a direct or indirect focus on poverty reduction. On average (unweighted mean) the proportion was about 26 per cent, though Finland's share was 50 per cent, Germany's 43 per cent, while the UK's was only 5 per cent. In *Zimbabwe*, the five

Table 4.2 Patterns of specific interventions (% of donor's bilateral portfolio) 1997

Country/Donor	Directly targeted	Indirectly targeted	Other
Zimbabwe			
Denmark	1	14	86
EC	16	7	77
Germany	0	35	65
Sweden	25	25	50
UK	0	51	49
Average	*9*	*31*	*60*
Zambia			
Denmark	3	27	70
EU	1	15	84
Finland	6	44	49
Germany	5	38	57
Netherlands	0	21	79
Sweden	3	11	86
UK	3	2	95
Average	*3*	*23*	*74*
India			
Denmark	21	42	37
Netherlands[a]	15 (29)	25 (51)	60 (20)
Sweden	16	47	37
UK	32	6	62
Average	*21*	*30*	*49*

Note: [a]The figures in parentheses refer to shares of Dutch project aid only; about half of all Dutch disbursements are for debt relief and thus qualify as 'other'. (Averages are the unweighted mean of the individual donors).

European donors had a higher mean of 40 per cent of their portfolios in PR. Two, the UK and Sida, had about 50 per cent of their country portfolio in the PR category compared with lower levels for Denmark (15 per cent), the EC (23 per cent) and Germany (35 per cent). In *India*, there was evidence of an increasing emphasis by development agencies on poverty-reducing interventions and, if anything, the table understates the proportions by including a number of older projects. The mean proportion of interventions with a direct or indirect orientation was 51 per cent and exceeded 60 per cent for Denmark and Sweden. The UK had the highest share of directly targeted interventions (and also the highest share of unfocused ones). Clearly, there is a huge variation between agencies in the same country and across different countries. This suggests that there is ample scope for donors to increase the share of their country programmes that have a demonstrable link with their PR goals.

Few external agency interventions are directly targeted on the poor

It is not always clear what the donors' individual strategies are with respect to the targeting of their interventions. Danida's new policy seems to be that where there are no pro-poor macro policies it will focus its efforts on targeting poor regions and peoples (Udsholt, 1997: 43). Sida proposes to continue with specifically targeted projects with greater efforts at participation of the poor. Both Finnida and the EC seem to be more doubtful about pursuing interventions at grass-roots level in future. The UK's 1997 White Paper emphasizes that UK interventions should have a demonstrable link with PR, but its preference for budgetary aid and sector-wide approaches suggests that the bulk of its interventions in future are likely to fall into the 'indirect' or 'other' classification.

It was unclear from the case studies what conditions prompted the agencies to focus or target directly as opposed to relying on broader or indirect approaches. The agencies revealed no tactical approach similar to that favoured by the World Bank, which has a policy, though not necessarily a practice, of narrow targeting in countries where there is good capacity and poverty is concentrated, and wider targeting where this is absent.

Table 4.2 indicates that in practice the degree of *direct targeting* was very low, with the average proportion of the total bilateral portfolio of five major European donors to Zimbabwe standing at 9 per cent, although Sweden's total was far higher at 25 per cent. In Zambia for seven European donors, the directly targeted proportion was only 3 per cent, while in India it was far higher, at 21 per cent. Systematic information on the whole of donor portfolios is not available for the other countries.

From *Ad hoc* projects to sector programmes for PR?

European development agencies have largely pursued their poverty objectives through *ad hoc* projects. Although there has been some shift towards sector-wide interventions especially in Africa, this has not yet become a predominant mode of intervention. Several agencies are shifting partially towards a more sectoral mode of aid delivery, though not always with PR objectives in mind.

In *Zimbabwe*, the Nordic donors have been especially interested in sectoral interventions in sectors of interest to the poor like agriculture, education and health and sometimes land reform and water supply. The European Commission has provided budget support to the Ministries of Health and Education for buying essential supplies such as medicines, textbooks and furniture. However, it was not clear how far this had a poverty focus and monitoring the poverty impact was made difficult because of problems of fungibility of the funds provided. No donors have so far given support to the Zimbabwean Government's own Poverty Alleviation Action Plan (PAAP).

In *Zambia*, the health sector is becoming increasingly coordinated through sectoral programming with a focus on basic aid care and health management. Denmark, Finland and Sweden have been involved in programmes of health care management and decentralization, as well as primary education. Germany has remained predominantly in the project mode, but the UK has recently ventured out of the project mode for PR into sectoral programming in health and population. Few donors, however, are currently seeking to make it their predominant mode.

In *Burkina Faso*, there has been some sector-wide budget support linked to reform by donors such as the EC, as well as coordinated rural health programmes led by Germany, basic education led by France and rural development and food security led by the Netherlands.

In *Tanzania* the Nordic donors, the Netherlands, the EC and the World Bank have become interested in supporting sectoral development programmes in health, education, roads and agriculture as well as other essential reform programmes covering fiscal management, the civil service and local government. In all of these, PR has been an implicit objective. Their main features have been Tanzanian ownership and coordinated donor support through administrative channels with operational responsibility in Tanzanian hands. In the education sector, the level of government ownership has actually been undermined by the high level of donor interest, coupled with the weak administration of the Ministry of Education which finds it impossible to cope with the weight of studies, papers and recommendations submitted by over 50 donor-funded consultants, resulting in delays in the sector reform process and reduced ownership.

In *India* donor sectoral strategies have been weak, though there is growing interest in this mode of intervention. The EC and the UK have supported the government's District Primary Education Programme in Madhya Pradesh and Andhra Pradesh/West Bengal respectively, though it is the World Bank which has provided the vast share of resources. The same donors, including the World Bank, have also supported the emerging Reproductive and Child Health sectoral programme, and it is likely that other European agencies will wish to be involved. The European agencies are enthusiastic about developing partnership directly with State governments, and it is likely that significant sector reform programmes will develop here. The UK is already funding a reform programme in the power sector and a health sector programme in Orissa, and is finalizing the details of an urban poverty sector programme with the Government of Andhra Pradesh.

In *Nepal* Danida has been a strong advocate of sectoral approaches and has succeeded in attracting other donors (the EC, the World Bank, the Asian Development Bank, Japan, Finland and Norway), as well as the rather reluctant Government of Nepal, to engage in sectoral programmes. In *Bolivia*, GTZ supported a wide public health programme via regional health authorities on a long-term basis.

Overall, however, despite some rethinking and a partial shift in direction by donors, sector-wide programmes involving budgetary and institutional support remain relatively rare as a mode for poverty reduction and *ad hoc* project interventions remain the dominant mode. This is an important issue for a future intensified PR effort by donors (the pros and cons are discussed in more depth in Chapter 7). The evidence on effectiveness and the lessons from the past of donor interventions, largely project mode, are examined in Chapters 5 and 6. It should be added, however, that donors such as the European Commission and the UK have recently stated their desire to shift increasingly towards a sectoral reform model wherever the institutional and monitoring capacities permit and, in the UK's case, where commitment to PR is demonstrated.

Decentralization and poverty reduction

The European agencies seem to be largely at one in pursuing a policy of government decentralization in virtually all the seven countries. Decentralization may be seen as a necessary but not a sufficient condition for promoting greater official responsiveness to the needs of the poor and improved access for them. There are also risks associated with decentralization, since the result may be the empowerment of local elites who may be even less motivated than national elites to promote PR reduction. Finally, it should be noted that the sectoral approach described above may, in practice, be in conflict with the decentralization imperative, since sectoral approaches have thus far mainly involved the central government ministries, which have tended to be reluctant to devolve responsibility to the regions.

It is ironic that, despite their vocal support for decentralization reforms by governments, the donor agencies themselves very often bypass the newly created local authorities in implementing their interventions, creating donor funded enclaves of excellence (or otherwise). There are at least three explanations for this. First, local authorities often remain very weak, and when donors balance their desire to support decentralization with the imperative to show results, the latter wins out. Second, decentralization does not necessarily guarantee concern for the poor, and anti-poverty interventions may, it is thought, be better implemented outside of the local power structure. The final reason is quite possibly the most important, namely that lukewarm support for decentralization reflects old habits which die hard. Most donors have traditionally retained high levels of direct control over the implementation of projects and programmes, and some are even accused of micro-management.

Thorough decentralization implies a more 'hands-off' approach to which donors take time to adjust. It requires replacing direct control with a system of agreed targets and an appropriate monitoring mechanism which enjoys the confidence of both parties. That said, there are nonetheless a range of examples of agency support for decentralization from the seven country studies, which are discussed later.

The ambivalence is well illustrated by the case of *Tanzania*. Here, it was the World Bank which blazed the trail, making decentralization of basic health and education management (and cost sharing) a condition for the disbursement of its large social sector credit. The major European bilateral donors initially objected to this, but ultimately relaxed their objections. The Dutch, the Danes, the Finns have begun to prepare the way for decentralization though their programme of 'District-based support to Primary Education', as well as through their support to the Local Government Reform Programme.

In *Burkina Faso*, the recently launched national decentralization programme has an explicit focus on poverty reduction. In *Zambia*, donors are highly critical of the failure to implement decentralization effectively, with few resources and decisions being devolved to local level. The central government remains extremely weak and local government institutions are even weaker. The Burkinabe and Zambian experience and the Tanzanian *Ujamaa* policy show that decentralization of funds and devolution of decision-making powers to the local level, a crucial element, often lag behind and thus limit the potential positive impact. The result may be that responsibility for services needed by the poor is transferred to weak local governments, but without their gaining the corresponding resources or the authority to tax. This can lead to a situation where donors support decentralization in general, but try to bypass the newly created local authorities, which are more interested in their own survival than in the fate of the poor.

In *Nepal*, Danida and UNDP in particular have played a leading role in promoting decentralization. In general, direct cooperation with NGOs at a local level has a long history, and has been adopted by donors as a means of avoiding top-down implementation of aid and corruption. Opportunities to disburse aid through this channel multiplied, with community or village-based NGOs mushrooming in the last decades. However, experience has shown that the lack of pro-poor aid implementation also remains a problem for this form of decentralized cooperation, with many NGOs being 'hijacked' by the well-to-do.

In some more recent donor-supported interventions in *India*, a significant role is envisaged for the Panchayati Raj Institutions (PRIs), which have been strengthened since 1992. However, it is too early to be sure that these will take account of the interests and needs of the poor because the PRIs mirror the general power structure and tend to be dominated by landowners, upper castes and men. Also, the outcome is likely to vary a great deal from place to place and State to State. In the case of *Bolivia*, some donors seem to have contributed substantially to the implementation of administrative and political decentralization as well as the Public Participation Law.

On the whole, the information available from the case studies provides little evidence on the effects of decentralization policies on poverty reduction. There was a consensus that a diversification of aid channels and direct cooperation with authorities or organizations at the local level can allow for a better targeting of aid, because of their proximity to poverty groups. However, there were strong doubts about the effectiveness of decentralization policies in countries that are pervasively poor and where central government institutions are chronically under-funded. While decentralized cooperation was seen as a potential option for targeting aid to poverty groups in Asia and Latin America, there was a feeling that, in some African countries in particular, decentralization was implemented half-heartedly by the central government.

Summary

At the country level most donors have not made a deep analysis of the poverty situation with an precise identification of poor groups. Nor do they have a precise idea of what constitutes a pro-poor strategy for each partner country. The external lead on this has largely been left to the World Bank and UNDP.

The European agencies have had little meaningful bilateral dialogue with their partners at the national/macro level on poverty issues and policies nor have they worked together collectively to seek a consensus on an appropriate 'single strategy' with their common partners. There was not much evidence of a lead from the European Commission. This implies that, in a country like Zambia, for example, where the policies for the poor are weak, the donors are depending on 'trickle-down' to assist them, despite their rhetoric on 'pro-poor' growth. However, there have been some exceptions: the Netherlands and the Nordic donors in Tanzania (with the UNDP and the World Bank), the UK in India and some of European donors taking a position on social policies as a counterweight to the World Bank in Consultative Groups in Nepal and Bolivia. There have also been cases of regular dialogue on issues relevant to poverty at the meso/sectoral level; Germany and Denmark in India and Nepal and Germany and the Netherlands in Burkina Faso. There is clearly a need for the European agencies to play a significant role in dialogue not only on the formation of pro-poor policy but even more importantly on its implementation. There is considerable scope especially at the sectoral level and especially as these countries are very dependent on external resources. There is scope even in India which is less aid-dependent. However, it sometimes requires a difficult search to locate the appropriate focus within government structures to be effective.

The agencies' own bilateral aid strategies have generally lacked a sharp operational poverty focus and a clear identification of the groups they intend to benefit. With a few exceptions, these strategies have been drawn up in a 'top-down' way with limited consultation with the wider civic society. The PR interventions constituted a modest 26 per cent of total bilateral portfolios in Zambia, 40 per cent in Zimbabwe and a substantial 51 per cent in India where donors have increased their poverty operations in recent years. Directly targeted PR interventions were the minority. European donors in general do not seem to have a clear strategy on their desired balance between direct and indirect targeting 'in-country'. There was also considerable variation in involvement among the individual donors. Despite rhetoric on 'ownership', there were very few examples of donors supporting locally owned and initiated poverty programmes. While *ad hoc* project approaches remain the dominant mode, some donors are shifting towards sectoral approaches to aid delivery. Finally, all European donors are at one in seeking and supporting greater government decentralization in their partner countries. Some advances have been made but there remain considerable constraints on effective financial devolution and local institutional capacities. There is as yet no systematic evidence that even successful decentralization of responsibilities is favouring the poor.

5
Have the Poor Benefited? Evidence on Effectiveness and Impact

There is surprisingly little evidence available to indicate the type and extent of the impact of donor-funded interventions on the poor. First, most monitoring and evaluation reports tend to concentrate on physical outputs or on management processes rather than on the actual impact on beneficiaries. To assess impact would require the use of more sophisticated techniques and would cost more. Baseline surveys, which are very rarely conducted, would be needed, as well as the use of 'control groups' to compare the well-being of people in 'with-project' areas with non-benefiting areas, for instance. Also, only a small minority of interventions have been evaluated, thus sharply reducing the information base available to assess the benefits flowing to the poor. Finally, when monitoring and evaluation studies were carried out, they usually made little attempt to disaggregate impact, or even access to outputs, by socio-economic group. Although they may be a useful source of information on general implementation effectiveness, they are unsatisfactory guides to the impact on poor groups in particular.

It is against this background that this chapter tentatively seeks to provide some insights into whether interventions funded by European donor agencies have been successful in benefiting the poor. A series of 90 interventions were selected and assessed from across the seven country case studies. The focus was on identifying examples of good practice in order to learn lessons from experience. Donors were asked to select those projects and programmes which they considered to be the most poverty-oriented. The sample is therefore a biased one, and is likely to over-estimate the positive impact of externally funded interventions on the poor. However, by systematically assessing the design, approach, and estimated impact of some 90 cases, it provides insights into the strengths and weaknesses of a large sample of interventions which the agencies themselves considered to be pro-poor. The next chapter concentrates on the lessons learned, and provides more detailed examples drawn from the case studies.

Method and approach

Case study methodology

The researchers sought to assess a wide range of characteristics of agency projects (and a few programmes). These included the extent to which projects were specifically targeted at the poor, the degree of participation, the attention to gender relations, and the level of monitoring and evaluation. Impact was given particular attention, and efforts were made to estimate the likely benefits for poor groups in terms of impact on their livelihoods, their access to resources, their level of knowledge, and their rights, as well as the overall impact.

The agencies were asked to provide project documents, monitoring reports and evaluation studies to facilitate the review, supplemented by visits of several days to each of the projects, usually by local researchers. Rapid and participatory appraisal techniques were used to interview intended beneficiaries, project staff, donor and local government officials, and often non-beneficiaries as well. Attempts were made to ensure that poorer groups were not marginalized, sometimes by using individual or small group interviews in addition to village meetings. The process was facilitated by the substantial cooperation from the donor agencies, who did not seek to compromise the independence of the analysis. Consistency of approach was ensured by providing each team with a common methodology. In India, where particularly extensive use was made of local researchers, a workshop was held to ensure that the objectives and tools used were understood in the same way by all.

In each country, a reasonably even balance of projects was sought for each of the four or so major European development agencies. The sample was intended to reflect the sectoral and regional emphases of each donor and sought to avoid domination by any one sector. A balance was also struck between interventions which had been in progress for five or more years and newer interventions. The latter were assumed to be more likely to reflect more recent thinking and approaches to poverty reduction, while the former might furnish more evidence of impact. The full sample, broken down by country, donor, and broad sector, is contained in Annex 5.

Clearly, the limitations of the agencies' monitoring and evaluation reports, outlined above, together with the limited time available for visiting individual projects, made it difficult to make definitive assessments. The judgements, therefore, are best described as 'perceived' impact rather than actual impact, which in any case may not be apparent until some time after the agency's withdrawal. It must also be stressed that, in making comparison between European agencies on the basis of this cross-country aggregation of interventions, it needs to be borne in mind that the sample for a particular donor may not necessarily be representative of its overall operations.

The tables below indicate the overall performance with respect to targeting, participation and other dimensions, taking account of both design and implementation, with the latter being weighted more heavily. Annex 3 sets out the key to the criteria which were used to judge performance on these various aspects. Where performance at the implementation stage varies considerably from that at the design phase, the data are cited in the text but not in the tables. The results and the overall picture emerging suggest that a substantial gap remains between the stated agency policies on how they identify, design and implement pro-poor projects and their actual practice. There are some encouraging signs and trends, and the following chapter confirms that there are important examples of projects which have been highly effective in benefiting the poor, or which were successful in particular aspects.

Poverty orientation

Table 5.1 provides an overview of the broad approach taken by agencies when designing interventions to benefit the poor. It assesses whether the project design reveals clear and direct linkages with delivering benefits to the poor, or whether these linkages are more indirect, long-term, and contingent on other factors. Three categories are indicated; direct, indirect, and other. These vary both in the degree of directness of the linkages, and in the extent to which the poor are benefiting disproportionately. The definitions

are given below, although it is recognized that the boundaries
between them are sometimes blurred.

- *Direct PR projects/programmes*: interventions which seek to target
  the majority of benefits to poor groups, and where the linkages
  between design and benefits to the poor are clear and expected in
  the short to medium term.
- *Indirect PR projects and sector/policy reform interventions*:
  - interventions which are expected to bring substantial benefits
    to the poor, although others may benefit, and where the link-
    ages are less immediate but plausible;
  - measures which may bring benefits to non-poor groups, but
    which are designed to promote pro-poor policy reform or
    increase institutional capacity to benefit poor groups.
- *Other projects/programmes*: interventions which may bring benefits
  to the poor, but where the linkages between design and benefits
  to the poor are less clear, are long-term, and contingent on other
  factors.

Table 5.1 shows that over three-quarters of the sample had either a
direct or indirect focus on the poor, and that only 23 per cent had

Table 5.1 Type of poverty orientation of selected interventions (% and
number of projects)

Donor	Type of poverty orientation				Sample size
	Poverty-oriented total	of which		Other total	
		Direct	Indirect		
Total %	77	29	48	23	100
Total number	69	26	43	21	90
Donor					
Denmark	17	4	13	2	19
EC	5	2	3	4	9
Finland	4	0	4	1	5
Germany	13	6	7	2	15
Netherlands	9	2	7	3	12
Sweden	5	3	2	3	8
UK	9	7	2	2	11
Other	7	2	5	4	11

no particular focus on the poor. It is striking, however, that little more than a quarter of the sample, selected by donors as pro-poor, could be described as directly focusing on reaching the poor. This suggests that projects and programmes with less clear and immediate linkages with poverty reduction are considered by donors as being a particularly effective means for achieving their poverty reduction objectives. The UK was a major exception with nearly two-thirds of projects classed as direct, although the sample is not representative. It is, of course, perfectly possible for interventions with an 'indirect' or 'other' focus to have a significant impact on the poor, but the evidence presented later in this chapter would appear to show that the greater the degree of poverty orientation, the larger the expected benefits for poor groups.

Targeting of the poor

Whereas Table 5.1 examined the agencies' broad approach to pro-poor interventions, Table 5.2 is based upon a more detailed consideration of both the design and implementation of 82 interventions for which information was available. A project may be intended to have a direct or indirect poverty orientation, but this may be

Table 5.2 How well targeted were donor-supported interventions? (% and number of projects)

Donor	Degree of targeting				Sample size
	Total with significant effect	of which		Negligible total	
		High	Moderate		
Total %	62	21	41	38	100
Total number	51	17	34	31	82
Donor					
Denmark	13	4	9	6	19
EC	3	1	2	5	8
Finland	4	2	2	1	5
Germany	11	4	7	2	13
Netherlands	5	1	4	5	10
Sweden	5	2	3	3	8
UK	6	2	4	4	10
Other	4	1	3	5	9

Note: Data were unavailable for eight interventions.

irrelevant *unless mechanisms are built in to ensure that a substantial share of the benefits accrue to the poor.*

For each of the 82 projects a judgement was made as to how seriously the donor-government partnership had included targeting mechanisms in the project design and to what extent these had been put into practice. Particular weight was given to actual implementation.

The table indicates that no particular efforts were made to target benefits to the poor in 38 per cent of the sample. Only 21 per cent of projects were highly targeted on the poor, with 41 per cent demonstrating a moderate level of targeting. The full data indicate that the share of highly targeted projects was lower at the implementation than at the design stage, presumably because of either technical constraints or a lack of prioritization by agencies and partners.

Among the agencies, Germany had the best record, with 11 out of its 13 projects having moderate or high levels of targeting. This was mainly attributable to GTZ projects, which financed all 4 projects with high levels of targeting and 5 of the 7 projects with moderate levels. 2 KfW projects had moderate levels and the remaining 2 revealed negligible use of targeting mechanisms. The majority of interventions supported by Denmark, Finland, Sweden and the UK demonstrated some degree of targeting, whereas half of all Dutch projects and 5 out of 8 EC projects used no targeting mechanisms.

Participation, gender, sustainability and impact

Participation

Adopting participatory approaches throughout the project cycle is generally seen as good practice, and this would appear to be borne out by the analysis at the end of the chapter. The picture which emerges here from a sample of 89 projects is rather mixed. Table 5.3 shows that nearly two-thirds of interventions were significantly participatory in design and implementation. However, only a quarter of these (or one in six of all projects) were highly participatory. This is quite at variance with the project documentation, which often highlights participation as a major priority. One-third of the sample showed negligible participation by poor groups.

When the level of participation at the design and implementation stages is analysed separately, the full data suggest that nearly

Table 5.3   How participatory were the donors? (% and number of projects)

Donor	Degree of participation				Sample size
	Significant total	of which		Negligible total	
		High	Moderate		
Total %	65	17	48	35	100
Total number	58	15	43	30	89
Donor					
Denmark	16	3	13	3	19
EC	5	0	5	4	9
Finland	4	2	2	1	5
Germany	8	3	5	7	15
Netherlands	6	0	6	5	11
Sweden	6	1	5	2	8
UK	7	5	2	4	11
Other	6	1	5	5	11

Note: One intervention was excluded for which data were unavailable.

two-thirds of all interventions excluded any participation by the poor at the design phase. This is worrying, given that some form of involvement of poor groups when projects and programmes are being designed is likely to lead to interventions which are more 'in tune' with their needs. In addition, involvement at each stage of the project cycle is usually considered to foster a greater level of ownership by beneficiaries.

The degree to which a participatory approach appeared to be the norm, according to the sample of 89 interventions, varied considerably from one donor to another. Nearly 85 per cent of Danish projects were participatory, while the UK had the largest share of highly participatory projects (45 per cent). The Netherlands and the European Commission had no projects which were ranked as being highly participatory, whereas Germany's projects were fairly evenly split between high, moderate and negligible levels of participation.

One particularly positive point is that there appears to be a clear trend towards higher levels of participation. When the sample is divided between those interventions which were completed by the end of 1997 and those which were ongoing, only 9 per cent of the older projects were judged to be highly participatory compared with 21 per cent of the newer projects.

Gender

It was often difficult to determine the extent to which gender relations informed project design and, in particular, project implementation. Impact was rarely disaggregated by gender in project monitoring and evaluation reports. Judgements were possible for 75 of the 90 projects, and indicated, perhaps not surprisingly, a similar result to that for targeting. Of all projects, 37 per cent paid little attention to gender relations (Table 5.4). However, nearly half (45 per cent) of all interventions which paid attention to gender relations, revealed a high degree of gender sensitivity, a considerably higher proportion than for targeting or participation.

The full data suggest that gender was given *greater* weight at the implementation than at the design phase, perhaps because during the time that has elapsed since the projects were designed, gender has enjoyed an increasing profile within development agencies, and perhaps within some partner governments as well. This would appear to be borne out by the data, since if projects due to finish by 1998 or earlier are compared with those which are ongoing (and more recent in design), the proportion of projects which integrated gender relations to a high degree rises from 15 to 37 per cent.

Table 5.4 How well were gender relations integrated? (% and number of projects)

Donor	Degree of gender sensitivity				Sample size
	Significant total	of which		Negligible total	
		High	Moderate		
Total %	63	28	35	37	100
Total number	47	21	26	28	75
Donor					
Denmark	15	5	10	3	18
EC	3	2	1	5	8
Finland	4	3	1	1	5
Germany	7	3	4	4	11
Netherlands	7	3	4	1	8
Sweden	4	2	2	4	8
UK	6	3	3	3	9
Other	1	0	1	7	8

Note: 15 interventions were excluded for which data were unavailable.

Although there are some indications of improvement, it remains disappointing that only 28 per cent of all project spending took thorough account of the fact that poverty is usually experienced differently by men and women, and that special measures may be required to maximize impact for women in particular. No individual agency emerges as a leader in this field.

Sustainability

The evidence for sustainability must be treated with caution, since in most cases interventions were ongoing or only recently completed, and thus judgements as to likely future sustainability have to be considered tentative. The evidence suggests that a full two-thirds of interventions reveal some degree of sustainability, though in practice this tends to be highly dependent on the intervention having generated enough political commitment for governments to continue funding where agencies have left off (Table 5.5). Less encouraging is the fact that researchers estimated that fewer than one in five interventions were highly likely to be sustainable. This probably reflects the fact that the sample covers relatively poor countries, with limited resources to maintain recurrent costs once

Table 5.5   How sustainable were projects? (% and number of projects)

	Estimated degree of sustainability			Sample size
	Significant total	of which	Low total	
		High	Moderate		
Overall sustainability					
Total %	64	19	45	36	100
Total number	43	13	30	24	67
Productive vs Non-productive					
Productive	78	26	52	22	23
Non-productive	57	16	41	43	44

Note: 15 interventions were excluded for which data were unavailable. Productive sector included watershed, irrigation, forestry, some women-in-development, some NGO, some IRDPs, and some credit interventions. Non-productive included education, health, urban poverty, drinking water, among other interventions.

donor agencies have withdrawn. This may explain why productive sector interventions were judged to be significantly more likely to be sustainable than non-productive interventions. Non-productive interventions, in this case mainly social-sector interventions, tend to require very substantial budgets to cover recurrent costs, such as teacher or hospital staff salaries and maintenance.

Impact assessment

The above analysis has sought to consider how far the European agencies and their partners have addressed important dimensions of project design and implementation with a view to maximizing the benefits for the poor. The rest of this section asks what the benefits for the poor have been. It also tries to assess whether approaches such as targeting and participation were associated with higher impact on the poor.

Overall impact has been judged across four dimensions; impact on *livelihoods* through job creation or productivity improvement, on *access to resources,* and on the level of *knowledge.* The fourth dimension concerns any evidence that the poor have been *made aware* of their needs and rights and see themselves as becoming more confident, competent, and less risk-prone in managing their own affairs. It has been possible to make some attempt to judge the significance of the benefits to poor people in 73 interventions across the seven country case studies. The judgements are largely based on evidence of project outputs and interviews with those involved with, and who are intended to benefit from, the projects. The absence of monitoring or evaluation reports, or their lack of information on the distributional impact of interventions, together with the limited amount of time available, means that the results are somewhat impressionistic.

Table 5.6 summarizes the overall impact for the 73 projects, and reveals that *over 70 per cent of all interventions brought or are likely to bring some benefits to the poor. Of these, a third are estimated to be likely to generate a large impact.* This suggests that donor interventions are far from having been a failure as a means of reaching the poor. However, the figures also underline the considerable scope for improvement, given that a greater number of projects had a negligible rather than a strongly positive impact. In addition, it is necessary to bear in mind that the sample of donor projects reflects those projects considered by the agencies to have had a pro-poor focus.

Table 5.6   Estimated or potential impact on poverty (% and number of projects)

Donor	Estimated impact				Sample size
	Significant total	of which		Negligible total	
		Large	Moderate		
Overall impact					
Total %	73	25	48	27	100
Total number	53	18	35	20	73
Dimensions of impact %					
Livelihoods	60	24	36	40	72
Resources	91	34	57	9	77
Knowledge	80	31	49	20	71
Rights	67	15	52	33	72

Note: Interventions 17, 18, 13, 19 and 18, respectively, were excluded for which data were unavailable.

From the four dimensions – livelihoods, resources, knowledge/ skills and rights/empowerment – it appears that donor-supported interventions were most effective at increasing the access of the poor to resources. Over 90 per cent of all interventions contributed to a large or moderate increase in access. In contrast, agency-supported interventions were least effective at promoting a large improvement in the rights dimension, only 15 per cent of the sample, or one in seven projects, generated a large impact, although overall two-thirds were associated with an improvement. About 60 per cent of interventions were perceived to have enhanced livelihood security, the lowest of the four dimensions assessed. However, 40 per cent of these generated a large impact, compared with under a quarter for the rights dimension.

Donor-supported interventions made a significant impact on levels of knowledge, defined in terms of education or skills learnt. Nearly a third of all projects improved levels of knowledge and skills, and only 20 per cent made no contribution at all.

That agency-supported interventions should have a differential effect on the various dimensions of poverty impact is not surprising. External agencies are less likely to be able to influence the structure of power relations of another society so as to increase the bargaining power and rights of the poor, than to improve access to resources and services or knowledge through financial and technical cooperation. Furthermore, bilateral donors are constrained in how far they are able or willing to offend national government partners. Efforts to improve the access of the poor to resources and knowledge may be less unpalatable to vested interests than attempts to alter the fundamental balance of power in the poor's favour. This suggests that, if development agencies are to live up to their ambition to address poverty in a multi-dimensional fashion, they need to work more closely with partner governments to increase the rights of poor groups and enhance their livelihood security.

Exploring factors behind impact

How far can particular elements of intervention design and implementation be associated with levels of impact? The data are not susceptible to econometric analysis, since the three-way categorization used (high, moderate and negligible) does not provide sufficient degrees of freedom. However, the graphical presentation below strongly supports three conclusions: the more direct and immediate the linkages with poverty reduction, the greater the perceived impact; the more targeted the intervention, the higher the perceived impact; and finally, the more participatory the intervention, the higher the estimated impact. Chapters 6 and 7 explore in more detail some of the qualifications which might be attached to these conclusions.

Poverty orientation and impact

Figure 5.1 suggests that those interventions where the linkages between approach and poverty reduction are more direct and immediate are strongly associated with high or moderate levels of impact. Under 5 per cent of interventions with a direct poverty orientation had negligible levels of impact (1 out of 22).

Those interventions where the linkages with poverty reduction were least clear and most long-term, the 'other' category, were associated with the lowest levels of perceived impact on poor groups. No interventions classed as 'other' were associated with high levels of impact, 29 per cent were associated with moderate impact, while over 70 per cent were perceived to have brought negligible benefits for the poor (12 out of 17).

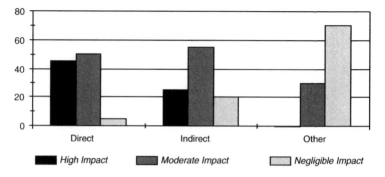

Figure 5.1 Relationship between poverty orientation and impact (direct, indirect and other interventions rated by degree of impact (%)).

Figure 5.1 indicates that 'indirect' projects generated moderate levels of benefits for the poor, somewhere between 'direct' and 'other', with 56 per cent (19 out of 34) delivering moderate impact. This would tend to suggest that an approach which sets out from the start to address poverty reduction directly, and attempts to target the majority of benefits to the poor, is particularly effective at reaching the poor. However, it does not alone resolve the question of what is the satisfactory balance in a donor's portfolio between direct, indirect and other projects, since these results do not indicate the scale of benefits. It tends to be the case that more direct approaches tend to be smaller in scale, benefiting fewer total numbers of beneficiaries. These figures say nothing about the relative sustainability of the benefits delivered.

Targeting and impact

Figure 5.2 suggests an even stronger association between the degree to which interventions include pro-poor targeting mechanisms and the level of impact on poor groups. Almost three-quarters of projects (11 out of 15) with a high degree of targeting were estimated to have had a high level of positive impact on poor groups. No projects which were highly targeted had a negligible impact. In contrast, an almost identical proportion (71 per cent) of projects with negligible use of targeting mechanisms were judged to have had a negligible impact on the poor (12 out of 17). No projects lacking targeting mechanisms delivered high levels of benefits. The association

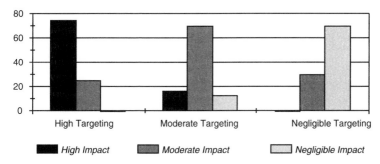

Figure 5.2 Relationship between targeting and impact (highly, moderately, and negligibly targeted interventions rated by impact (%)).

between moderate levels of targeting and moderate benefits is equally strong, with 71 per cent associated with moderate impact (22 out of 31). A similar qualification applies, namely that this evidence does not take account of the *scale* of benefits delivered; more highly targeted interventions tend to have a smaller total number of beneficiaries than less targeted interventions.

Participation and impact

Figure 5.3 reveals a similar pattern to Figures 5.1 and 5.2. All 12 projects with high levels of participation were associated with high or moderate levels of impact. However, only 8 per cent of interventions

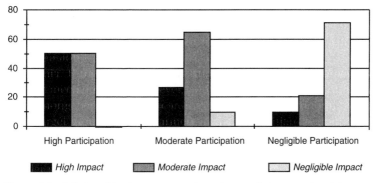

Figure 5.3 Relationship between participation and impact (participatory interventions rated by impact (%)).

(or 2 out of 24) with negligible levels of participation were estimated to have generated high benefits for poor groups, and 71 per cent had no benefits at all. Again, moderate levels of participation were linked with moderate benefits, the exact share being 65 per cent (24 out of 37).

Summary

Very little is known about the impact of agency interventions on the poor, since evaluations have either neglected distributional issues or focused on inputs or outputs rather than impact. The sample of interventions drawn upon here provides a supplementary source of information, although it was possible only to assess perceived impact, due to the lack of baseline data and the limited time available. In addition, the results obtained were not necessarily representative, given that they included those interventions identified by donors themselves as being poverty-reducing. Despite these qualifications, a number of conclusions emerged.

- Over 70 per cent of projects had a positive impact on the poor, of which a third had a high impact.
- Agency-funded interventions were more successful at addressing some dimensions of poverty than others. In particular, agencies were most effective at improving the access of the poor to resources and knowledge, with between 80 and 90 per cent of the sample having a positive impact. They were less able to improve the livelihoods and rights of the poor very significantly.
- Only one-fifth of the 90 interventions were highly targeted at poor groups, even though the sample covers projects identified by donors as poverty-focused. Indeed, 37 per cent made negligible use of targeting mechanisms.
- Though two-thirds were participatory, only 17 per cent of projects were highly participatory.
- Two-thirds of projects revealed moderate or high levels of gender sensitivity and the figure is higher for more recent projects.
- Only a fifth of projects were judged to be highly likely to be sustainable after donors withdraw.
- The evidence from this sample suggests that interventions targeted on the poor and involving their participation are systematically associated with greater impact on them.

6
Good and Bad Approaches: Case Study Evidence

In each of the country studies a common approach was followed based on an agreed methodology. The depth of analysis varied across the studies depending on the resources available, with most involving field studies of one or two weeks, many of them conducted by local researchers. The case studies were not designed to be yet another round of 'quick and dirty' evaluations of aid effectiveness, but to provide analyses of good practice (and of factors leading to failure) based on the perceptions of a wide range of stakeholders. These included both 'insiders' within the government and donor organizations and 'outsiders', namely, intended 'beneficiaries' and 'non-beneficiaries', 'opinion formers' and poor individuals and groups themselves. Information was gathered from project and programme documents, monitoring and evaluation reports (where available), interviews at a regional or national level, and through visits to project and programme sites.

This chapter looks in more depth at the approaches which lie behind the summary statistics presented in Chapter 5. It highlights good practice approaches to targeting the poor and ensuring their participation, and successes in promoting greater sustainability of benefits. It also examines some of the weaknesses which emerge from the case studies and, discusses the implications of these for the poor, and in some cases how they might be rectified. In Annex 2 a number of recommendations are made, drawing on insights gained from case studies in India.

The evidence presented in this chapter for the UK reflects experience under the Overseas Development Administration (ODA) and the Department for International Development (DFID), which succeeded it in May 1997. For the sake of convenience, the term DFID is used throughout.

Targeting the poor

The overwhelming impression from the country field studies is that European donors have made only limited use of highly targeted approaches, though the majority of interventions have included some degree of targeting. This was illustrated in Table 5.2 which showed that one in five of the sample of 82 cases were highly targeted, with a further 40 per cent showing moderate targeting. Here we examine in more depth what a successful targeted approach looks like, as well as highlighting some weaknesses in practice on the part of agencies and their partners. More detail on some of the cases discussed in this chapter are provided in Annex 4.

Increasing emphasis is being given to the concept of partnership between agencies and, usually, government bodies. Effective targeting depends on the attitudes of both the development agency and its partner or partners. Thus, in Nepal some share of responsibility for the lack of effective targeting lies with the government, which until recently discouraged targeting of particular groups, including indigenous, ethnic and low-caste groups. However, the agencies have considerable scope either to reject proposals which they consider to be unlikely to deliver benefits to the poor, or to work closely with partners to improve the approach and to strengthen the capacity of the delivery organizations. It may be the case that line ministries operating at the local level, local government bodies and NGOs lack the experience and capacity to implement a targeted approach. Yet the evidence suggests that there is plenty of scope for development agencies to place greater emphasis on a capacity-building phase prior to service delivery. Two interventions by Danida in Burkina Faso provide an example of this being put into practice, with some 25 per cent of the budget being spent on participatory activities, which gave particular attention to the needs of women and sought to identify both the villages in greatest need and the individuals within those villages (de Boisdeffre, 1998b).

A relatively straight forward approach relies on broad geographical targeting whereby the poorest regions of a country, or the poorest districts within regions are prioritized. This has been the policy of the Indian Government in its District Primary Education Programme. Although the intention is to provide improved primary education to all, in the initial stages funding has tended to be directed to those districts, and those villages within districts, which have the lowest literacy levels. This approach has been supported by a range of donors, including the European Commission and the UK's DFID. A somewhat more sophisticated approach, though operating on a far smaller scale, has been supported by Finnida in a rural water supply and sanitation project in Nepal. Project allocations have been prioritized on the basis of a village hardship index, favouring those communities suffering the greatest hardship. This has included an impact analysis which, unusually, disaggregates impact by gender and socio-economic and ethnic groups, to lead to a better understanding of the opportunities and constraints facing women, low castes, and ethnic minorities (Gsaenger and Voipio, 1999).

Interventions may also be effective in reaching the poor by identifying particular groups which are disproportionately poor. Sida has supported this approach in Zimbabwe with considerable success, through a health scheme which targeted commercial farm workers and their dependants, who are among the poorest groups. The objective is to improve their health status and to train one or two workers per farm as health workers.

A further approach involves self-targeting. This requires careful design in order to create an incentive structure which leads poorer groups to self-select. The Norwegian agency, NORAD, funded a microcredit institution, PRIDE, in Tanzania which used self-targeting effectively to prevent the benefits from the scheme leaking to richer individuals. Drawing on the Grameen Bank's experience of methods shown to include poorer groups but exclude the rich, PRIDE provides only relatively small loans and requires borrowers to attend compulsory training for one hour each week. A study shows that in 1995 over 75 per cent of all borrowers in the Arusha branch had either no education or only primary level education, compared with 0.4 per cent with university education and 23 per cent with secondary education. Given that educational level tends to be a reasonable proxy for socio-economic status, these figures suggest that the self-targeting mechanisms used were effective in directing a greater share of the benefits to poorer groups.

Approaches which seek to prevent leakage of benefits to non-poor groups may not necessarily be desirable or effective. Instead, it may be an appropriate goal to deliver a service to all sections of the population, but to ensure that population-wide delivery does not mean neglecting poor groups. This usually requires particular attention to be given to the needs of the poor, yet may help create the expectation among the poor that they have the right to demand services from the same (national or municipal) bodies which meet the needs of the better-off. In this vein, the GTZ has worked very effectively with the Burkinabe National Water and Sanitation Office (ONEA) to provide drinking water to the poor and non-poor alike. The intention has been to ensure that the normal drinking water network works better and meets the needs of *all* the urban and semi-urban population. Meeting the needs of all its potential clients, however, required careful analysis of the constraints in accessing drinking water facing poorer groups, particularly women as primary users, and resulted in pro-poor targeting mechanisms being built into the financial planning process. Equity considerations have been taken into account for the first time, resulting in a pricing policy which provides for cross-subsidization from richer or larger clients to poorer or smaller consumers, from metered users to users of public fountains, and from richer to poorer urban centres. This has been effective due to the systematic use of socio-economic studies as an instrument of planning to assess the needs, consumption patterns and payment capacities of the National Office's customers. Analysis showed that the urban poor were reliant on public fountains and water sellers; priority was therefore given to investment in public fountains over metered connections, which tend to benefit the rich. Complementary measures have tackled maintenance and more demand-side aspects such as the value of hygienic water supply, led by NGOs and targeted at poorer sections of the population.

Approaches which seek to deliver benefits to poor groups only may in some circumstances be less effective and may also stigmatize the poor. The KfW has supported the social marketing of condoms in Burkina Faso, concentrating on a range of groups most at risk from HIV infection rather than concentrating solely on the poor, both in order to ensure maximum effectiveness and to avoid stigmatizing the poor by creating the impression that AIDS is a disease of the poor. Its national focus has had the advantage of raising awareness across the population as a whole, with market research indicating that 70 per cent of the population recognized the programme's brand of condoms after being exposed to its advertising. It makes a positive contribution to poverty reduction both by benefiting the poor along with everyone else, and by tackling a significant route of transition into poverty, namely, developing AIDS or being orphaned as a result of AIDS.

However, such a broad focus presents some risks. The strategies developed to reach the various target groups, such as miners, lorry drivers, prostitutes and migrant labourers, sought to differentiate *within* each group, to take account of the particular constraints facing the poor. Yet the evidence indicates that the programme mainly reached urban and semi-urban populations, with very limited sales of condoms to income-poor rural populations. The targeting mechanisms did not take sufficient account of the fact that even highly subsidized condoms were considered to be a 'luxury good' for the great majority of the rural population, and thus out of the reach of the large proportion of the rural population living below the poverty line (Loquai and van Hove, 1997). In addition to the cost factor, PROMACO's own studies show that the rural poor's awareness of the importance and means to protect themselves from HIV was lower than for other groups. These results do not undermine the legitimacy of a national approach which seeks to avoid stigmatizing the poor, but they do suggest that understanding the particular constraints and mindsets of the poor needs to be given higher priority, as well as perhaps exploring whether cheaper traditional methods might be promoted.

The evidence in Chapter 5 pointed to a strong association between the degree to which interventions included pro-poor targeting mechanisms and the level of impact on poor groups. The above analysis indicates that a wide variety of approaches to targeting may be effective, and that the precise method needs to be carefully tailored to the context. Unfortunately, the positive examples outlined above were outweighed by the number of poor practice interventions. These fell into two main categories. In some cases, attention to the poor went little further than a statement of intent in the project document. In such cases the design and implementation failed to consider whether the poor were likely to be among the main beneficiaries, or whether particular mechanisms might be required to ensure that they shared in those benefits. The other main category included those interventions where some consideration had been given to identifying the poor, their particular needs, and means to reach poor groups, but weaknesses in design or implementation resulted in few actual benefits for the poor.

The experience of Denmark, the EC, Germany and the UK in the watershed sector in India points to the particular importance of including targeting mechanisms in productive sector activities. Watershed development projects are land-based activities, so it is necessary to try to avoid the landowners and the slightly bigger farmers becoming the major beneficiaries simply because they own more land and are generally more powerful in securing their own interests. Although all the projects examined in the India case study tried to reach the economically weaker sections (marginal farmers, landless labourers, scheduled castes and tribes, women, and so on), the following approaches would help increase the benefits for the poor as well as meeting environmental and productivity objectives:

- poverty reduction should explicitly be the primary objective (or one of them);
- the emphasis should be shifted – at least partly – from land-based to biomass-based activities and from privately owned land to common lands;
- the poor should get equal or (preferably) preferential access to the usufructs from common lands;
- treatment of the watersheds should always start from above, both because of ecological considerations and because more poor people tend to live in the upper regions;
- in selection of watersheds for treatment emphasis should be put on the prevalence of poverty, in addition to ecological factors;
- watershed development projects should have a component of non land-based activities, specifically targeted at the poor;
- the poor should have preferential access to the employment created under the watershed schemes.

Sometimes the needs of the poor are marginalized by technical concerns. This is more common among projects with a long history, and whose first phases were designed at a time when the current emphasis on poverty reduction was weaker in donor thinking. Thus

Sida's programme of support for soil conservation and agroforestry extension in Zambia dates back to 1984 and reveals a largely technical approach to targeting, relating to soil quality, farm size, and favouring innovative and women farmers. In what appears to be a hangover from the earlier period, even the most recent agreement in 1994 does not reveal a strong poverty orientation.

More fundamentally, marginalization by technical concerns may be the end result of a conflict between poverty reduction and other objectives of an agency. The Zambian project, to some extent, and others point to a possible tension between the poverty and environmental objectives supported by agencies (and governments). While some interventions have sought to combine support for environmental improvements with a poverty focus, others have treated these two objectives in isolation. Thus while GTZ's support to the fisheries sector in Zambia sought to combine an environmental objective (reducing the consumption of declining wood reserves) with a poverty objective (focusing on small-scale fisherfolk), another recent project (by the same donor in the same country) focuses on environmental concerns without making any reference to poverty reduction. The latter project, GTZ's Zambezi teak forest project, although it dates from as recently as 1995 (running until 2010), does not clarify the expected target groups, and makes no attempt to differentiate between different socio-economic users of the forest and what their respective needs may be. This failure to consider the priorities and needs of poorer groups, together with ineffective management, has resulted in the project having a negligible impact on poorer groups.

What is particularly disappointing is the failure to use even broad geographical targeting of the poor in several projects. The European Commission's scheme to stabilize export earnings from coffee in Tanzania, through its Stabex instrument, includes no pro-poor targeting mechanisms whatsoever, and does not attempt to differentiate among beneficiaries according to their socio-economic status. The target group is coffee farmers in the Kilimanjaro region, one of the least poor regions, and few of the coffee farmers belong to the poorest segments of their communities. The programme does fund feeder roads which have generated some employment, thus generating some positive benefits for the whole community including the poor. However, the lack of targeting mechanisms means that, despite the programme's substantial inputs and outputs, the benefits to poor groups are very limited.

A second EC project, supporting micro-projects in Zambia, pays little attention to how it might reach the poor. The EC programme requires financial contributions from those communities which benefit. The World Bank, which runs a similar programme, is prepared to reduce the level of contributions for poorer communities from 25 to 15 per cent, but the EC's project allows no such flexibility. The EC also dismisses attempts to reach the poor who are located in remote areas, where they are disproportionately concentrated, on the grounds that low population densities in these areas make the programme unviable. This attitude may be changing, since the EC programme has recently financed an NGO campaign to raise awareness of the resources available from the programme in poorer areas. An official in the European Commission office in Delhi indicated that there was no clear strategy for prioritizing poorer areas, and that the personal enthusiasms of individual staff were often the greatest determinant of where aid was focused. Similarly, a UK project document in Zambia commended the choice of region for the project on the grounds that it was easily accessible by road. Such factors occur in a range of agencies and help explain why even broad attempts to reach the poor by selecting poor regions are not more common.

A further factor is the pressure to succeed, both in terms of disbursing funds at a pace which will generate recognition by senior management, and in terms of being able to point to concrete achievements satisfying demands for accountability in donor capitals. This places a premium on working in areas where the donor has a history of effective partnership and areas with strong institutional, including delivery, structures. Often these are not among the poorer regions of a country, which explains why the pattern of European aid allocation in India bears little relationship to levels of human development (Cox *et al.*, 2000).

In some cases, the lack of attention to targeting is a symptom of a lack of guidance within the development agency concerned. A clear example of this is an ostensibly poverty-focused agricultural training project financed by the French Ministry of Cooperation in Burkina Faso. This was located in one of the least disadvantaged agricultural regions, and access to training was made available only to the literate.

The literate are typically less poor and represent only 10 per cent of the potential beneficiary population. Except for some women-specific components, only men were eligible. This example reflects the general lack of awareness within the French development coop-eration system of good practice approaches, with a few exceptions, such as the latest phase of a rural development project funded by the Caisse Française de Développement (de Boisdeffre, 1998b). Dutch and Danish-supported drinking water projects in India also revealed a lack of broad targeting in the sense of not selecting poorer villages, and also paying little attention to ensuring that the poorest enjoyed full access within the villages. However, more recent Dutch and Danish projects reflect new guidance and a new approach, and do recognize the importance of a more participatory approach in order to safeguard the interests of poorer groups (Cox *et al.*, 2000).

Gender sensitivity

Most of the European agencies involved in the case studies had poli-cies which state that the goal of gender equality should be sup-ported in its own right but also that it is of instrumental benefit in achieving effective poverty reduction. The latest DAC guidelines highlight the following links between poverty and gender equality (OECD, 1998):

- the lack of income, food, health care, education and opportuni-ties that characterize poverty affect women more than men;
- women's efforts to overcome poverty are further constrained by discrimination in access to social and economic resources.

The guidelines set out a gender and development strategy, recogniz-ing that gender equality is not a 'women's concern', but a broad societal issue that women and men have to address together. The evidence from the case studies, summarized in Chapter 5, indicates that more than two out of three projects gave some consideration to the fact that poverty tends to be experienced differently by women and men, and that special measures may be required to ensure maxi-mum impact on poor women and girls in particular. However, overall only one in five projects made this a high priority and the case stud-ies reveal a large amount of lip-service being paid to the gendered nature of poverty. There were, for instance, very few examples of impacts being assessed in a gender disaggregated way, making it hard to assess the success of interventions in benefiting poor women through promoting gender equality. Nonetheless, newer projects tended to give a higher priority to poverty and gender linkages (37 as opposed to 15 per cent), and the examples below illustrate some successes, including shifts between phases of projects reflecting lessons learnt.

The CARE-PUSH urban poverty project in Zambia, part funded by DFID, identified women as particularly vulnerable, and designed the largest component of the project, food for work, to take account of this. The scheme involved a four-hour working day, instead of the eight-hour day characteristic of formal work. The shorter working day removed a major impediment to female participation, due to their other family-based obligations. The modest rates of pay (in-kind, in food) also served to discourage men from participating. Both factors combined to achieve a highly targeted approach, whereby at least 90 per cent of beneficiaries were women. The fact that payment was in terms of food rations tended to increase the women's control over their earnings, since it is they who usually control food resources.

GTZ's support to small and medium enterprises in Burkina Faso developed indicators designed to reveal constraints and impacts in a gender-disaggregated way. This provided the information for efforts to increase the access of women to traditionally male crafts, and also promoted the standing of activities traditionally practised by women, such as street-selling of food, by facilitating their representation in trade fairs, for instance. Targeting women artisans was shown to have particular value as a PR measure, since studies conducted in collaboration with the University of Ouagadougou showed that far more of the additional income of female artisans was spent on the nutrition, education and health of their children than was the case for male artisans. However, successfully addressing gender equity issues does not necessarily imply that the project had a highly poverty-focused approach. In fact, one estimate suggested that only 10 per cent of the project's resources directly benefit poor individuals.

KfW-PROMACO experience of the social marketing of condoms in Burkina Faso showed the importance of looking at gender in a holistic way, rather than simply concentrating resources on either women or, in this case, on men. Until 1995, promotional and awareness-raising activities were concentrated on men, as experience had shown that men were particularly hard to reach and to convince of the value of barrier contraception. However, a gender disaggregated impact assessment revealed that, in fact, women, particularly in rural areas, were far less aware of the dangers of HIV and of the options for protection. As a result, the programme reoriented its activities to focus more on women, including awareness-building sessions for women and promotional campaigns which sought to strengthen their negotiating powers *vis-à-vis* their partners. Greater emphasis was given to distribution channels designed to reach women, such as female retailers and more female programme staff (Loquai and van Hove, 1997).

An approach which focuses on gender relations between men and women rather than the needs of either sex, was shown to be important even where women were the principal target group. An example of the care taken by agencies and their partners to ensure that men were brought into the process concerns a women's self-help network in Burkina Faso, supported by Dutch and German NGOs (funded by their respective bilateral agencies). It concluded from experience that many of the problems faced by its members were linked to the nature of relations between women and men within the household, and could not be treated effectively by working with the women alone. After analysing these constraints and the scope for change, the network's trained social mobilizers have sought systematically to inform and consult husbands and partners, with the result that there has been increased acceptance and support of their wives' or partners' activities. Activities concerning birth control and responsibility for child-care, for instance, have been organized as a social event for the whole family, and men have been invited to some sessions and asked to provide labour when required. By promoting the economic and social empowerment of women while facilitating the communication between the sexes, the impact of the project has been increased (Loquai and van Hove, 1997).

There were many examples of gender relations not being considered in project design or implementation, which usually reduced the intervention's impact on poverty. The European Commission's microprojects programme in Zambia, despite its length of operation, appears to have failed to identify women as a priority group among the poor and thus did not develop mechanisms to target them. As a result, an assessment of beneficiaries underlined that women tended to be assigned inferior roles in project implementation. They were not expected to attend project meetings, and when they did attend, their contributions tended not to be valued, and men emerged as the dominant decision-makers. Although all agencies have formally subscribed to the DAC guidelines on gender equality, this commitment is seldom effectively translated into practice.

Seeking the participation of the poor

Chapter 5 indicates that of the sample of 89 projects only one in six were highly participatory, and this figure was even lower at the design phase, where it was rare for the poor to be involved. On the positive side, two-thirds of all projects *did* involve some kind of participation, and the trend is clearly for growing participation, with double the share of newer projects (21 per cent) being highly participatory compared with those interventions completed by the end of 1997. This section will examine evidence pointing to an increasingly participatory approach, resulting from agencies and governments learning from experience. The various benefits of participatory approaches are explored, both in their own right and as an instrument for reaching the poor and ensuring greater ownership and sustainability. Some weaknesses are analysed, particularly the lack of focus on generating demand. The question is raised, 'participation by whom?', and some of the complexities of decentralization are examined.

The data referred to above pointing to increasingly participatory approaches over time probably underestimate the trend, since a more detailed examination of the project documentation covering the various phases of projects dating back two decades reveals a large number which became significantly more participatory in the later phases. This tendency may not only apply to official donors, as the same was found to be true of a number of agency-financed NGO interventions, such as the UK-funded PUSH project in Zambia. In Tanzania there has been a distinct shift from a top-down to a more participatory approach since 1992, usually in the second or third phase of a project, in a range of rural development and forestry interventions financed by Denmark, Finland, Germany and the Netherlands. Similarly, in India, there was considerable emphasis on more participatory approaches in Dutch and Danish water projects and in the UK's natural resource projects.

As emphasized in the preceding section, the responsibility for assessing the degree and nature of participation which would be beneficial lies with both development agencies and their partners. Part of the reason for the growing prominence of participatory approaches is that more developing country governments, both national and local, are themselves convinced of the merits of greater participation. This implies a responsibility on partners to reject top-down ways of working by agencies. There are a few instances of this happening, such as a women's solidarity network in Burkina Faso, funded by the Dutch programme and a German NGO. This firmness on the part of the local NGO owes much to the conviction of its staff that they were in the driving seat, making their own decisions, and thus felt able to reject support which was felt to be excessively 'hands-on'. Although ownership by the staff of an implementing organization does not necessarily imply ownership and participation by the beneficiaries, it is a necessary condition for this. Such firmness by local partners is rather rare, which in part reflects the inequality of their relationship, given the financial dependence of partners on agencies. Arguably donors also have a responsibility beyond their own bilateral programme to bring influence to bear with respect to good practice approaches to poverty reduction, such as participation. There are examples of this, like the success of Sida in working with UNICEF in Bolivia, ensuring a shift away from a rather bureaucratic approach to one which is more responsive to the needs of the communities where it is working.

Promoting greater participation of the poor in decision-making, resource allocation, and implementation processes is seen as a good in itself by the poor themselves and by development agencies. Indeed, projects can fail according to conventional criteria and yet still be considered as having had a positive impact on the poor. The German-funded rural development/self-help project (VARENA) in Burkina Faso provides a good example. There were divergent opinions of the success of the project in improving livelihood security, but widespread agreement that it had increased knowledge, partly through training in better production techniques, and had generally bolstered the poor's sense of their rights and scope to participate in local political processes. These less tangible benefits were apparent in many other projects, including the Danish-funded natural resources project in Iringa District in Tanzania. Its highly participatory approach, which involved local people in problem identification and planning, had, according to officials, created a stronger awareness among local communities of the problems of poverty and helped them to identify and plan for the required solutions, and participate in their implementation.

The evidence from the sample studied suggests that highly participatory projects which operate outside of existing institutional structures may have value and may tackle a rights/empowerment dimension of poverty, but they are highly unlikely to be sustainable following donor withdrawal (see below). A key priority for agencies therefore is to work with the existing structures, governmental and non-governmental, to try to ensure that they are more genuinely representative of the poor. This may involve working with line ministries at a national or, more often, a local level to enhance their capacity to deliver services in a more consultative fashion. It may also involve taking a long-term perspective, and trying to create a situation where poor groups have sufficient representation within national and local democratic structures to ensure that their views and needs are taken into account in the process of decision-making and resource allocation.

Participatory approaches can be an effective vehicle for generating high levels of ownership within partner-implementing organizations and among actual beneficiaries. This is clearly illustrated by the social marketing of condoms in Burkina Faso by a Burkinabe organization (PROMACO) funded by KfW. Evidence from interviews suggests that it is widely perceived as being a locally owned initiative, and that this has helped increase the social acceptability of condoms. PROMACO was rarely criticized as being a vehicle for the propagation of Western values, unlike many other similar initiatives in the field of family planning and sexually transmitted diseases (Loquai and van Hove, 1997). Some of the factors which helped create this sense of local ownership include:

- PROMACO's staff are all Burkinabe (with the exception of the director), and KfW has remained in the background;

- low awareness of the high level of donor subsidy;
- the strong involvement of members of the local community in condom distribution and awareness-raising activities;
- the success of the programme in adapting the distributional channels and promotional activities to the needs of the various target groups;
- the popularity of the advertising gimmicks.

The District Primary Education Project (DPEP) funded by DFID in Andhra Pradesh and elsewhere in India by the European Commission progamme also highlights how participatory approaches can result in high levels of ownership. This has been achieved in large measure by decentralizing elements of the decision-making process down to district and village level. Each school and each teacher is given an annual lump sum which can be spent following consultation with Village Education Committees. The DPEP in Andhra Pradesh has been particularly successful in mobilizing local people in even the poorest villages to contribute labour, time and money to school construction or extension. This has generated a new conviction that it is their school, and not the government's, and that they have the right to insist that teachers attend regularly. The extent and type of contributions have been decided at the village level, with the result that a sliding scale has often been used to ensure that the poor can make a fair contribution (Cox *et al.*, 2000). Part of the success of DPEP lay in the strategic decision at national level to promote local participation through decentralization, but part of the particular success in Karimnagar District in Andhra Pradesh lay in the personality of the DPEP coordinator. The importance of individuals was apparent in a wide range of case studies, and this provides few systematic lessons for development agencies and government beyond the value of working with high quality, well motivated partners.

Donors and partners often face difficult dilemmas when trying to ensure the participation of the poor, while still working with structures that are sustainable. Attempts to 'legislate' for the participation of poor groups may simply result in unsuccessful attempts to impose egalitarian structures in a context where discrimination is institutionalized. A GTZ-funded forestry project in Zambia hand-picked village committee members without understanding the social and power relationships within the villages. The members received no guidance as to their role, and the committees failed to represent the interests of the poor, or indeed to function effectively. Similar weaknesses are apparent in a number of projects in India which sought to achieve a minimum quota representation of low-caste members in village committees. A DFID-funded urban poverty project at Visakapatnam concluded that it was more effective to work with existing local urban groups, which might be undemocratic but more sustainable and effective than setting up parallel depoliticized organizations. Unusually, the project sought to involve local government from the outset and to 'mainstream' it among other government urban projects, though this was partly compromised by the strong interventionist role played by DFID. DFID's experience showed that parallel organizations which might be more democratic were unsustainable and in reality ended up being concerned with non-critical issues (Cox *et al.*, 2000).

The lesson would appear to be that the precise type of participation is highly dependent on the context, but that some kind of involvement of the poor or their representatives is likely to increase effectiveness. A project financed by the European Commission (GARDP) in Nepal illustrates some of the risks of a non-participatory approach and also underlines a long-standing weakness of both development agencies and governments – namely, an excessive preoccupation with supplying inputs and a lack of attention to meeting and stimulating demand. GARDP supported education, drinking water, irrigation, feeder roads and women's development, but with minimal levels of community participation. Each sectoral component was formulated centrally and ownership lay with the donor experts or government ministries rather than the intended beneficiaries. School buildings were provided, but the lack of any social mobilization activities resulted in limited utilization and thus a limited impact on literacy and educational learning. There was little or no attention to strengthening the capacity of local bodies to implement or maintain project activities, with the result that few judge the project to be sustainable.

The above is simply an example of a general preoccupation with supplying physical inputs to development, such as school buildings, health clinics or urban housing, without sufficiently considering whether they genuinely meet the priority needs of the poor and whether complementary demand-generation (often awareness-raising) activities are required. A DFID-funded health and family welfare project in Orissa, India, concluded that it was difficult to discern any impact at all on health service efficiency or quality of care despite nearly two decades of UK support. In part, this was a result of concentrating on infrastructure rather than addressing institutional weaknesses *and* a lack of attention to information, education and communication activities (Cox *et al.*, 2000). Similarly, a number of Dutch, German, and one UK-supported, urban poverty projects concentrated heavily on providing housing, yet various studies have shown that housing by itself is low on the list of priorities of urban poor groups, especially the poorest, compared with employment opportunities or access to clean water. One 'beneficiary' who had been resettled and had then returned to her original slum said, 'If I have a job and food here, I can sleep on the footpath. What do I do with a golden house 16 km away?', highlighting that she and others had not been involved in deciding what kind of intervention would best meet their priority needs. A French project in Burkina Faso was intended to provide primary education, yet failed entirely to recognize the importance of trying to understand the constraints preventing the poor from attending school. No efforts were made to design mechanisms to counteract these constraints. This lack of concern about participation and the demand-side aspects of poverty is characteristic of French procedures, which concentrate on political aspects rather than the developmental considerations (de Boisdeffre, 1997).

It should not be concluded, however, that straightforward responsiveness to local needs is a recipe for success. 'Local needs' are far from homogeneous and reflect a diverse range of interests. Even if only the interests of the poor are considered, their demands are also likely to be wide-ranging and may be impossible to meet sustainably all at the same time. These risks are illustrated by a Finnish-funded integrated rural development project in Tanzania, which was so responsive to local demand that the resulting programme spread its resources across too many activities (Voipio and Hoebink, 1999). The first phase had foundered due to the very limited participation by intended beneficiaries and local government bodies. Phase two addressed this by increasing participation. Participatory rural appraisal methods were used to enable people: to analyse their own situation, resources, problems, and opportunities; and to decide what their objectives are, organize and manage the activities and institutions and, through monitoring and evaluation, to take decisions on the direction of activities.

One result of this participatory approach was that the programme in Tanzania initiated a wide range of productive and social sector activities. These are recognized by officials and recipients alike as having had positive impacts, and that the more participatory approach had enhanced the beneficiaries' self-esteem, self-confidence and ability to plan and implement activities. However, the benefits were felt by many to be unsustainable. The diversity of programme activities appeared to have hindered attempts to ensure that they were integrated effectively into the existing district government administration. In fact, parallel structures were created (or maintained from Phase 1) which bypassed the existing regional authorities, which are intended to be the overall coordinators of development plans in the region. This resulted in muddled accountability between the programme structures and district and village government, which hampered efforts to improve the performance of government bodies. Officials and others concluded that the demands generated by the participatory approach could not all be met and that greater sustainability could only be achieved if the programme concentrated on supporting a narrower range of productive sectors, on the assumption that less dispersion would generate greater success within the remaining sectors. Support to the social sectors should be maintained, or even stepped up, but only on the basis of a far fuller partnership with the government authorities, whose active involvement should protect the gains realized (Voipio and Hoebink, 1999).

The above example illustrates that, although the participatory approach may well be a vital component of success, it can generate difficulties of its own, and sustainability may require it to operate within boundaries. Participatory approaches may carry a heavy opportunity cost for beneficiaries in terms of time or activities and income forgone. The demands on the scarce staff resources and expertise of development agencies may also be considerable. Therefore, a judgement usually has to be made as to the type and extent of participation which will be most beneficial. GTZ's support to the National Water and Sanitation Office in Burkina Faso illustrates both the value of a participatory approach and that a positive impact does not require full participation at every point. In providing water fountains in poor urban areas the National Office located fountains according to a norm of one for every 500 people, without consulting water users. However, the decision as to who would operate and maintain the fountains was delegated by the Office to a committee drawn from the local community. Full participation might have brought benefits – indeed in some circumstances, such as where caste hierarchies predominate, the precise siting of water pumps can be critical – but in this case it appears that the National Office and GTZ had identified the critical areas for participation (Loquai and van Hove, 1997).

Effective participation at a national level demands that appropriate analytical skills and capacity exist within the relevant ministry. The India case study suggests that donors could do more to help ease capacity constraints in the Ministry of Health and Family Welfare whose expertise is seriously overstretched, by funding Indian and international consultants. Since the rates of pay of national (and international) consultants have been inflated often by extensive use by donor agencies, the agencies could 'top up' aid payments to allow the governments to employ additional expertise themselves. This would ensure a greater equality in the donor–national government dialogue (Cox *et al.*, 2000).

The Holy Grail of sustainability

Achieving sustainable benefits for poor people is one of the greatest challenges facing development agencies and their partners. OECD DAC guidelines (OECD, 1992) highlight the various dimensions of sustainability, and from a pro-poor perspective they may be summarized as follows.

- *Institutional sustainability*: broadly interpreted this involves ensuring that policies and incentives take full account of the needs of the poor; that there are sufficient management and other relevant skills; that effective delivery mechanisms are in place to reach the poor; that participatory approaches take account of the potential conflict between poor and dominant groups.
- *Financial sustainability*: ensuring that sufficient funds are available to allow the activities to be continued following donor

withdrawal; ensuring the affordability of replicating or scaling up pilot projects.

- *Technological sustainability*: ensuring technology which is effective and affordable and acceptable to poor groups.
- *Environmental sustainability*: ensuring that the potential conflict between short-term gains and long-term needs is resolved, taking account of the needs of the poor.

This section concentrates on the institutional and financial components of sustainability. Of the sample of 67 case studies for which an assessment of likely sustainability was possible, less than one in five were judged to have a high likelihood of being sustainable both institutionally and financially (see Table 5.5). One reason for this may be a disinclination among development agencies to take a sufficiently long-term view, though a number of examples below suggest that there are no short cuts to institutional sustainability. This section also argues that agencies and their partners need to accept and admit that financial sustainability may be illusory, particularly (but not only) in the case of social service delivery in the poorest countries.

Analysis of the sample of interventions examined might appear to belie the assertion that an insufficiently long-term view is taken, since many have been operating for more than ten years, sometimes for two decades. However, it is clear from project documentation and from discussions with agency officials that most interventions have in fact been designed as five-year projects and then renewed phase by phase, sometimes by different donors. Many officials would admit that a more realistic assessment of the likely time needed to deliver institutionally sustainable benefits would have led to those interventions being designed differently. The Orissa Health and Family Welfare Project discussed above is a good example of an intervention which, with hindsight, should have sought to tackle institutional weaknesses, such as developing an adequate training institution or promoting a greater decentralization of resources and responsibility to local levels, before spending huge sums on clinics which were destined to be underused. Indian partners, who share in the responsibility for the project's failure, argue that the infrastructure 'cart' was placed before the institutional reform 'horse'. After nearly two decades, DFID is funding a Phase 3 which is centred on building capacity within the State government ministries to analyse policy options and put in place an appropriate incentive structure designed to form a solid basis for the effective provision of health services, particularly for the poor (Cox *et al.*, 2000). The growing awareness among agencies and their partners of the importance of making a far longer-term commitment has generated increased enthusiasm for sector-wide approaches (see Chapter 7).

Too often sustainability appears to be remembered by agencies and their partners only towards the termination and 'handing-over' of activities to local authorities. A good practice approach would be to start planning for sustainability from the very beginning of the design phase of an intervention. This would also imply a more collaborative approach between agency and partner government or organization at the design phase, as opposed to the rather donor-driven approach which is common. The Finnish-financed forestry project in Zanzibar provides a positive example of what can be achieved when sustainability is considered from the outset and a long-term commitment is made. The importance of building institutional capacity was recognized at quite an early stage, with the second phase (1989–92) concentrating on this by transferring the management of the project from a separate body to within the Forestry Department itself. Heavy investments were made in human resource training and participatory extension. Up to 90 per cent of the operational costs were carried by Finnida during Phases I and II, while in Phase III the revenue collection capability of the Government of Zanzibar was strengthened through increased sales of forest products, logging permits and taxation. Operating costs were cut by privatizing part of the activities. After 17 years of external assistance the strategies laid for self-sustainability appear promising, but will be tested over the next decade without donor support.

Another example of positive experience of institutional strengthening is CARE's Project Urban Self Help (PUSH) in Zambia, largely funded by DFID. In its second phase it has sought to increase collaboration with city councils, and to strengthen the councils' relationship with community-based organizations such as the Resident Development Committees. Its experience showed that some of these committees were political in nature and gave poverty reduction a low priority. However, rather than abandon trying to work with these bodies, PUSH has sought to strengthen the committees by working with the government in drafting legal terms to govern them and thus increase their impartiality, representativeness and legitimacy. The project is also actively involved in providing training to city council officials in how to strengthen community-based organizations. This reveals a long-term perspective, and one which is likely to result in the enhancement of existing structures, promising far greater sustainability than the creation of parallel ones, and their gradual reorientation or development of capacity to take better account of the needs of poor groups.

The perils of a short-term perspective, which places quick results over longer-term considerations of sustainability, are clearly illustrated by a European Commission microfinance project in Zambia. The donor deliberately excluded district councils and line ministries on the basis that they would introduce bureaucratic delays. This had negative implications for sustainability and for quality, since there was, not surprisingly, no commitment from local institutions to supervise the programme's projects, with the result that many were of a very poor quality, with only 37 per cent rated as 'good' in 1993. This 'quick-fix' approach appears very short-sighted, though there are similar examples from many other donors. Recently, since 1996, district councils and other local authority officials have been more closely involved and have conducted project supervision missions, resulting in enhanced quality and improving the prospects for sustainability.

A recurrent theme in many project case studies was the lack of financial sustainability even when institutional sustainability was achieved. In other words, there are a host of examples of agencies working closely with governments to increase the degree to which policies and incentives are consistent with the needs of the poor, to improve the quality of the delivery mechanisms, and to build capacity and successfully withdraw donor technical assistance, *without* the benefits being financially sustainable. The experience of Irish Aid in Kilosa District of Tanzania illustrates a highly successful approach to working within existing structures, building their institutional capacity, yet failing to achieve financial sustainability. From 1979 until the early 1990s the project was supply-led and rather non-participatory in approach. Project identification largely reflected the interests of the particular Irish Aid programme coordinator in charge at the time and project design was top-down and donor-led. In response to a situation of minimal ownership by local authorities and communities, characterized by passive recipients unwilling to contribute their own resources or labour, the programme was reoriented in 1996 and a participatory rural appraisal approach was introduced. Beneficiaries, teachers and local officials all welcomed the more participatory approach, noting its contribution to enhancing their own sense of control, ownership and responsibility for activities, and increasing capacity and accountability. The efforts made to integrate the programme into the existing council structure were highly effective, since with few exceptions almost all activities are directly implemented by the relevant departments within the Council. This approach, backed by technical cooperation, has helped build capacity within local government, and has reduced administration costs.

Yet, even where all those concerned agree that an exemplary participatory approach has been followed and where local ownership at district government level is now strong, financial sustainability following Irish Aid's withdrawal remains highly doubtful. Although the project exploited the scope for mobilizing contributions by beneficiaries towards the construction or rehabilitation of school buildings, for instance, there will be greater reluctance (and inability among the poor) to make an ongoing contribution to recurrent salary and maintenance costs. The new activities are thus ultimately reliant on the central government increasing its funding of district councils so that the enhanced quality of social services can be sustained. This appears unlikely in the context of highly constrained budgets at the national level.

A Danida-funded agriculture and natural resources project, also in Tanzania, reveals a very similar pattern of high institutional sustainability coupled with doubtful financial sustainability. In this case, the project achieved high levels of ownership by local government, being operated directly through three departments, down to departmental village-based extension officers. This increases accountability, and provides for more effective monitoring and supervision and significant reductions in project administration and management costs. Villagers who were interviewed testified that their participation in training, and in the planning and implementation of activities, had increased their knowledge, self-confidence, ownership and sense of responsibility for ensuring the success of these activities. This commitment was reinforced by the fact that most activities, such as tree planting aimed at improving soil fertility and providing fuel wood, were productivity-enhancing and income-generating, and their expectation of enhanced income increased their receptiveness to the message of forest and soil conservation and water source protection. Yet, while these factors all have a positive bearing on sustainability, there was considerable pessimism as to the financial sustainability of many activities despite their integration into the existing government structure. Again, the prospects were seen as highly dependent on the Government of Tanzania increasing the allocation of funds to district councils as part of the decentralization initiative from region to district. Without this, and without increased rights of tax revenue collection at district level, the local authorities would be unable to continue to provide the subsistence and fuel allowances to maintain the extension services. There were, in late 1997, signs of the extension and training system being run down even before Danida's withdrawal (Voipio and Hoebink, 1999).

Increasingly development agencies are thinking in terms of forging long-term partnerships with developing country authorities or actors. This implies making a longer-term financial commitment, which would appear to be realistic given the kind of problems highlighted above. It may also imply an integrated approach which addresses constraints at the national, sectoral and local level:

- working at a national level to achieve budgetary reform aimed at a balance of public expenditure which better reflects the priorities of the poor;
- working to achieve policy and institutional reform within particular sectors, including better cross-ministerial cooperation and coherence; also seeking a more progressive tax system, including charges for tertiary education and health; and
- encouraging effective decentralization of revenue-raising powers to local bodies.

The importance of making a long-term commitment is reflected in several other case studies, including in Burkina Faso, where problems of financial sustainability were found to be at least as acute as in Tanzania. Two brief examples reveal Germany's GTZ and KfW responding to this challenge by openly admitting that financial sustainability is an impossibility in the short to medium term, and making a corresponding commitment to provide financing for longer than usual. The GTZ recognized that financial sustainability without continuing donor support was unrealistic in the medium term for its drinking water project, because of the enormous investment needs coupled with the low purchasing power of the majority of clients, and the need to subsidize the low-income groups in order to ensure broad access to drinking water and sanitation. Similarly, KfW entered into a long-term partnership with PROMACO to ensure the sustainability of the social marketing of condoms. In its view, sustainability in a country as poor as Burkina Faso entailed ensuring an institutional delivery system which was almost totally staffed by Burkinabes, and which had a market-oriented approach which generated incentives for wholesalers and retailers to increase sales, and left PROMACO well-placed to attract financing from other sources to reduce dependence on donors (Loquai and van Hove, 1997).

Replicating success?

Part of the measure of the success of agency-supported interventions in reaching the poor depends on the extent to which these interventions have introduced new and better approaches and that such approaches have been 'scaled-up' or replicated. External agencies can usefully play the role of risk-taker, in a context where bureaucracies tend to be risk-averse, shouldering the blame for failed approaches, with partners taking the credit for those which succeed. Agencies can help to accelerate change or to tilt the balance slightly in its favour, though not unless innovation resonates with an important section of a ministry, for instance. Some interventions, such as the UK programme in India, state that support for innovation is a vital element of their rationale. A number of examples of agency–partner good practice in replicating success are briefly indicated below, but the overriding conclusion is that innovative approaches are not common, and that successful scaling-up and replication have to date been the exception and not the rule. The picture from Nepal was particularly gloomy, with Gsaenger and Voipio finding few examples among their sample of successful replication on a nationwide basis of donor-funded pilot projects.

Several interesting example of insights gained from donor-funded approaches having an impact on the poor beyond the confines of the original project emerge from the India case study. The positive contribution of Dutch- and Danish-funded interventions designed to address the needs of women provided individuals within a department of the Ministry of Agriculture with a convincing illustration of how taking account of gender relations could improve impact on disadvantaged women, in particular. This positive model was invaluable in strengthening the hand of advocates for change and contributed to a recent directive requiring gender analysis of many Ministry of Agriculture interventions. A further example is the UK's support of a watershed programme in Karnataka which is widely recognized as being highly innovative, particularly in terms of its emphasis on community participation and its attention to the needs of the poorest. It is seen by DFID as having influenced the approach to watershed management at State level. However, it should be noted that it required very lengthy and involved inputs from the Indian and the UK sides and these costs, including training, may limit its replicability. Although part were one-off costs, the approach hinged on extensive and prolonged negotiations with governmental and non-governmental actors, which would largely remain if the approach was replicated.

Small-scale pilot projects do not necessarily have to be replicated or serve directly as a model for scaling-up in order to have value. The initial project may provide valuable insights on the nature or causes of poverty which can then inform a decision to support a particular sector on a far larger scale. An example is the experience of the Dutch in financing a women's self-help network in Burkina Faso (AFSEN) which was an important influence in their decision to step up Dutch support for the urban poor. The original project provided insights into the extent and nature of the vulnerabilty of poor groups in the suburbs of Ouagadougou, who face a higher cost of living than those in rural areas and lack solidarity networks of equal sophistication and strength. They are unable to benefit from the potential advantages of city life, such as better access to health and education, since they are unable to pay for them as they lack secure access to land and face eviction at any time. As well as influencing the Dutch decision to prioritize the urban poor through larger-scale support, the project fed into the design of the new, larger urban-poverty programme.

There can also be dangers associated with attempting to scale-up successful approaches to PR. The District Primary Education Project in India has arguably been quite successful at expanding access to education to districts and villages with appalling levels of illiteracy. Its very success has attracted a huge inflow of donor funds, particularly from the World Bank, which is welcomed since it should mean that a similar expansion of educational opportunities is available to far more of India's poor and illiterate. However, several informed experts, both Indian and within bilateral agencies, highlight a number of dangers posed by the very rapid replication of DPEP to additional districts. The success so far has been based on reasonably effective decentralization of resources and decision-making down to district level, and below that, ultimately to villages. This has required a huge effort to train officials at district and lower levels, to ensure that they have the capacity to develop district and village-level plans that genuinely respond to the needs of the local community rather than reflecting the vision of State-level bureaucrats. Too rapid an expansion, according to some, has stretched the capacity to provide high quality training of district-level officials. Evidence suggests that a consequence has been a lowering of standards in order that district plans, for instance, are approved and future disbursements are authorized. Mitigating these risks is a responsibility of both development agencies and the responsible Indian government officials and may require a slower approach to scaling-up.

Conclusions and suggestions

Conclusions and suggestions below are drawn from the analysis above. In order to give a more detailed idea of the nature of fairly effective poverty-focused projects, Annex 4 provides a summary of 12 selected case studies. More detailed conclusions drawn from the India case study are included in Annex 2.

Targeting

- Although there were examples of lessons being learnt and applied, development agencies have given insufficient consideration to whether and what type of targeting mechanisms may be required in order to reach poor groups effectively. Broad targeting on poorer regions or districts, or by concentrating on particularly vulnerable groups, has been used effectively, but opportunities have been missed.

- Population-wide approaches, providing services to both poor and non-poor, may be a legitimate way for governments and agencies to ensure that the institutional norm incorporates the poor. However, unless the constraints facing the poor are taken into account, population-wide delivery all too often results in the poor benefiting little (GTZ project in Burkina Faso).
- Targeting mechanisms may be particularly important in the productive sector, where the concentration of assets (e.g. land) in the hands of the better-off will otherwise result in the more powerful securing most of the benefits (European donors' watershed projects in India). Interventions designed to supply services like primary health or education must also be matched by a targeted stimulus of awareness and the generation of demand for these services by poor people, otherwise utilization and benefits will remain very low (DFID, health, India).
- There is a danger that agencies' multiple objectives may result in a tension between PR and other objectives, for example the environment. A focus on environmental concerns in isolation from PR objectives, is likely to lead to a failure to consider the priorities and needs of poorer groups and may result in an anti-poor distributional impact (for example GTZ, forestry, Zambia).

Gender sensitivity

- Lip-service is often paid to the gender dimensions of poverty, with only one in five of the sample making it a high priority; newer projects were better.
- Careful design can result in the effective targeting of poor women, based on a careful consideration of the constraints facing women (CARE/DFID, Zambia).
- Focusing on gender relations between men and women even where the principal target group is women addresses the fact that constraints facing women are often linked to the nature of relations between women and men within the household.

Participation

- Only one in six projects in the sample revealed high levels of participation by the poor, but recent projects were more participatory than earlier ones. Both developing country partners and development agencies have a responsibility to reject top-down approaches which exclude the poor. Agencies can also seek to influence other agencies to promote a more participatory approach (for example, Sida, Bolivia).

- Promoting greater participation is seen by the poor as a good in itself, even if a project fails according to conventional criteria, such as directly increasing livelihood security. Less tangible benefits are often highly valued by poor groups, including those bolstering their sense of their rights, their capacity to analyse and articulate their own needs and possible solutions, and their confidence and ability to participate in local political processes (for example, Danida, Tanzania; GTZ, Burkina Faso).
- Participation by local implementers tends to result in greater ownership and helps generate demand for new services. It is not a panacea, however, and can result in pressure to dilute efforts over an unsustainably large range of activities (Finnida, Tanzania).
- Meaningful participation needs to be implemented in advance of infrastructure components rather than simultaneously, thereby influencing the design, location, and appropriateness of such physical investments.

Sustainability

- The picture on sustainability is mixed. Although only a fifth of the sample were estimated to be highly likely to be sustainable, there were many examples of projects becoming more institutionally sustainable in their most recent phases. Development agencies are increasingly wary of creating unsustainable parallel structures, favouring a longer-term perspective which seeks to build capacity within existing governmental and other bodies. This may require integrated action at national, sectoral and local levels.
- Some donors, notably GTZ and KfW, are prepared to admit that financial sustainability may be fanciful in the poorest countries, which instead require a long-term partnership and financial commitment combined with institutional strengthening measures. Many development agencies are moving towards this position, particularly in their support for sector-wide approaches through long-term budgetary support.

7
Options for Reaching the Poor More Effectively: Some New Thinking

In the last few years, and especially with the 1996 International Poverty Reduction goals for 2015, some rethinking on approaches has been emerging. Several donors – more especially Danida, DFID, Sida, the European Union; the SPA working group on poverty[1] as well as the OECD-DAC Secretariat in Paris – have espoused changed approaches to poverty reduction. Some new ideas are reviewed here: the concept of partnership, the consensus on a single country strategy, a shift towards using sectoral approaches to poverty reduction and mechanisms for linking debt relief to poverty reduction. At this early stage it is only possible to assess the options largely on *a priori* grounds although there is some relevant partial evidence.

The concept of a 'partnership' where the recipient is in the driving seat

The concept of 'partnership' itself is not a new one and has been the basis of EC development cooperation through the Lomé Convention for many years. However, there are new elements in the current concept of partnership being proposed by DFID, Sida and Finnida as well as the EC. These have quite a lot of common features.

The idea is basically a form of contract between equals – the donor and a partner – who share the same values and the same commitment to poverty reduction. These agencies envisage such partnerships with low-income countries (with Sida largely centred on sub-Saharan African poor countries). Each partner will have obligations to the other. The poor country partner is expected to:

- be 'committed to the international targets for poverty reduction by 2015' and more specifically 'to pro-poor economic growth, the conservation of the environment and the pursuit of appropriate policies' (DFID, 1997: Panel 14);
- observe civil, political and social rights and pursue accountable, open and responsive governance and to conduct consultation (and dialogue also for Sida) with civic society on national priorities and the representation of the needs of the poor.

The donor partner is expected by DFID to contribute a long-term commitment, an enhanced level of resources and greater flexibility in the use of these resources (DFID, 1997: 2.21).

Both sides envisage an arrangement that supersedes conditionality approaches which are seen to have been largely ineffective. A basic condition for an effective partnership is seen as a common view on policy, with full responsibility being taken by the recipient partner. Sida goes further in recognizing the need to involve the poor or the representatives of the poor, not just by official dialogue but also by bringing in civic bodies: NGOs, independent media and private business (Swedish Government, 1996–7; Carlsson, 1998).

These approaches are only in the embryonic stage and it is not yet clear what will be the nature of certain key modalities, quite apart from the likely effectiveness of this mode of approach. Nor is there any particularly relevant experience available on partnership in the past. There are therefore a number of points and questions to pose at this stage (see Maxwell and Riddell, 1998; Kayizzi-Mugerwa, 1998).

First, will there be transparent criteria applied equitably to all candidate partners in terms of the type of partnership and the amount of resources? Second, what will be the rules of the partnerships themselves? Will there be genuine negotiation and agreed contracts? Will there be a binding contract or a looser agreement? Will cooperation be based on targets and not detailed controls or hidden conditionality? Will multiple partnerships be avoided? Third, how stringent will the content be in relation to PR? How specific and important will pro-poor commitments be? How will the voice of the poor be strengthened – how will they be better equipped to enter into a partnership relationship? Without this element, a partnership based on dialogue with government authorities may lead to the marginalization of the poor. Fourth, what will be the procedures for monitoring the progress of both partners? Will this be based primarily on commitment or on performance? Who, if anyone, will arbitrate on shortfalls in meeting the contract obligations? Fifth, what will be the model for non-partner governments? Partnership implies considerable selectivity in aid allocation, so there will need to be models for action where governments are uncommitted to PR, or cannot meet human rights or good governance criteria.

There are a few indications from the European agencies of the possible approaches on these questions. DFID says there will be a range of relationships and it is not expected that any one partner will meet all the criteria. It also says that 'where there are weak administrations there is no need for separate country strategies to be negotiated by each donor', and it seems to envisage advocacy among its donor partners in search of a wider more unified partnership (DFID, 1997: 2.25).

DFID recognizes that it will not be possible to have partnerships with everybody, 'Where poor countries are ruled by governments with no commitment to helping the poor realise their human rights, we will help where we can do so through alternative channels. These will include institutions of civil society, voluntary agencies and local government' (DFID, 1997: 2.24). Clearly there is a high degree of selectivity between partner governments implicit in this approach in both the DFID and Sida formulations.

The DFID position is relatively precise. It expects to have partnerships with many poor countries, but it is looking for those which 'demonstrate their commitment to the elimination of poverty', and 'those whose governments show no commitment to the poor to realise their human rights' will clearly not be favoured. 'We have limited financial and human resources and it is right to concentrate our bilateral programmes on priority areas where the needs are greatest and where we can achieve results' (*ibid*: 2.23). The Finnish Government has taken a similar position.

The European Commission has had a partnership concept in its early Lomé Protocols where the ACP governments had a legal entitlement to funds and basically determined the strategy for their use.[2] In more recent years the Commission has moved towards a more conditional approach combined with an emphasis on the domestic ownership of policy formulation. The 1993 Council Resolution focused support on countries 'in which the principles and objectives of the national strategy correspond to the general guidelines defined by the Council'. At the same time the Council of Ministers recognized that this objective would have to be reconciled with the importance of helping development partners to define and introduce policies to combat poverty (Council, 1993: 224). The 1996 Council Resolution proposes consideration of increased support for countries showing a commitment to Human and Social Development (HSD) and registering improvement in HSD indicators (Council, 1996).

The Commission approach to structural adjustment funding favours ownership in the design of reform programmes and their timing and sequencing, but the conditionality relates to performance based on results achieved (outcomes), not measures implemented. However, it seeks to separate the macroeconomic elements of reform from equitable growth reform linked to budgetary or balance-of-payments aid. The latter would be optional. The Commission now gives strong emphasis to dialogue on poverty reduction, and political commitment domestically is seen as vital.[3] Within the context of National Indicative Programmes (NIPs) in the Lomé Convention countries, the guidelines now state that it should lead to reciprocal commitments on the objectives, priorities and instruments of the fight against poverty. The Commission is insisting on a much more participatory process for the formulation of NIPs in any future EU/ACP cooperation agreement. Although it seems to have an implicit policy of selectivity, the required degree of commitment by its partners to 'la lutte contra la pauvreté' remains somewhat vague (Loquai *et al.*, 1998: 47–8, 16).

Effective pursuit of a partnership approach to PR must meet important conditions for effectiveness inside the partner country. In particular, there needs to be a reasonable consensus among the government institutions and adequate linking between ministries to ensure an integrated approach. This institutional preparation is likely to take quite a long time and needs to be seen as a process which might be timetabled with milestones and which needs a special budget. None of this can be done in a hurry. As the European Commission recognizes, it must be seen as a medium-term objective and not an immediate reality. It also requires more coordination and consensus-seeking on PR strategies among the European agencies themselves.

Single-country strategies on poverty reduction

There are two senses in which there is scope for pro-poor 'single strategies'. First, there is the idea of all the partners (all donors and recipient governments) achieving a consensus on a 'single strategy' for a country which has a pro-poor character. Second, there is the idea of all the external agencies having an agreed collective strategy or division of labour in terms of their portfolio of interventions in pursuit of PR objectives. These two concepts of consensus on strategies are related but not the same.

Consensus on a single PR strategy for the country

It is desirable to aim for a 'single-country' strategy – designed and 'owned' by the recipient government and ideally approved by the Parliament of the country concerned – which all donors can 'sign up' to and support. Some donors in the SPA working group, in particular DFID, the European Commission and Finnida, favour this approach. It obviously makes sense for any 'partnership' arrangements to focus on a 'single strategy' and hence to be multi-donor in nature and reflect a collective consensus. Agreement on such a strategy would provide the basis for a commitment of budgetary support by external agencies for public expenditure as a whole or at least for sectoral budgets. The content of such an approach might include agreement to reorient public expenditure in certain directions which are more pro-poor, support for some intersectoral allocations of funds in a more pro-poor way, and greater responsiveness of governments and ministries towards all sections of society including the poor. There would also be agreement on wider economic policies which eliminate distortions or regulations that disadvantage the poor especially.

Quite a lot of work has been done on the nature of pro-poor policies in general, especially by the UNDP and the World Bank. However, little or none has been done by the European development agencies. The major need for the next few years is for the European agencies to give more thought to the appropriate economic, social, regional, and human rights policies, and the appropriate public spending and revenue-raising approaches and asset redistribution. They need to focus particularly on the appropriate policies in the specific countries where they hope to develop their partnerships. Collective effort by the EU donors would offer economies and a greater chance of a consensus on the content of such policy. The European agencies, which are currently working in an *ad hoc* way on these issues, could also work together more in the provision of assistance for the development of data collection and strategy formation which will benefit the poor in countries which lack this capacity.[4]

Since pro-poor policy formation and implementation are largely a function of the domestic political context, the external agencies need to give more attention than in the past to the nature of these political constraints and to what can potentially be done to counter political/patronage processes which work against redistribution in a pro-poor direction. The simple assumption that the introduction of more pluralist electoral systems will tilt in favour of the poor is almost certainly not valid. Parties and governments favour those who provide support in their constituencies but these are often not the poor. This is probably the most challenging area, since the external agencies need to keep a balance between encouraging domestic governments to own their own policies and programmes and at the same time playing the role of outside pressure groups seeking to tilt those policies and programmes in a pro-poor direction.

So far few poor countries have produced convincing poverty reduction strategies and costed programmes to benefit the poor. To attract medium-term budgetary support from the external agencies they would need a PR strategy to be integrated into a medium-term accountable budgetary framework. Three countries in sub-Saharan Africa have moved in this direction – Ghana, Mozambique and Uganda. Uganda, while not a perfect model, does provide some guide to how a PR framework and programming might stimulate increased budgetary support from the European and other aid agencies.

Consensus on the donors' collective strategy in the country

Next there is the donors' own need to search for a coherent set of interventions or portfolios. Whatever the strategy of the country authorities may be, and even if it should be an ideal agreed strategy, is there still the need for the different external agencies to deploy their own, often diverse resources and skills in a consistent way and with a suitable division of labour within the country? It is not a simple matter of whether they should support growth or redistribution, although there is an element of this in it. Clearly economic growth is pretty well essential for any prospect of achieving the PR targets. Even if the pattern of growth is broad-based and allows participation of the poor, the external agencies need to decide their pattern of contribution. A simple example will illustrate this. While support for basic social services and support for extension services to poor farmers and poor areas are both appropriate roles for some donors to play, nevertheless, they will not on their own achieve sustainable PR or development unless there is (for example) a satisfactory economic or physical infrastructure, such as roads, which will allow farmers, including poor farmers, to produce, transport and market their products. Hence, to take an extreme example, a set of donors which insist on spending all their funds on basic education and nothing else on PR grounds, would soon unbalance the country strategy if the agencies were a dominant source of finance, as they often are collectively.

There is little evidence of donors thinking about their respective roles. Currently it may not matter, since donors have not shifted their resources in any major way towards a common basket of support, say, for basic social services. Nevertheless, in the next ten years it will be a matter of some importance. One example of a division of labour might be between the European Commission taking the main role in economic infrastructure replacement and maintenance and others (for example, the Nordic donors) taking on the role of supporting the basic social services.

From *ad hoc* projects to sectoral approaches for poverty reduction

Recent shifts in opinion

So far most European agencies, with the possible exception of the European Commission, have relied largely on *ad hoc* project interventions. However, there are signs of a shift towards a wider sectoral or budgetary approach. Danida has been prominent in this, while both Sida and DFID are looking at a partnership to shift from project finance towards budgetary or programme aid funding priorities and management by the country authorities themselves. In particular, 'where we have confidence in the policies and budgetary allocation and the capacity for effective implementation in the partner government, we will consider moving away from supporting specific projects to providing resources more strategically in support of sector wide programmes or the economy as a whole' (DFID, 1997: 2.22). Danida has perhaps gone further than most donors in shifting from a project to a sectoral approach. The Danish position would seem to be one in which targeting poor districts or sections of the population will be pursued in countries where governments show less evident commitment or capacity for pro-poor macro policies (Udsholt, 1997: 39–43, 50). The Netherlands and Finland have also recently announced their intention to tilt away from a project approach towards sectoral budget support. A precondition is for the partner to seek poverty alleviation and to be gender sensitive and ecologically sound. Finland adds another precondition: the fiscal management system of the recipient government has to be sufficiently effective and accountable (Voipio, 1998). The Dutch also propose to transform a cluster of projects into a support programme for a specific organization which will be made much more responsible for implementation than in the past but with continuous policy dialogue on progress (Hoebink and Schulpen, 1998).

Ad hoc project approaches: potential weaknesses and strengths

Donors have focused most of their interventions for the poor through *ad hoc* projects but there are at least four major weaknesses in *ad hoc* interventions for PR.

- They tend to embody a philosophy of control and direction, a 'hands-on' approach in which outside agencies intervene in many management decisions ranging from identification, design, appraisal and staff incentives, to monitoring. Yet effective interventions in favour of poor people require their full involvement from beginning to end and procedures responsive to their needs. Official development agencies have often been remote and weak in their understanding of the local situation facing poor and vulnerable groups and especially those in remote backward areas – which is not likely to make for effective specific community-based interventions in particular.

- *Ad hoc* project approaches tend to encourage an enclave approach which bypasses the public sector system, and, often with off-budget funding, fragments the system and generates lack of accountability and inconsistency. More important for poverty reduction is the high risk that donors will set standards of development and service in their projects which are out of line with feasible local standards of affordability, performance and sustainability. They also tend to be associated with an excessive use of expensive expatriate personnel, neglect of locally suitable staff and stifling of local initiative and ownership.
- These types of projects are very expensive in the skills and administrative time required of external agencies. Any strategy to expand the scale of donor PR efforts faces this real constraint, which is more acute and damaging for some donors than others.
- Donors involved in projects often find that their functioning and impact are inhibited by the wider institutional management and policy weaknesses within the sector concerned.

Against this, *ad hoc* projects are potentially more easily focused or targeted on poor people and in poor districts. They can be 'community-rooted' and therefore very close to poor people. Moreover, in principle they offer scope for innovatory approaches by donors which are either replicable elsewhere or which can be scaled-up.

A sectoral approach to PR; potential advantages

A sectoral approach is likely to have the following main features which distinguish it from *ad hoc* projects. It is likely to focus on a whole sector or sub-sector which is relevant to improving the access of the poor to resources, knowledge, livelihoods and empowerment. It is likely to involve major domestic public sector institutions such as Ministries of Health, Education, Community Development and Agriculture, hence donors are operating through regular government administrative channels. It offers opportunities for donors to provide institutional support. Finance is likely to be in budgetary and transparent form. It is likely to require sectoral coordination of donor activities by the local authorities or by a 'lead' donor in the sector or sub-sector so that broad planning is possible and consistency is achieved between donors and domestic institutions.

Wider and more consistent framework for PR

Under a sectoral approach the upstream and downstream activities can be integrated in the attack on poverty; work at grassroots level can be complemented by a pricing or a marketing policy that is consistent with the resources devoted to it and efforts at the local level. Donors can have potential influence on relevant policy changes which they would lack via projects. The donor interventions are likely to be more integrated into the partner's own processes rather than being enclave interventions. The institutional capabilities can in principle be strengthened both upstream and lower down. Donor efforts can be coordinated and a critical mass of finance and technical assistance can be focused on PR objectives within a country.

Ownership, commitment and appropriate standards

Sectoral (budgetary) support can be based on national strategies designed and 'owned' by the domestic authorities, and ideally also discussed and approved in the national democratically elected Parliament. But even where the central government does not have a genuine PR strategy it is possible to find committed Ministries or committed people within them with the capacity to implement a strategy. Compared with *ad hoc* projects, support for Ministries with a clear policy, which really focuses on the poor in their spending and management policies, is preferable. The predominant use of local staff closer to the problems of the poor should be more effective than enclave projects using a lot of expatriate personnel and consultants. Standards of design are likely to be more appropriate to the resources and capacities of the country, and hence sustainable. There is also a potential advantage if donors working together can raise the status in the political hierarchy of Ministries (for example, Community Development and Social Services), which, though important for PR, sometimes suffer weak status and lack of domestic support. It must be stressed that these potential advantages depend crucially on a range of requirements which may not in fact be actually present.

The potential problems and risks of the sectoral approach

The sector-wide approach may offer promise, but it is neither a panacea nor easy to implement with the various modes of deployment of donor personnel, decision-making procedures and coordination problems being what they are today. The following problems and risks must be borne in mind when developing the sectoral approach further.

Impact, budgetary support and fungibility

A programme approach can cover a wide area of operations in which the donors would provide funds for the Ministry budget line or sub-items within it and have wider potential impact than with *ad hoc* project interventions. The external agencies will need to be willing to provide more budgetary support including funds for domestic recurrent budgets, which they have often been reluctant to support. While the impact can be potentially much greater from funding sectoral or sub-sectoral budgets, counterpart funds or direct budgetary support for certain types of spending such as basic health, education or agricultural extension services, will not necessarily be fully additional for that purpose. It will depend (as has long been known) on what the partner government is otherwise intending to do. Only where a single agency or a group of aid agencies saturate with funds a particular (poverty-relevant) line of expenditure, is there an assurance of some 'additionality', unless the partner government also desires to achieve such reallocation, which has so far been rare.

Centralization and lack of focus

Contrary to the general trend in favour of decentralization, the sectoral approach can lead to further recentralization of planning, decision-making and financial control in the poor recipient countries. The donors normally plan sector programme 'packages' with the central government Ministries of the recipient countries. There is a risk that the 'lion's share' of the aid funds, originally intended for the benefit of the rural poor, may 'leak' to the bureaucratic machinery in the recipient capital. There is a risk of a loss of focus on the poor and a lack of targeting mechanisms for this purpose in a more general, and perhaps more remote, centralized approach. However, this is not inevitable and mechanisms need to be in place to ensure adequate responsiveness to the needs of poor people.

Slow and cumbersome donor decision-making and coordination procedures

The coordinated multi-donor sectoral approach can lead to very slow and cumbersome arrangements if the decision-making rules of the donors require all or most major decisions concerning the sectoral programmes to be made in the donor headquarters. Only very few donors have competent sectoral expertise permanently in the embassies or country-level aid coordination offices. If the only chance for the recipient country authorities to seek donor views and advice is to meet the donors' headquarters-based sector specialists during the bi-annual or annual joint donor appraisals or reviews, the process becomes prohibitively slow. In many countries experience has already shown that it is no easy task for the recipient government sector ministries to coordinate the tight timetables of the donors' subject matter specialists, task managers and consultants to get them all around one table at the same time to plan and decide on the next steps of the sector reform process in a well coordinated manner.

Loss of the holistic, integrated approach

The advantage of many of the integrated rural development programmes (IRDPs) has been that the donors and local (for example, district) authorities have been able to take a holistic view and operate flexibly in any of the administrative sectors, as the local problems and opportunities often involve important interdependences, for instance between health, water, agriculture, education, roads, credit, and so on. The sectoral programmes are easily perceived as the 'acquired rights' of individual Ministries, which often may not be willing to share the resources with other 'competing' Ministries, even if an integrated approach were clearly in the interests of PR. There is a similar risk of competition instead of fruitful collaboration between the sector specialists of the donor agencies and consulting companies.

Ideological and political disagreements between donors

Good coordination and cooperation between the donors are key precondition for the success of the sectoral approach. The various donor countries and specialists may, however, have surprisingly different visions about the best way to ensure an ideal balance between, say, the efficiency and equality objectives of social service provision, or about the relative roles of central and local government, the private sector and NGOs in social service provision, or about the relative merits of tax-based versus user fee-based financing of services. The differences in views and visions may reflect the surprisingly large differences between the ways these things are organized in the domestic policies of the donor countries, even within the EU. There is a risk that the sector reform processes in poor countries may become battlefields between the competing European schools of thought, despite of all the rhetoric about 'recipient ownership' and 'single-country strategies'.

A flexible process approach

Recent thinking (see particularly Cassels, 1997) is that the conditions required for sector aid as an instrument to be effective are rarely met. Hence the need for a more flexible approach. While a sectoral focus is seen as desirable, it will be necessary to find sector partners who share the same (PR) goals and an 'intent' to pursue them. While dialogue not conditionality would be the key process it would be necessary to agree certain milestones for performance in terms of the use of budgetary funds committed over the medium term. The emphasis would be on a process – step-by-step – approach with a realistic recognition that the process could be quite a long one. It would be necessary to meet the requirements of accountability. An even more radical approach would be for the accountability for such funds to be achieved through the national parliament and its committees, rather than directly to the external agency.

Implications for external agencies

The challenge is to reconcile a sector-wide approach with a poverty focus. There are implications here for donors in the switch from their traditional project mode. For them to seek an influence on sectoral policies in favour of the poor requires a more sophisticated understanding of the impact of different aspects of sectoral policy, such as health or education, on the poor (for example, targeting of subsidies for hospital or primary care, distribution of health professionals, user fees, insurance arrangements, the balance of private and public care (Cassels, 1997). It also requires considerable attention and understanding of how to improve the delivery of basic services and not just changes in spending patterns. These aspects require a good understanding of the political constraints on the discretion of governments in this process. Methods for monitoring and assessing the effectiveness of the contribution of sector-wide interventions to poverty alleviation will need to be developed between donors and their partners. For the external agencies to play this changed role, they will need a somewhat different range of skills from those they have traditionally used for projects. These personnel will also need to be more continuously in the field and involved with local processes if they are to give much support or have much influence.

Sector or project approach to PR: some evidence

What light does our research throw on this choice of options? It throws only partial light largely because most of the case studies examined were *ad hoc* projects and only a small minority involved sectoral approaches.

The evidence on *ad hoc* projects set out in Chapter 5 does indicate that the European donors had a considerable positive impact and had shown some improvement in their management processes in recent years. However, the evidence does not point to an established advantage in this approach to PR. Given the scale of resources, the impact was not especially strong. The key point here is that donors or their agents did not fully exploit the potential advantage of this approach in terms of adequate local participation, particularly in the vital early stages of projects. They have often kept an excessive 'hands-on' management style which has not encouraged ownership. They also failed to introduce sufficiently effective targeting mechanisms to reach poor people disproportionately. Moreover, few of their projects promise to be sustainable. Although they have talked of their role in pilot innovatory approaches to PR, in practice they have made a fairly routine and not a particularly imaginative contribution. In a number of cases what they have piloted has not been particularly replicable. At the same time, there were a few cases of a sectoral nature which offered some insights on the scope for a more effective sectoral approach.

In *Nepal*, Danida has been the lead advocate of the sectoral approach. In the education sector it has done very good background work and has succeeded in attracting a range of other (larger) donors (for example, the EC, the World Bank, the Asian Development Bank, UNICEF, Japan, Finland and Norway) to join the education sector development process.

In *India*, it was generally felt that donors could be more effective with a sectoral strategy and more sectoral interventions. The Dutch aid authorities claim that one of their successful sectoral interventions was the Mahila Samaknya Programme aimed at enhancing educational opportunities for women (1989–94). The support of the EC and the UK for the Indian-owned sector-wide District Primary Education Programme has so far proved relatively successful, although it may be premature to judge its superiority (Cox *et al.*, 2000: especially Chapter 6). Nevertheless, it was a case of the donors (appropriately) buying into a locally owned sector-wide programme and did not owe much to the donors' sectoral initiatives or non-existent strategies. It is important, of course, to remember that the institutional capacity of the Indian Government is likely to be better than that in Nepal or in Africa. Yet it was also clear that where local expertise was overstretched in certain areas (for example, the Ministry of Health and Family Welfare) donors with specialists in the field could make a major contribution.

In *Tanzania*, about 20 sectoral donor coordination groups have been facilitated by a lead donor (for example, the Netherlands for the environment, forestry and education) with an exchange on plans, programmes and experience. What is more important, there has been some shift of ownership and coordination to the Government of Tanzania, including the sectoral as well as the central ministries. However, while machinery is in place, local capacity is limited. There is an absence of sectoral plans and public investment programmes. Moreover, coordination has worked less well in the social sectors (compared to, say, physical infrastructure) where donors have different 'inherited models' of how to proceed.

Differences in donor perceptions have posed a challenge in sector coordination. In Tanzania for example, they fell into three major 'schools of thought' on approaches to the development process in the education sector. The World Bank initially advocated a major shift away from the long Tanzanian tradition of state-provided universal primary education, towards a 'demand-driven' approach where state subsidies to primary schools would be provided largely on a 'matching grant' basis (for example, 50 per cent state subsidies to those schools which were able to contribute the other 50 per cent themselves). The idea was to provide the funds directly to the school committees, bypassing the district education offices. Denmark, Sweden and the Netherlands objected and defended the role and capacity strengthening of the district authorities and the ideal of universal provision. A third view of a 'pure' central government-led education sector programme was advocated by the European Commission and DFID. A constructive compromise has since emerged. Currently, the EC and the UK focus their support on the national education sector development programme, managed by the Ministry of Education and Culture (MOEC). The Danes and the Dutch, as well as the Finns and the Irish, now direct most of their education sector aid through the 'District Based Support to Primary Education' programme (DBSPE), which is fully in line with the MOEC's principles of the national reform process and with the government's reform process to give the districts an increasing role in managing education and health service provision. The World Bank continues its support to the school-level matching grants, but now accepts that the district authorities have a role to play in coordinating the process at the local level.

The Tanzanian health sector reform process has progressed more smoothly. From the point of view of poverty reduction and equality in the framework of sectoral programmes, an important challenge for the donors as well as the recipient governments is to create mechanisms for targeting the central government's (often donor-funded) subsidies disproportionately in favour of the poorer and more deprived districts, villages and population groups. In Tanzania, the World Bank has proposed a two-tiered system whereby schools and health centres in the poorer districts would receive their matching grants on $2:1$ basis (against the normal $1:1$ basis). Much more work needs to be done, however, to develop finer-grained allocation criteria and systems.

In *Zimbabwe*, some doubts have emerged about whether sectoral approaches can really reach poor people effectively. The main concern focused on a central government with little commitment to PR as well as on whether donor sectoral support for Ministries can really promise more for the poor even though they may have the institutional capacity, since they lack a clear policy on reaching poor people. There is seen to be a risk that the central upstream focus of donor efforts will not effectively trickle down to the poor, who probably need to be targeted.

In *Zambia*, a very weak public institutional framework and poorly integrated social service delivery systems at local level mean uncertainty about implementation to assist the poor. Also, the Ministries of Community Development and Social Services and Education rank low in political status and budgetary resources, and hence lack a constituency. Lobbying for increased budgets to help the poor through greater collective donor support as well as greater donor assistance for institutional development might be dynamic enough to change this. Finally, the EU, which has provided sectoral aid for supplies of medicines, text books and furniture for basic health and education, could not ensure that these would be focused on the poor.

In *Burkina Faso*, there has been some donor sectoral coordination and division of labour in relation to health. With Germany in the lead, there was exchange of information and coordination and complementarity of donor operations. The European Commission provided budgetary aid, with Member States undertaking basic health care projects in a number of provinces. The sectoral coordination took place within the Bamako initiative and a national decentralization policy for the health sector. One aim was to make basic health more affordable and accessible to the rural population (Loquai and van Hove, 1997: 20 and Table 4).

On the issue of fungibility and additionality some light is thrown by evaluation studies on the impact of counterpart funds from EU programme aid for the education and health sectors in three African countries. In Ghana and Uganda the funding did not change the domestic government's priorities for these areas, but in Côte d'Ivoire it was very effective, especially in the supply and distribution of essential drugs and in measures designed to improve working conditions in the medical profession and measures to protect the most vulnerable groups from deteriorating economic conditions. This greater EU effectiveness in Côte d'Ivoire was partly due to the high concentration and relative quantitative importance of EU funding in these areas as well as strong domestic political commitment. Moreover, compared with Ghana and Uganda, the European Commission participated in policy dialogue as a leader, supporting health and decentralization programmes and playing an extremely active role in defining areas of operation and targeting recipients specifically through improvement of the budgetary process (Caputo, 1997).

Linking debt relief and poverty reduction under HIPC II: emerging ideas

The Cologne Summit in June 1999 proposed linking the provision of increased debt reduction with a poverty reduction framework and increased social spending by the eligible Heavily Indebted Poor Countries (HIPCs). The mechanisms for effecting this in the next stage of the HIPC scheme are still under discussion. Poverty reduction is a long-term task, though the HIPC initiative could be implemented in a period of up to 3 or 4 years for many of the eligible countries. Once a country has qualified for relief, the reduced debt service payments will effectively release domestic budgetary funds over a significant period of time in the future. Debt relief is only one resource for assisting PR objectives, but the ideas that emerge for the PR link in this particular context will have considerable relevance for the approach of the external agencies to budgetary support for PR in their ongoing and future involvement beyond debt relief.

A specific recent proposal for such a link (Foster *et al.*, 1999) takes a comprehensive view of the process and places the focus on the assisted country's medium-term budgetary framework. The latter is seen as an essential structure for open and accountable planning, prioritization of government spending in relation to pro-poor objectives, as well as for monitoring of outcomes and impact. It would envisage a government which develops a PR strategy and a rolling 3-year plan for achieving a more pro-poor pattern of government spending and services. The government, and not the external agencies, would be at the centre of a process to draw up plans and budgets for poverty reduction in a way which is more responsive and accountable to domestic society and parliamentary institutions and especially the needs of the poor than in the past. There should be no pre-set menu for judging the pro-poor content of each government's strategy, plan and budgets. Intra-sectoral shifts in education and health spending (subsidies) and improved quality of such services may often be a priority in African countries, but equally there may be cases where greater priority attaches to infrastructure improvements to enhance the livelihoods of poor regions and poor groups or provision of more effective safety nets for the vulnerable.

Broad PR benchmarks are proposed to judge performance and there would be regular review processes involving all stakeholders – domestic civil and external. These benchmarks might include the development of an anti-poverty strategy, a genuine poverty reduction action plan with costed programmes; improvements in monitoring procedures and data for tracking expenditures, outputs and outcomes for PR; improvements in transparency and participation etc. While a certain minimum level of performance would be essential, countries would tend to be assessed against changes or improvements over time. In this sense it is a process approach to creating a comprehensive poverty reduction framework and not a set of micro poverty-oriented conditions and targets.

Summary and conclusions

The new partnership idea offers an approach which in principle reconciles the concept of ownership with a positive role for the external agency. It is still at an embryonic stage in terms of its modalities. A major concern is whether enough partners can be found which are mutually committed to shared values on poverty reduction. There are two particularly key requirements for effectiveness. First, the external agencies need to avoid multiple partnerships and therefore need to proceed in a more collective and coordinated way themselves. Effective partnership requires them to seek consensus on single-country strategies for PR with all their partners, and also to seek a sensible division of labour among themselves within that strategy. There has so far been a major gap here which needs to be filled. Second, the external agencies need to approach partnership for PR as a process and not as a blueprint. It cannot be undertaken in too much of a hurry, especially as a consensus is necessary between different parts of the recipient government institutions. At the same time, without the use of conditionality the impetus to achieve the poverty targets will require a 'selective' approach to partners in the medium term. There is only a case for longer-term support to those authorities which continue to show some degree of commitment to their own poor.

Ideas for a *comprehensive approach* to PR where governments are expected to produce PR strategies and medium-term pro-poor rolling plans integrated with annual budgeting, offers more chance for domestic ownership and accountability to both domestic civil as well as external stakeholders. If a convincing framework of this kind is established, donors could channel more substantial flows of budgetary support on a medium-term basis. This is the ambition of the Comprehensive Development Framework approach, set out by the World Bank in late 1998.

There are considerable potential advantages in a *sectoral approach* to PR but certain important conditions must be met for it to work effectively. First, there needs to be an effective partnership with sectoral organizations and much better donor coordination. This includes seeking a consensus or compromise on their approaches to, for example, the education or health sector to benefit the poor; developing a division of labour; and being equipped locally with the expertise to play a useful role and, where necessary, to take the lead. There are some cases where this has indeed happened. Second, there remains a major risk that sectoral approaches will be over-centralized and unfocused on the poor. The challenge (especially in sectors like health and education) is to combine upstream policy and systems-oriented interventions with downstream interventions which directly involve communities in the improvement of their own health or education status. There is a need for targeting mechanisms to be devised and built-in for services to reach poor areas, communities and groups disproportionately. There are few examples of this in practice so far.

Ad hoc projects have shown major weaknesses, but a considerable proportion of the poverty-oriented European projects have nevertheless provided benefits to poor people, especially where they were initially well identified, targeted and participatory. There remains much scope for more effective approaches to this type of intervention. While exploration of sectoral approaches is desirable, there should be caution about the speed of the shift away from projects until sectoral approaches have been validated as more effective by careful monitoring and evaluation of how well they actually work.

8
Poverty Reduction: Organization and Management of the European Agencies

There has been a clear shift among the European development agencies in the 1990s towards greater commitment to poverty reduction objectives and only a few donors have bucked the poverty trend, the most obvious examples being France and Spain. The 'committed' donors have also shown a growing consensus on their stated operational aims for PR. Yet, the experience set out in the earlier chapters, if representative, also reveals surprisingly few examples of 'good practice' approaches being realized by these donors in their own poverty assessments, in their country strategies and dialogue processes or in their direct interventions on the ground relating to poverty reduction. A clear analysis of what poverty means, who the poor are, and which interventions are likely to benefit the poor most, is often strangely lacking. Even where poverty has been well conceptualized at headquarters level, as is the case for Denmark, Germany and Sweden, donor country strategies remain disappointingly short on strategic thinking. Part of the explanation for this seems to lie in the organizational structure and management systems of the donor agencies themselves.[1]

How well organized are donors for poverty reduction? It is difficult to prove a direct link between particular donor organizational structures and the level of PR impact the donor may achieve, particularly since there are many powerful determinants, such as the local context. Of course, the quality of management and organization is a major factor in the effectiveness of any aid delivery, whatever the objectives. We therefore concentrate on those aspects that seem to us, *a priori*, to be the most significant in making delivery mechanisms more effective in reaching and benefiting poor people.

Three particular organizational or management features are examined here. First, there is the question of the *central direction and guidance* given to personnel in undertaking aid delivery for PR purposes. Even more important are the systems for motivating or disciplining the actions of personnel to achieve the poverty objectives, including systems for identifying and screening interventions and, of course, assessing performance in implementing PR objectives.

Second, there is the *level of personnel, the balance of appropriate skills and the deployment* to perform these tasks effectively. Especially important is the degree to which donor organizations decentralize their personnel and their decision-making responsibilities in the field or at the country level (from headquarters in the donor capitals). This is highly relevant to understanding the local poverty situation, to flexibility in responding to it and to effective coordination with other donors in the country concerned.

Third, there is the related issue of donor *coordination*. Systems for ensuring adequate *learning and feedback on the lessons of experience* are particularly important in tackling poverty issues because of the inherent difficulty of this process. In organizational terms this raises the question of the degree of focus in monitoring and evaluation systems on poverty-reducing effectiveness.

Transmission mechanisms: weaknesses

Central directives and operational guidance

There is generally a lack of central directives and clear operational guidelines for agency staff and implementing consultants on poverty reduction. Even among donors with explicit PR objectives, there are few which seem to drive these objectives operationally from the top of their organizations. Moreover, the country studies reveal a weakness in the mechanisms for transmitting to field staff the central policy frameworks on poverty of most donors.[2]

Some agencies have divisions or departments with specialist staff responsible for conceptualizing the poverty, gender and social aspects of their activities. Some have coordinating committees and scope for exchange of experience among staff. More recently one agency, Sida, has established a permanent task force on PR. Efforts have been made to make staff aware, providing training and guidance manuals. Nevertheless, the general impression is that management approaches have not been particularly corporate, but instead rather informal or at least permissive. There was usually some sense of uncertainty among agency staff about what precisely they were expected to do in practice to meet the objectives. Indeed, sometimes the extent of PR initiatives tended to depend rather on the individual programme manager and his/her attitudes, perceptions, knowledge and motivation.

Some examples will illustrate what donor agencies are doing and what they lack. The German Federal Ministry, the BMZ, has a permanent division which is responsible for the conceptualization of poverty and gender issues. The GTZ, responsible for technical cooperation (TC), has created separate administrative units charged with the implementation of PR policy and there is an inter-disciplinary working group in the planning department to support operational departments. This helps to promote self-help and NGO activities, for example, in all German agencies. There is also a staff panel on PR to help orient German TC better towards these objectives and to clarify the problems of implementation overseas. This is intended to promote PR as an objective in all GTZ activities and improve coordination between headquarters and overseas offices. KfW, responsible for capital aid, has no specialized units for PR. These are helpful management mechanisms in the BMZ and GTZ, but the German agencies appear to provide no central directives; the focus is on exchange of experience through working groups and training. In the absence of clear guidance or even handbooks to draw upon, the concept of PR is seldom meaningful for managers and staff who often feel the poverty concepts are too broad and abstract (Weidnitzer, 1997: Chapter 4).

In the European Commission, DGVIII has made some efforts in recent years to generate interest in PR activities. In its policy division it has established a unit for human and social development and gender issues, which includes a social policy (poverty) adviser and health and education expertise which is potentially highly relevant. This unit can take initiatives and submit policy proposals. There is also a food security unit. Administrative guidance and training have been provided to improve staff awareness.

However, there remains considerable uncertainty among Commission staff about the practical implications of the EU's poverty focus.

Clear directives from senior management and incentives for staff are lacking: an important precondition for ensuring greater focus. In DG I B, management systems are weaker still. There are no official guidelines or criteria on how to determine which are the poorest areas and groups, nor is there a requirement to use poverty assessments nor any manuals for staff to follow in pursuing PR interventions (Loquai *et al.*, 1998: 42–3, 59).

During the first half of the 1990s, Denmark, Finland, Sweden and the UK have also shown a lack of a corporate approach or central drive in translating their poverty objectives into systematic and effective operational guidance to personnel. However, all four agencies have recently made renewed efforts on this. In Danida, where guidance and translation of objectives into practice were weak (COWI, 1996: Chapter 7), there has been increased focus on the operationalization of its poverty objectives, especially through sector instead of project approaches. Finnida's evaluation unit has started a similar forward-looking review and new procedures are being developed. Sida has reviewed its strategy and has established a permanent Task Force on poverty to drive its own programme with new more explicit guidance. The UK introduced a more ambitious poverty elimination strategy in late 1997. Its management drive to achieve this has only just started. Clearer guidance has been provided for the poverty orientation/country strategies and the advisory structure is being reviewed. It is essential that direction and guidance are clearly unambiguous and that the programme managers have to account for the implementation of these intentions.

In Finnida operational guidance, training and incentives for personnel and consultants to develop their knowledge and skills in poverty work have been weak, with no clear roles, working definitions, logical frameworks or guidance on standards for poverty assessment available for personnel. However, plans were drawn up in 1997 to improve guidance and monitoring (Voipio, 1998: 17–19).

Those agencies like France, Italy and Spain, which have not had significant PR aims, not surprisingly provide little or no guidance or direction to staff on poverty issues. French officials both in Paris and in the field were often puzzled by what 'poverty reduction' means or what other donors mean by it. This, of course, partly reflects a basic difference in the general French conception or perspective on the poor and the need for a special strategy. The Italian agency, recognizing its lack of internal capacity, has tended sensibly to work with multilateral organizations for interventions of this kind, using the personnel of UNDP, WHO and IDA for the execution of certain programmes which it has partly financed and supervised. However, there is a limit to a strategy of this kind for a big bilateral aid programme.

A key component of the transmission mechanism concerns *donor country strategies*. Several agencies now provide clear and similar instructions to programme managers on how to prepare country strategies for PR (for example Sida, Danida, KfW and DGVIII). These usually require identification of the poor in the country, commitment on the part of the government, assessment of the likely poverty impact of the proposed interventions, and compliance of the country aid priorities with PR objectives.

Yet experience suggests that these requirements are rarely implemented in practice. Thus for Danida, an evaluation (COWI, 1996) judged that there was little clear link between the country situation and the Danish intervention and there were no indicators for monitoring the performance of country programme managers on PR. Nevertheless, Danida is seeking to initiate the country strategy process at recipient country level and there is a strong drive for this from headquarters (Udsholt, 1997: Chapter 5).

In DFID, a review of the country strategy papers of recent years (admittedly before the new strategy was introduced) showed that the poverty content was disappointing and the poverty analysis superficial. Out of 18 Country Strategy Papers (CSPs), the coverage of poverty issues was high in only 4 and moderate in another 7, and they rarely identified the target groups or gave much of an operational lead. More important, it had been rare for them to justify the whole portfolio of interventions in relation to the poverty strategy. CSPs have not generally been structured within a framework which regards PR as the overriding objective of the aid programme which it has more recently become.

Country observations revealed some examples of donors commissioning background papers, such as poverty assessments, or state, sector or gender analyses, but this happens only rarely. In terms of content, a fundamental weakness is that the country strategy papers usually provide little information on the various opportunities and constraints for effective PR, and the pros and cons, in PR terms, of different geographical or sectoral concentrations. Donors' country strategies were nearly always drawn up in a 'top-down' and rather bureaucratic way with limited opening up of the process to outside knowledge by involving local stakeholders such as governments, local NGOs and the private sector.

Country strategy and programming could become a far more effective instrument for transmitting the PR objective through changes in approach and motivation. Some recent moves by the UK and Sida indicate a more positive focus on country strategies, and a more effective participatory approach to country strategy formation is now being pressed. Nevertheless, the gap so far between the requirements specified for country programme managers and the actuality suggests a basic weakness in management incentives and performance accountability.[3]

Getting the incentives right

The extent to which PR is prioritized in practice is likely to reflect the motivation and incentives for programme managers and their staff. The incentive system is poorly adapted to encourage managers to grapple with the difficult problems of designing interventions which are likely to provide genuine benefits for poor people.

First, donors seem to lack a set of benchmarks for judging the PR performance of their managers, so that those who make a more serious attempt to develop a programme of incentives to increase poverty impact are thus unlikely to be recognized or rewarded for their efforts. One aspect of this is to have a system for monitoring the performance of country programmes according to the aims that they set themselves – for example, in terms of the shift towards a more poverty-oriented portfolio of projects or more dialogue on strategy and policy locally. Yet there is little or no evidence of this kind from any of the European donors. In fact, Chapter 4 indicated how extremely difficult it is to know retrospectively how much poverty-focused activity donors have been involved with in any single partner country. With accountability lacking, how can the performance of programme managers be assessed and, indeed, why should they bother too much to pursue this difficult objective if no one is taking any notice of the results? Nor does the personnel performance appraisal system seem to be closely related to a judgement on the quality of the programme managers' work.

Second, there need to be procedures for requiring personnel to ensure that all their proposed specific interventions take account of the agency's objectives. These systems are now being introduced by agencies like Sida, where 'all projects should define their target and participatory groups and indicate their planned impact on poverty'. Follow-up studies are intended to investigate poverty impact (Carlsson, 1998: 46). DFID has not so far revised its procedures but senior management messages seem clear. Finnida's new design guidelines require the planners to assess and report on the compatibility of each new intervention with the main strategic goals of Finnish aid, including PR. DGVIII now has a Quality Support Group for project proposals under the European Development Fund which screens new proposals above a certain threshold for compliance with priority objectives including poverty. There are some doubts about how effective this system has been but the longer planning horizon and lower disbursement pressure under the EDF 8 (compared with EDF 7) may help incentives and the effectiveness of the screening process (Loquai *et al.*, 1998: 49–50). The DGIS in the Netherlands also has a screening system for projects to meet gender and poverty objectives – the O-toets. In the case of the Spanish International Cooperation Agency, which has defined PR as one objective of its programme, there is little evidence that this receives much attention at middle management level. It is unclear whether the poverty objective influences the identification of projects, and there is no unit which systematically analyses projects for PR or other development criteria (Freres and Corral, 1997: 15).

Third, the effective use and motivation of consultants are perhaps neglected issues. Two agencies – Finnida and the European Commission – rely heavily on consultants for design and implementation especially. Consultants are a valuable resource and source of experience and knowledge, particularly where agencies use 'generalist' staff who revolve rapidly. This is particularly important in PR efforts. In Finnida, however, it has been observed that there is no incentive for these consultants to hand over early to local people or to seek local institutional ownership. It is important, for the management of poverty oriented aid, that incentives and performance assessment indicators are constructed so that the consultants and consultancy companies are rewarded for recruiting local consultants and handing over rather than staying on in the developing country (Voipio, 1998: 98).

The European Commission is extremely dependent upon consultants for the design, implementation and monitoring of its programmes. However, the system for tendering for consultants is universally acknowledged to be highly unsatisfactory. A separate unit, outside the technical unit and the country desk, is charged with managing the tendering process, with a representative of the technical unit as one of the evaluators. The emphasis is on the transparency of the selection process, resulting in legalistic considerations predominating over technical quality. There is no pre-qualification procedure to ensure a minimum standard of technical excellence, and the pool from which the EC can draw is severely limited by the fact that it pays significantly lower rates than other donors (approximately 30 per cent below the going rate). The importance of ensuring a 'fair' balance of nationality in the allocation of contracts among the Member States arguably compromises the quality of technical expertise provided. In the health sector, the cost of preparing bids, which may amount to Euro 20,000, and the lower rates offered have drastically reduced the scope to involve institutes of public health, which may well have more appropriate expertise than many of the consultancy firms which do tender. Perhaps the most serious flaw in the procedures is that those technical experts who have been involved in project or programme design are automatically excluded from competing at the implementation phase. While intended to ensure fair competition, this can have extremely negative effects on effectiveness. An example is the reproductive and child health sector programme in India, to which the EC has allocated Euro 200 million. The team of EC consultants which spent about nine months in India working with other donors and the Indian Government on the programme design was ruled out from tendering for programme implementation. Given the EC's very limited staff resources at the Delegation and in Brussels, their departure signals the loss of a huge bank of knowledge, including relationships and trust built up between the consultants and the government and other donors. In addition, the re-tendering process is slow, resulting in a significant loss of impetus. EC officials are understandably frustrated by a system which fails to support them in their attempts to deliver an effective aid programme (Cox *et al.*, 1999: Chapter 5).

Fourth, an effective approach to PR usually needs to be a highly participatory one, benefiting from an extended preparation phase and a strong 'software' component. But participatory approaches tend to be time-consuming which runs directly counter to another incentive characteristic of donor agencies – the need to disburse aid within the allotted time. Several senior bilateral aid officials have spoken openly of their frustration at having to cut corners or compromise their poverty focus in order to satisfy the demand for meeting spending targets from headquarters. As long as promotion opportunities are quite closely linked to disbursement rates in some measure, without a commensurate emphasis on quality and impact, the PR objective is likely to be squeezed or to become rather dependent on the personality of the individual managers. This argument is less important for some donors where disbursement pressures may be less, leaving more management time for PR. In German technical cooperation, under the so-called ZOPP or objective-oriented system of project planning, for example, a sort of logical framework, the early and decisive phases of project identification and design are carried out without direct participation by the target group from the developing country. Hence there is need for a more flexible, less strict and more relaxed preparatory phase procedure for programme managers if they are to identify and design projects – especially self-help projects – in a genuinely participatory way (Weidnitzer, 1997: 39). A similar reconsideration may be necessary for other donor agencies as well. Finnida has recently developed new guidelines for its project management systems which are more sensitive to PR and gender and which favour participation by beneficiaries in planning at all stages of the project cycle. There have been some encouraging examples of participatory interventions.

Appropriate personnel

Assessing the appropriate level of personnel to achieve effective aid delivery is a hazardous task, and information and comparable classification are not available. Nevertheless, observation suggests that some donor agencies markedly lack enough staff to carry out the rather sophisticated operations required by an effective PR strategy, nor do they often have the right balance of skills among them.

In the European Commission, despite the recent efforts of DGVIII and DG I-B to build capacities, it is evident that skills and expertise for PR and social development are rather scarce and they appear inappropriate for an aid administration that has a focus on these issues (Loquai *et al.*, 1998: 45). DGVIII's range of skills still reflects more traditional concerns – concentration on economics, civil engineering and agriculture (Cox *et al.*, 1997: Chapter 2 and Table 2.2). The Commission has made some efforts to build up in-house capacity on poverty and Human and Social Development (HSD) aspects in the 1990s and there is a unit for HSD including gender in the policy division of DGVIII, with one expert each for health, education and training, gender, vulnerability and human empowerment. The first social development and poverty adviser was appointed in 1993 to contribute to the formulation of a PR policy, guidelines, training and advice to specific country desks. There is a directorate of health with 5 specialist staff and a unit for education staffed with 8 experts. Nevertheless, the balance is not right, and the majority of Commission officials consulted in the study gave priority on PR to the recruitment of staff with specializations and expertise in the 'soft areas' (social development, self-help promotion, decentralized cooperation and participatory approaches). DGVIII also lacks adequate institutional, health and education expertise.

DG I of the Commission, responsible for Asia and Latin America, is undoubtedly understaffed in the numbers and balance of skills in relation to the funds it controls. 'DGVIII has one desk officer for Guinea Bissau while DG I-B has one person responsible for the whole of Brazil' was the comment of one stressed official. The rather complex and unclear organization and management structure of DG I-B makes it difficult to trace where the responsibilities lie in terms of the integration of EU policy objectives on PR. It lacks specialist departments for health and education, and coordination by a cross-cutting North-South internal unit for gender and population has limited impact on implementing departments. Staff are weighed down by the management of large budgets and have limited time for training and coordination, and the initiative is left largely to desk officers who rely heavily on external experts (Loquai *et al.*, 1998: 45).

On the other hand, DFID in the UK has always had a good range of skills, and it has developed a more appropriate range of skills in the last decade with social development and institutional as well as health planning skills which are highly relevant to PR work. Nevertheless despite this well established multi-disciplinary approach, there are some signs that the particular professional management structure DFID has established may not necessarily ensure the maximum multi-disciplinary cooperation.

One thing is clear; with any shift from project to sectoral approaches to PR interventions, the skill requirements will need to shift towards those who have more institutional and policy skills for reforms in the social sectors, and in fiscal management and central and local government. For example, these will include skills to compare the costs, outcomes and distributional impacts of different social sector initiatives and policy choices, skills to assess the incidence of different taxes and charges, expertise in user-friendly computerized public accountancy and reporting systems, and training in budget planning at local levels. These will tend to differ from the needs of the project mode and may need to be found in other developing countries or in other Ministries and municipalities in the donor countries.

Decentralization of donor organizations

Among the European donor agencies there are considerable differences in the organizational structure and location of personnel. Yet the degree of decentralization is a vital issue in the effectiveness of aid delivery, especially poverty-focused activities. Decentralization can have several components depending on the proportion of local staff located at the country level, the range of their skills and their degree of autonomous decision-making capacity. One practice is for headquarters to remain the nodal point for top-down policy and decision-making, with minimal country-level capacity to channel back information and maintain daily management of the aid portfolio. A second partly decentralized practice involves the partial division and partial replication of the country capacity between headquarters and the country-level office. The formulation of country-strategy sectoral programmes and decisions on the country portfolio remain at headquarters with country-level inputs. A third practice involves the decentralization of personnel and decision-making competence to the country, with only the overall budget and donor policy framework determined at headquarters. All these models are represented in India for example, with even some variations on each of them.

At one extreme, Germany has most of its aid personnel centralized at headquarters. The BMZ, responsible for country strategy and
dialogue, has no overseas offices and is not well represented overseas. Decision-making is also centralized in Berlin. GTZ, the TC
implementation agency, uses contracted long-term experts in the
field, while KfW has no overseas offices and relies on short-term
missions. Finnida's personnel and decision-making power is also
highly concentrated in Helsinki. Of 180 staff members, only 15 were
resident in the field in 1997. There is limited devolution of authority and resources to the embassies and regional offices. With conse-
quent problems of communication, 'headquarter staff have very thin
personal exposure to the nature of life realities of the poor'. Recent
Finnish evaluations have systematically indicated that a weak point
of their interventions has been insufficient understanding of the
broader cultural, economic, political and social situation in the societies and communities where they operate (Voipio, 1998: 44–5).
This is a criticism that no doubt could be made of the headquarters
staff of other agencies as well, and the feedback of insights on
poverty is particularly inhibited when staff do not revolve much
between headquarters and the field or when there is a high turnover
of staff in the field. Finnida depends quite heavily on implementation by consultancy companies, and the consultants develop a good
fund of knowledge and experience on development and poverty
issues. However, this experience is not fed back into the central policies or procedures. The European Commission, which also relies
very highly on contracted consultants for implementing its aid
delivery, has similar problems.

The European Commission's DGVIII is well represented overseas.
In 1996, 60 of the 71 ACP countries had a delegation, with an average staff of 4.2. However, decision-making responsibilities are not so
well delegated from Brussels. Delegations are heavily burdened with
administrative and financial tasks and lack analytical capacities to
pay more attention to strategic issues; staff often tend to have relatively little direct experience or insights on concrete problems of
poverty at the programme and project level. There is also limited
turnover of staff between the Delegations and Brussels, which must
inhibit the feedback of experience from the field into central policy
and decision-making. DG I-B has Delegations in 15 of the 39 Asian
and Latin American countries, but these have more restricted

responsibilities than those in the Lomé Convention countries, with no financial responsibilities, and they appear to play a more political and commercial than a development role. However, the draft mandate for ACP/EU negotiations signals a certain willingness to devolve responsibilities from the Community headquarters to the Delegations and their partner organizations (Loquai *et al.*, 1998: 43–4, 59).

The UK is probably the most decentralized of the European agencies in terms not only of its staff but also its decision-making responsibilities. The overseas regional and country offices play a major role in the formulation of country strategies and it has been estimated that some 50 per cent of bilateral expenditure decisions are made in the field. The UK has always circulated its staff between headquarters and the field which helps headquarters' understanding of local situations. The decentralized system has offered considerable scope for local PR initiatives particularly in sub-Saharan Africa, India and Bangladesh (though these have been more permissive rather than directed from headquarters in the 1990s). For example, in Bangladesh 'the very existence of DFID personnel on the ground generated its own impetus for a shift away from the big infrastructure projects of old and into the social sectors of education, health and micro credit. The presence of social development advisers on the ground inevitably strengthened commitment to these areas and facilitated the subtle process of dialogue with the recipient government. Decentralisation was felt to offer not just better local knowledge but a greater ability to "chase up" and monitor individuals and organisations particularly important where large sums were channelled through indigenous NGOs' (Cox, 2000: 20).

The French system is also quite decentralized and field missions have competence in relation to the initiation and implementation of projects and responsibility for preparing the country strategies. However, the central administrations in Paris (Ministry of Cooperation, Caisse Française, etc.) which finally determine the budgets and strategies for the country programmes, are not focused on poverty reduction. In addition, the main location of expertise is Paris and not the field mission, if Burkina Faso is representative (de Boisdeffre, 1998b: 16).

The Spanish International Development Agency has its Technical Cooperation Officer (OTC) in each Latin American country, though important decisions are still taken at headquarters. The OTC coordinators are responsible for the formulation and execution of bilateral projects but always under headquarter supervision where PR has not been a major priority. The coordinators' better appreciation of local needs and initiatives can seldom be brought to bear because of the lack of institutional mechanisms; their incentives are geared more to day-to-day management and cost control and their jobs are short-term and precarious (Freres and Corral, 1997: 26).

Nordic donors like Sida and Danida have been shifting towards more decentralized organizations but through mergers with their diplomatic service in the field. Unfortunately, Sida has been seeking to reduce its staff levels, especially field staff (Carlsson, 1998), which if successful cannot really be helpful to its new poverty initiatives. For Danida, Udsholt (1997: 35–6) observes that the move to address poverty issues more seriously may place heavy demands on the capacity within the Danish Ministry of Foreign Affairs, where poverty experience and general experience with strategic planning and policy dialogue are limited and of recent origin. He adds that there will probably be a need to devolve competence from headquarters to the embassies overseas to achieve a more effective division of labour. For the Netherlands also, since the merger of the DGIS with the Ministry of Foreign Affairs, responsibility for the bilateral programme, including selection, appraisal, monitoring and evaluation of projects and programmes, has shifted from The Hague to the embassies. These have gained personnel, though one implication has been a tendency for generalists to have priority over experienced development staff and specialists in staffing decisions (Hoebink and Schulpen, 1998).

There are strong grounds for arguing that greater decentralization of donor staff resources and decision-making powers to the recipient country level may make interventions more effective, especially in trying to reach the poor. There are a number of aspects to this.

First, the greater the proximity of donor agency personnel to the local situation in the partner countries, the better should be their understanding of the local political, cultural and social context bearing on poverty and on effective ways of intervening to benefit poor people. Scope is offered for greater awareness and sensitivity to local thinking and for close local contacts based on personal relationships. There is more likelihood of ensuring some knowledge of what has been tried before. However, it is not enough for the staff to be in partner country capitals; they should be familiar with the situation in the rural as well as urban areas where the problems of poverty prevail. Reaching the poor is a highly ambitious enterprise which is associated with developing innovative, appropriate and replicable approaches to poverty. This requires the careful nurturing of relations with government and project partners and often the participation of intended beneficiaries over a period of time. All these factors, we would argue, are associated with having a sufficient level and range of expertise, ideally at the country level, and being empowered to take decisions swiftly and flexibly.

Second, the availability of a range of competence in-country can improve the quality of project proposals formally received, since there is considerable scope for an informal pro-active role in the design of projects, especially as many of the proposals received are poorly conceived and designed. When local needs are best resourced by local experts there is a special need for donor competence in selecting and supervising them. Third, the development of sectoral approaches to PR necessitates working closely with the central and (in India) the State Governments, and the policy reform process and negotiations are more effective if there is strong country-based sectoral expertise present all the year round. Fourth, and relatedly, if donors are going to coordinate among themselves and with their partners in specific countries for the exchange of experience and consistency of approach and actions, they need to have personnel who can communicate with each other on the ground, especially regularly in working groups.

There are some counter-arguments in favour of a strong headquarters-based country capacity and sectoral expertise. It is seen as facilitating the learning of lessons across the whole donor programme, and especially at the regional level, since sectoral expertise is often organized in regional units at headquarters. The accumulation of knowledge can then be 'sent out' to individual countries when the need arises. It may be easier to ensure that full account is taken of state-of-the-art thinking on PR. However, it is not entirely clear why these functions cannot be performed by a slimmed-down headquarters staff. A more decentralized organization is undoubtedly more costly though not necessarily less cost-effective; in India, DFID believes that the higher costs (moderated somewhat by the use of local staff) are justified by greater effectiveness. Perhaps a more powerful point is that it lends greater political weight and authority to the negotiations with partner governments and ministries.

It is not easy to make a judgement on which model is likely to achieve more effective PR in aid. However, three of the country operations examined, in India, Nepal and Burkina Faso, revealed that the more decentralized donors – those better represented in the field – were more effective. They learned quicker and were equipped with monitoring capacity and local expertise. In India, the research team favoured decentralization, and in particular because of the sheer size and institutional structure of India and the demands this places on a donor. The weakness of the Delegation of the European Commission in India, in particular, was clearly manifest, compared with some other donors who were better represented on the ground (see Cox *et al.*, 2000: Chapter 5 and further below). In Nepal, for example, the GTZ office in Kathmandu – with highly competent German and Nepalese professionals – was running the German country programme independently and effectively. In fact, there had been no official visits from Germany to the field for three years, while the UK had a weak programme partly because of the lack of local presence of development aid professionals (Gsaenger and Voipio, 1999). The study of Burkina Faso (Loquai and van Hove, 1997: 8) concluded:

> for those donors that have a general poverty reduction strategy, awareness of this strategy in the field and the capacities for implementation seem to vary in line with the degree of decentralisation of the aid system. This means that donors that delegate competence and human resources for policy formulation to the field seem better placed to translate their general policy into a country strategy and contribute to a policy dialogue on the country level.

The limitations of overall numbers of personnel in-country are compounded by the often limited *range of specialist skills* which can be drawn upon. There are very few donors with significant numbers of social development advisers and even fewer with institutional development skills, though the UK and Germany are to some extent exceptions to this, while the European Commission, France and Spain clearly are not. The European Commission in India is an acute example of this weakness. It is nothing short of scandalous that the Commission, with such a large annual programme of expenditure,

Box 8.1   What donors can learn from each other in Tanzania

Most donors whose decision-making procedures are heavily centralised at headquarters can learn from the Dutch in Tanzania, who have a strong team of experts working year round in the Dar-es-Salaam embassy with sufficiently independent decision-making authority. This puts them in a very strong position in the new sectoral and institutional reform pro- grammes, which they can influence far beyond their relative share of funding, simply because they are always available to discuss with and to advise their colleagues in the Tanzanian ministries, and not just during the bi-annual joint donor planning, appraisal or monitoring missions like most of the other donors.

Most donors can learn from the Norwegians and the Irish, who have people among their staff who have spent most of their professional careers dealing with Tanzania, as field consultants, embassy staff, or as Tanzania desk officers at headquarters. The personal memory on Tanzanian issues is a great asset compared with many other donors whose staff circulate rapidly from one posting to another, never developing a deep enough understanding about the society whose development they are supposed to serve.

Many European donors can learn from the Danes and the British, whose 'embassy grant facilities' make it possible for them to pledge support at very short notice to various small demands (quick studies, workshops, pilot projects) when there is a need for such inputs to keep the ball rolling in the sectoral or institutional reform processes. Many other donors spend much more money but make a smaller impact because their decision- making procedures (involving headquarters) are too slow and cumbersome.

Donors which deploy large funds in Tanzania but have weak contacts with the field-level realities of poor Tanzanians, can learn from the expe- riences and perspectives of the Nordic States, the Dutch, the Irish, the Swiss, UNICEF and some of the international NGOs (including the mis- sionaries), who may have less money but have a longer institutionalised memory and more deeply rooted field-level experiences, of Tanzanian local realities. All other donors can learn from the way the Irish have made participatory poverty profiling a routine procedure in all Irish funded interventions.

The best results in poverty reduction in the view of local Tanzanian observers have been achieved by those European donors who have focused their assistance on the rural areas of Tanzania and funded activities such as clean water supply, health, education, vocational training, rural roads, small business development, agriculture, livestock and environmental protection. More important than the areas of focus has been a long-term commitment (for example 20 years); doing the basic things right and not being carried away by new fads or always seeking new innovations.

(Extract from Voipio and Hoebink, 1999)

has the equivalent of only 7 full-time staff to implement its mandate. They are also expected to administer the EC's aid programme in Nepal, where there is practically no resident EC representation apart from the private consulting companies who manage the EC-funded projects. None of the EC delegation staff are sectoral experts in health or education, the two largest programmes in the EC portfolio. The Delegation lacks both sectoral and cross-cutting (gender, institutional development and social development) expertise. Its staff are therefore reliant first on technical support from Brussels, and secondly on consultants. However, the EC Technical Unit for the whole of Asia comprises only 12 people, who collectively provide about 1.5 'person equivalent' for the India programme. There is a single specialist on education for all Asia, and similarly for health, and a few experts cover the 'horizontal' issues, such as the environment, forestry, and women and development. The Unit can therefore offer only very limited inputs into the India programme, again due to the impossible scope of its remit. In addition, there is a desk officer responsible for India, who takes a lead in strategy development, but whose mandate is to spend at least half his time on political and trade-related activities as opposed to development cooperation. The Commission is therefore extremely dependent upon consultants for the design, implementation and monitoring of its programmes, and the system for tendering for consultants is universally acknowledged to be highly unsatisfactory. The main burden of responsibility for this lies with the Member States, who have long been sceptical of the Commission's ability to implement its aid programme effectively, and have thus favoured reliance on consultants. The Member States have also not supported the decentralization of decision-making authority and personnel to the country level, preferring to retain greater control through their representation on the Brussels-based Councils and Committees. A significant expansion of staffing levels in Brussels and at the country level is essential if the Commission is to fulfil its mandate effectively.

The UK's experience in India suggests that increasing the numbers of cross-cutting advisers, whose role it is to ensure that social, institutional and economic aspects are systematically considered at the design and implementation phases, and locating them in the programme country itself, have indeed increased effectiveness. Such an organizational structure would also seem likely to address a number of the weaknesses outlined earlier, notably with respect to gender and deepening the conceptualization and understanding of poverty.

Even where there is representation on the ground, often little *decision-making authority* is devolved to country-based staff and the decision to initiate an intervention or to adapt it during implementation rests with the headquarters staff. In the case of the European Commission's aid programme, this lack of delegated authority is even greater for the Asia, Latin America and Mediterranean (ALA/ MED) programmes, than for the Africa, Caribbean and Pacific regions. Although German aid is arguably even more centralized, it is the Commission's organization structure which is more problematic, especially in the ALA/MED programmes. This is because governments are obliged to deal with the Commission Delegations, even though they may have little direct authority, rather than directly with Brussels, whereas in the German case it is expected that government officials will contact their opposite numbers directly in Frankfurt, for instance.

Coordination in-country on poverty reduction

Field evidence confirms that coordination among donors, even at the most basic level of information exchange, is usually given a low priority. In part, this is related to donor levels of decentralization and devolution since coordination is likely to be meaningful only when it reflects and influences the realities on the ground and is thus essentially a country-based activity. Since many donors have low staffing levels in-country or lack particular specialist skills, they may simply not have sufficient time, or the right kind of knowledge, to engage in constructive coordination. Also they often require greater delegated authority for this purpose than they already have. Burkina Faso is an example of a country where European donors' coordination is rudimentary and needs to be extended to policy level and dialogue. Tanzania, on the other hand, is a country where several donors have relatively larger numbers of staff and where aid coordination – initially only among the donors but nowadays also including representatives of the Government of Tanzania – has functioned relatively more fruitfully than in many other countries where the donors have only very few staff present.

There are three obvious areas where greater coordination could help address some of the shortcomings identified in this study. The first is with respect to improving *donors' understanding of the nature and causes of poverty* within a particular country. This is a weak point for virtually all donors, yet remarkably little joint work is undertaken and there are instances of a reluctance to share what has been learned. For example, Danida has conducted an exemplary evaluation of the PR impacts of its country programme in Nepal but – amazingly – has never shared the reports with any of the other donors working in Nepal. A few donors have worked with the World Bank or the UNDP, providing either funding or staff for poverty assessments, public expenditure reviews and other missions, but this happens all too rarely. Carrying out such assessments, or building up government capacity to do so, is a large task which may require a range of skills or an investment of time which may be beyond an individual donor. Nevertheless success would benefit all parties. While there are bound to be difficulties, since bilateral donors may not share a common analysis with each other or with the World Bank, this remains a prime candidate for greater coordination efforts. Even an open exchange of information and experience about different approaches and experiences in poverty activities would be an advance, for example, in Burkina Faso.

A second valuable area for cooperation relates to *sectoral reform*. Here, there are a greater number of positive examples of donors cooperating on the design and funding of health, education and other sector reform programmes. There are also a few examples of recipient governments doing the coordinating, insisting that donors subscribe to a common framework, as with the District Primary Education Project in India. However, a great deal more could be done, and greater efforts made to see the 'big picture' rather than pursuing sectional interests.

A third related area is for donors to work towards a *consensus* on 'a single strategy' for PR between themselves and the domestic authorities especially in sub-Saharan Africa (there is an initiative of the UK in the SPA framework which is strongly supported by Finnida and the EC). Joint donor strategic dialogue with recipient representation from the central administration, local administration, project staff, NGOs and private bodies is a need which emerges, for example, from experience in Burkina Faso.

In all these areas of potential cooperation, the presence of sufficient numbers of well qualified staff in-country is perceived by many donors and by government officials as being a distinct advantage, if not essential. The evidence from the research team also suggests that recipient governments value being able to draw upon donor sectoral expertise, particularly if provided in the form of specialists familiar with, and permanently located in, the country rather than visiting experts who may change from one year to the next (see Box 8.1).

Feedback and learning lessons

Monitoring has in general improved in the 1990s and some innovatory approaches to monitoring at village level have been introduced for some projects, for example, DFID in Joint Forest Management and Planning (JFMP) in Karnataka and the Finnida-funded Rural Integrated Programme Support programme which is providing monitoring services for all foreign donors and NGOs working in the Mtwara and Lindi regions of Tanzania. Certain agencies are currently shifting towards greater examination of poverty aspects and are setting up research units in poor countries to do this more effectively (for example, the Dutch in Tanzania and the Germans in Nepal).

Nevertheless, the external agencies know too little about the impact of their PR activities on the poor themselves or the processes which assist the involvement of the poor. Despite the fact that nearly all of them have evaluation units and have carried out substantial evaluation work and monitoring, very little attention has been paid to the impact of their interventions on the poor or on income distribution (for example, Sida, Danida, DFID, EC, France and Spain). Hence the state of knowledge is inadequate and there is not enough evidence on what works and what does not work to benefit poor people effectively. It is the lack of priority given by external agencies to this aspect that is basically at fault, and this is particularly puzzling in the light of the PR rhetoric they have frequently deployed in the 1990s.

Summary

In general, the organization and management systems of the European development cooperation agencies are not particularly well adapted to translating their PR goals and aims into effective practice. Even among the more 'committed' agencies there has been a lack of central or corporate drive and clear guidance to programme managers. The management systems have been fairly informal and permissive, leaving much to individual discretion and motivation. Recently more vigour is being applied to the operationalization of poverty aims, especially for Sida, Danida and DFID with its new poverty strategy. Country strategies and programming have not been used so far as the effective instrument for PR which they could be. However, some agencies (for example, Danida, DFID, DGVIII, KfW and Sida) are now providing more guidance on the PR orientation of country programmes and the vetting of these at higher levels to sharpen them up. A weakness has been monitoring of performance to ensure that programme managers plan their country portfolios to meet the PR aims of the organization. Although the Netherlands and the UK have used poverty and gender screening systems for projects, this practice is only slowly spreading. Personal incentive systems could be better geared to encourage the long-term, patient and participatory approaches required for effective PR interventions, which are sometimes inhibited by incentives to achieve timely disbursement targets. New incentives and better procedures are necessary for selection and use of consultants, especially for those agencies like the EC and Finnida that rely heavily on them.

More effective poverty interventions will require a new balance of appropriate expertise with the incorporation of more institutional, social development and social sector skills, especially with the introduction of sectoral approaches. Some donors (for example, Germany and the UK) have increased their range of skills, but a number lag behind. DGVIIII, despite some efforts to widen its skills, is lacking in the essential institutional, health and education skills, while DGI is seriously understaffed for the roles it is supposed to play. There are powerful advantages for PR management (and probably a net balance of advantage) in having an organization that decentralizes personnel and decision-making responsibilities to the field offices or embassies, and which ensures that there is a wider range of skills there. Only the UK has a fully decentralized system of this kind, though other agencies, such as those of Sweden, Denmark and the Netherlands, are moving in this direction with some questions about adequate specialist staffing levels. DGVIII has substantial overseas Delegations but does not decentralize decision-making and lacks a range of appropriate skills. DGI is quite inadequately staffed overseas. Some agencies (most obviously the German BMZ and KfW, as well as Finnida) remain highly centralized in their national capitals. A more general shift to decentralized organization among European agencies may well be the key to improving the rather weak degree of in-country coordination and cooperation on poverty issues and interventions. This will become even more important with a shift towards sectoral approaches.

Finally, the European agencies have not developed a sufficient knowledge base on the nature of poverty in most partner countries, nor have they developed their own analytical and policy capacities in this area to match that of the World Bank, for example. They have started, but could do much more to support their partners' capacity on these issues locally, especially in the formation and implementation of appropriate pro-poor strategies. Although monitoring of agency interventions has improved in the 1990s, more effective built-in monitoring and evaluation work is needed to assess the impact of interventions on poor people and to provide lessons on what types of intervention work best to help them.

9

Conclusions and some Suggestions for Reform

The context of poverty

This review of seven poor countries reveals a wide range of opportunities for external agencies which seek to support or influence the pursuit of poverty reduction (PR). These include the need for:

- more effective economic policies to promote employment-creating growth;
- a shift of resources and services into rural areas;
- a reorientation of public social services and an improvement in their quality at basic levels;
- the creation of mechanisms to assist poorer regions and districts;
- better targeting of credit and other measures to help the poor;
- a redistribution of land ownership and use;
- strengthened institutional capacities at local levels.

Most of these countries have moved towards some degree of greater political freedom and pluralism, which is potentially helpful. Yet in terms of political processes and cultures, formidable obstacles remain to the redistribution of public subsidies, and even more so to the redistribution of assets like land, and the reduction of discrimination against (particularly poor) women.

Unfortunately most governments have little incentive to protect or promote the interests of the very poor. This is not simply because of the weakness of the poor and the indifference of elites. Certain groups such as civil servants or urban working class groups (who are often fairly poor, at least temporarily) demand more attention to their needs and predictably resist government attempts to re-target subsidies and social programmes such as education and health to benefit the truly needy. The key question then becomes the conditions under which governments are nonetheless likely to adopt pro-poor measures. Competitive democratic elections are no guarantee of influence for the poor. Domestically, political alliances with more influential groups can provide the poor with some benefits through broader-based programmes, though the poor usually remain the subordinate partners.

However, it is clear that there remains a powerful potential role for outside agencies as an 'external lobby' on behalf of the really poor within these countries. This is particularly so in countries which are highly aid-dependent. The manner in which this advocacy role is pursued raises important questions concerning the nature of partnership and dialogue (see below).

Poverty reduction goals and strategies of the European development cooperation agencies

All the European agencies have adopted the international development goal of halving the proportion of the poor by 2015, a goal which is enshrined in the OECD/DAC document, *Shaping the 21st Century*. They do not, however, share a common strategy on its achievement. Denmark, Finland, the Netherlands, Sweden and the UK have poverty reduction as their overarching goal, while for the European Community, Germany and (more ambiguously) Italy it is one priority among others. France and Spain do not have an explicit strategy for PR. French agencies do not consider that there are identifiable groups of poor people for whom a special strategy is required. The European Community programme has a number of Resolutions related to poverty, but is only slowly elaborating operational strategies.

Those agencies where poverty reduction represents an overarching objective make the strongest commitment to 'mainstream' all their activities in terms of it. There is some risk nevertheless that every activity will be presented as poverty-reducing, without real justification in all cases. Those agencies for which poverty is one priority among others, rarely reveal the weight to be given to the PR aim. This makes it harder to judge whether their implementation performance is adequate.

Virtually all the European agencies regard poverty as a multi-dimensional concept. It is no longer viewed as simply a lack of monetary income or consumption, important as these are. The poor tend to be defined and identified in rather general terms. There are also differences between agencies. For example, for Germany the poor are defined in absolute terms, while the European Commission tends towards a relative concept of poverty. Only two agencies (the UK and the Danish) focus on the rural population. Most agencies concentrate on the (often ethnic) groups which are marginalized and discriminated against, such as women and female-headed households (though not all agencies specify poor women). Denmark and the Netherlands focus on smallholders and small enterprises (not always necessarily poor farmers or poor entrepreneurs), and the Netherlands on the landless in Asia. Finland and the EC also give special attention to the disabled and the aged. Italy has tended to focus on those groups which need help arising from 'special situations' (conflict, emergencies, refugees and migrants and their rehabilitation). These formal positions of the agencies may not necessarily indicate the focus of their actual operations.

There has been a clear increase in the commitment of a group of agencies to poverty objectives during the 1990s with greater attention to more effective operationalization, especially Denmark, Sweden, Germany, the Netherlands and more recently the UK. These now form a distinct group of like-minded agencies on poverty issues. Finland and Italy have shifted their positions a little, the European Community is slowly working out its own position and operational guidelines, but France and Spain have not obviously shifted their stance.

For the like-minded group of agencies at least, there is a considerable consensus on economic and social aims to achieve their goals. Economic growth, though vital, is not seen as sufficient in itself to achieve adequate reduction in the degree of poverty especially in slow growing areas like sub-Saharan Africa. They share the notion of economic policies for 'broad-based' or pro-poor growth to provide opportunities for the poor, especially through greater employment. Their approach includes measures to improve access of the poor to credit and knowledge to boost their productivity as well as improved basic infrastructure for rural development. Priority is given to the provision of more and better quality basic social services especially primary education, health, drinking water and sanitation to offer easier access for the poor. Some agencies focus on the need to reorient public expenditure in this direction in their partner countries. Questions remain about the feasibility of the real scope for of significant employment creation for the unskilled poor while inadequate attention is being given to the redistribution of assets (especially land and land-use rights).

In their approaches to interventions, the agencies have increasingly recognized that the key to an effective poverty reduction strategy is a strategy that is 'owned' by the partner countries, with specific 'programmes' owned locally and not imposed from outside. Conditionality for poverty reduction is not favoured, although the European Community, for example, has not ruled it out. There have been few cases where the agencies have applied pro-poor conditionality. In their specific interventions since the early 1990s, most agencies favour approaches that allow local communities (including poor potential beneficiaries) more participation in both their ongoing projects and new ones.

More fundamentally, the agencies now see political reform, multiparty elections, pluralism, better central administration and decentralization as essential for more effective poverty reduction. Yet they are seldom explicit about how these reforms will promote greater responsiveness to the needs of the poor or will counter gender discrimination and increase popular participation. The agencies have helped with some decentralization in practice. Nevertheless, quite apart from the considerable constraints on effective financial devolution and local institutional capacities, there is as yet no systematic evidence that even successful decentralization of responsibilities is favouring the poor.

Country operations and poverty reduction

At the country level, most European donors have failed to make an in depth analysis of the poverty situation with a precise identification of poor groups. Nor have they a precise idea of what constitutes a pro-poor strategy for each partner country. The external lead on this has largely been largely left to the World Bank and the UNDP. The European agencies have had little meaningful bilateral dialogue at official level with their partners on the national/macro-level aspects of PR policies, nor have they worked together to seek a collective consensus on an appropriate 'single strategy' with their common partners. There has been little evidence of a lead from the EC on dialogue. The challenge is for the external agencies to do much more 'homework' on these issues and also for them to locate the appropriate focus within government structures where dialogue is likely to be productive.

However, there have been some exceptions; the Netherlands and the Nordic donors in Tanzania (with the UNDP and World Bank), the UK in relation to the Indian State governments, and some European donors taking a position on social policies as a counterweight to the World Bank in Consultative Groups in Nepal and Bolivia. At the sectoral/meso level, there have also been cases of regular dialogue on issues relevant to poverty; Germany in India, Denmark in Nepal, and Germany and the Netherlands in Burkina Faso. There is clearly a need for the European agencies to play a role in dialogue not only on the formulation of pro-poor policy but even more importantly on its implementation. There is considerable scope especially at the sectoral level. Ideally the domestic authorities should take the lead, but where this is lacking individual donors have a lead role to play provided it is played sensitively and in a participative way.

Although comprehensive information is not available, the importance of poverty-focused interventions in the portfolios of several European agencies has almost certainly increased in the 1990s. On average, probably about a quarter of their bilateral country spending is on projects with clear direct or indirect linkages with poverty reduction. However, this obscures considerable variation both between donors and in different countries. In India, half of the spending of four major European donors was clearly poverty-focused, while in Zambia it was about a quarter. In both cases the figures for individual donors varied significantly. Thus scope exists for lagging donors to do more to reach the poor. Despite rhetoric on 'ownership', there were very few examples of donors supporting locally owned and initiated poverty programmes. While *ad hoc* project approaches remain the dominant mode, some donors are shifting towards sectoral approaches to aid delivery (see below).

The effectiveness and impact of poverty-oriented projects

Very little is known about the impact of agency interventions on the poor since evaluations have either neglected distributional issues or focused on outputs rather than impact. From a sample of 90 interventions in the seven poor countries studied it emerged that over 70 per cent of projects had a positive impact on the poor, of which a third had a high impact. Interventions were more successful at improving the access of the poor to resources and knowledge. They were less able to improve the livelihoods and rights of the poor significantly. The managements of projects were participatory in their processes and showed moderate or high levels of gender sensitivity. However, a minority of projects were highly targeted at poor groups and they made very limited use of targeting mechanisms. This was significant because the most targeted projects seemed to make the greatest impact.

Finally, there remain considerable questions about the sustainability or prospective sustainability of these poverty-focused projects.

Good and bad approaches

Targeting

Although there were examples of lessons being learnt and applied, development agencies have given insufficient consideration to whether and what type of targeting mechanisms may be required in order to reach poor groups effectively. Broad targeting on poorer regions or districts, or concentration on particularly vulnerable groups, has been used effectively, but opportunities have been missed. Population-wide approaches, providing services to both poor and non-poor, may be a legitimate way for governments and agencies to ensure that the institutional norm incorporates the poor. However, unless the constraints facing the poor are taken into account, population-wide delivery all too often results in the poor benefiting little (GTZ success in Burkina Faso). Targeting mechanisms may be particularly important in the productive sector, where the concentration of assets (for example, land) in the hands of the better-off will otherwise result in the more powerful securing most of the benefits (watershed projects, India). Interventions designed to supply services like primary health or education, must also be matched by a targeted stimulation of awareness and demand for these services on the part of poor people, otherwise utilization and benefits will remain very low (DFID, health, India). There is a danger that agencies' multiple objectives may result in a tension between poverty reduction and other objectives, for example, the environment. A focus on environmental concerns in isolation from poverty reduction objectives, for instance, is likely to lead to a failure to consider the priorities and needs of poorer groups and may result in an anti-poor distributional impact (for example, GTZ, forestry, Zambia).

Gender sensitivity

Lip-service is often given to the gender dimensions of poverty, with only one in five of the sample making it a high priority; newer projects were better. Careful design can result in the effective targeting of poor women, based on consideration of the constraints facing women (CARE/DFID, Zambia). Focusing on gender relations between men and women even where the principal target group is women addresses the fact that constraints facing women are often linked to the nature of gender relations within the household.

Participation

Only one in six projects in the sample revealed high levels of participation by the poor, but recent projects were more participatory than earlier ones. Both developing country partners and development agencies have a responsibility to reject top-down approaches which exclude the poor. Agencies can also seek to influence other agencies to promote a more participatory approach (for example, Sida, Bolivia). Promoting greater participation is seen by the poor as a good in itself, even if a project fails according to conventional criteria, such as directly enhancing livelihood security. Less tangible benefits are often highly valued by poor groups, including bolstering their sense of their rights, their capacity to analyse and articulate their own needs and possible solutions, and their confidence and ability to participate in local political processes (for example, Danida, Tanzania; GTZ, Burkina Faso). Participation by local actors tends to result in a greater sense of ownership and helps generate demand for new services. It is not a panacea, however, and can result in pressure to dilute efforts over an unsustainably large range of activities (Finnida, Tanzania). Meaningful participation needs to be implemented in advance of infrastructure components rather than simultaneously, thereby influencing the design, location, and appropriateness of such physical investments.

Sustainability

The picture on sustainability is mixed. Although only a fifth of the sample were estimated to be highly likely to be sustainable, there were many examples of projects becoming more institutionally sustainable in their most recent phases. Development agencies are increasingly wary of creating unsustainable parallel structures, favouring a longer-term perspective which seeks to build capacity within existing governmental and other bodies. This may require integrated action at national, sectoral and local levels. Some donors, notably GTZ and KfW, are prepared to admit that financial sustainability may be fanciful in the poorest countries, which instead require a long-term partnership and financial commitment combined with institutional strengthening measures. Many development agencies are moving towards this position, particularly in their support for sector-wide approaches through long-term budgetary support.

Options for reaching the poor more effectively: some new thinking

The new partnership idea (recently proposed by Sida, DFID and the DAC) offers an approach which in principle reconciles the concept of ownership with a positive role for the external agency. It is still at an embryonic stage in terms of its modalities. A major concern is whether enough partners can be found which are mutually committed to shared values on poverty reduction. There are two particularly key requirements for effectiveness. First, the need for the external agencies to avoid multiple partnerships and hence for them to proceed in a more collective and coordinated way themselves. Effective partnership requires the external agencies to seek consensus on single-country strategies for PR with all their partners and also to seek a sensible division of labour among themselves within that strategy. So far there has been a major gap here. Second, the external agencies need to approach partnership for PR as a process and not a blueprint. It cannot be undertaken in too much of a hurry, especially as a consensus is necessary between the different institutions of the recipient government. At the same time, without the use of conditionality the impetus to achieve the poverty targets will require a 'selective' approach to partners in the medium term. There is only a case for longer-term support to those authorities which continue to show some degree of commitment to their own poor. This is formally recognized by the UK, Sweden and the Netherlands.

There are considerable potential advantages in a sectoral approach to PR but certain important conditions must be met for it to work effectively. The first is the need for the external agencies to coordinate their activities better. This includes seeking a consensus or compromise on their approaches to health or education for example, to benefit the poor, developing a division of labour and being equipped locally with the expertise to play a useful role and, where necessary, to take the lead. There are some cases where this has happened. Second, there remains a major risk that sectoral approaches will be too centralized and unfocused on the poor. An important challenge therefore is to ensure that targeting mechanisms are devised and built-in for the services provided to reach poor areas, communities and groups disproportionately. There are few examples of this so far in practice.

Poverty reduction: organization and management of the European agencies

In general, the organization and management systems of the European development cooperation agencies are not particularly well adapted to translating their PR goals and aims into effective practice. Even among the more 'committed' agencies there has been a lack of central or corporate drive and clear guidance to programme managers. The management systems have been fairly informal and permissive, leaving much to individual discretion and motivation. Recently more vigour is being applied to the operationalization of poverty aims, especially for Sida, Danida and DFID with its new poverty strategy. Country strategies and programming have not been used so far as the effective instruments for poverty reduction which they could be. However, some agencies (for example, Danida, DFID, DGVIII, KfW and Sida) are now providing more guidance on the PR orientation of country programmes and vetting these at higher levels to sharpen them up. A weakness has been the monitoring of performance to ensure that programme managers plan their country portfolios to meet the PR aims of the organization. Although the Netherlands and the UK have used poverty and gender screening systems for projects, this practice is only slowly spreading. Personal incentive systems could be better geared to encouraging the long-term, patient and participatory approaches required for effective PR interventions, which are sometimes inhibited by incentives to achieve timely disbursement targets. New incentives and better procedures for the choice and use of consultants are necessary, especially for those agencies like the EC and Finnida that rely heavily on them.

More effective poverty interventions will require a new balance of appropriate expertise with the incorporation of more institutional social development and social sector skills, especially with the introduction of sectoral approaches. Some donors have increased their range of skills (for example, Germany and the UK) but a number lag behind. DGVIII, despite some efforts to widen skills, is lacking in the essential institutional health and education skills, while DGI is seriously understaffed for the roles it is supposed to play. There are powerful advantages for PR management (and probably a net balance of advantage) in having an organization that decentralizes personnel and decision-making responsibilities to the field offices or embassies and which ensures that there is a wider range of skills there. Only the UK has a fully decentralized system of this kind, though other agencies, such as those of Sweden, Denmark and the Netherlands are moving in this direction with some questions about adequate specialist staffing levels. DGVIII has substantial overseas delegations but does not decentralize decision-making and lacks a range of appropriate skills. DGI is inadequately staffed overseas. Some agencies (most obviously the German BMZ and KfW, as well as Finnida) remain highly centralized in their national capitals. A more general shift to decentralized organization among European agencies may well be the key to improving the rather weak degree of in-country coordination and cooperation on poverty issues and interventions. This will become even more important with a shift towards sectoral approaches.

Finally, the European agencies have not developed a sufficient knowledge base on the nature of poverty in most partner countries nor have they developed their own analytical and policy capacities in this area to match those of the World Bank, for example. They have started, but could do much more, to support their partners' capacity in these issues locally, especially the formulation and implementation of appropriate pro-poor strategies. Although monitoring of agency interventions has improved over ten years, more effective built-in monitoring and evaluation work is needed to assess the impact of interventions on poor people and provide lessons on what types of intervention work best to help them.

How to strengthen agencies' effectiveness in reaching the poor

The picture that emerges suggests certain areas where the agencies could greatly improve their effectiveness.

1. Commitment

- France and Spain should make greater formal commitment to poverty objectives and the EU should move faster to turn Council Resolutions relating to poverty reduction into an operational strategy.
- Denmark, Finland, Germany, the Netherlands and the UK must make greater efforts to operationalize their PR objectives and to mainstream poverty reduction effectively in their management systems.
- There should be more inter-agency dialogue on differences in the conceptions of poverty and of their identification of the poor as well as their poverty reduction aims.

2. Pro-poor aims

- Concepts of broad-based or pro-poor growth and how it is to be achieved need to be sharpened, especially with regard to the choice of countries on which the agencies focus.
- More attention should be given to the inadequate implementation of avowed priorities for spending on primary social services.
- There should be a sharper focus on the neglected issue of redistribution of assets in some partner countries.
- There should be more specific focus on *how* political liberalization, more participatory electoral political systems and decentralized government are to ensure greater attention to the needs of the poor and weaker sections of society.

3. General organization and management

- Clearer central management direction/orientation and guidance to programme managers in the agencies should replace the current rather uncertain, often informal and permissive systems because of the conceptual and operational difficulties in implementing a PR strategy.

- Better personal incentives and performance monitoring systems are required to ensure that staff PR activities are recognized and rewarded, especially because of the difficulty and time-consuming nature of PR initiatives and the potential conflict with other management objectives such as rapid disbursement of funds.

- Incentive performance monitoring needs be applied particularly to:

  a) the drawing up of country strategies in conformity with agency PR objectives and aims;
  b) more meaningful and regular dialogue with partners on poverty issues;
  c) more effective targeting and greater participation of beneficiaries in specific interventions;
  d) longer-term, prior institution-building at central government, community and local levels;
  e) greater use of local consultants and ensuring that all consultants hand over ownership in a timely way.

- Attention should be given to the provision of adequate and appropriate personnel for PR strategies in response to the shifting balance of skill requirements towards (for example) those who can contribute to understanding the social situation and planning the appropriate choices in social sector activities; strengthening of central and local institutions as well as better fiscal management; and tax and user charge reform, land reform, gender issues, etc.

- More appropriate personnel should be located in the field offices and more responsibilities for decision-making devolved from headquarters to assist in improving local understanding, continuity and trust in dialogue, flexible and quick response as well as more effective coordination.

- There should be more monitoring and evaluation of interventions intended to help poor people with special attention to the impact on them.

4. Country operations

- More work should be done to improve understanding of the local/cultural/historical context of poverty and likely effective interventions, including more agency cooperation in commissioning local research on poverty and pro-poor policy in which they have a common interest.

- There should be more precise formulation of the agencies' own country strategies for achieving poverty reduction, drawn up with wider local consultation processes rather than the current rather top-down approach of many agencies.
- Clearer priority should be given to the mix of the agencies' own interventions, with an increase in the fairly modest proportion of poverty-related interventions in their bilateral programmes.
- More attention should be paid to the division of labour between donors on appropriate portfolios/activities, especially to keep a balance between growth-inducing interventions and those more directly or indirectly focused on poverty reduction.
- There should be more independent, work including assistance to specific partner governments on the formulation (and even more importantly the implementation) of pro-poor strategies.
- There is a need for more dialogue on poverty issues between the agencies and their partners at the national and sectoral level and especially for a greater effort to find a consensus view on a single strategy for each country.
- There is a need for coordination with the domestic authorities in the lead, but, in the transition, with certain individual donors taking the lead on issues where they have a comparative advantage.
- The new concept of partnership based on mutual commitment and ownership should be pursued preferably by all the agencies and not just unilaterally. Moreover, continued commitment in the medium term should depend on actual performance by all partners on PR aims.

Better practice approaches

- To address the needs of the poor more immediately, interventions generally require mechanisms to ensure that the poor benefit substantially and swiftly, especially in the productive sectors where those with assets like land and water have tended to corner the benefits.
- The poverty objectives of interventions and the identification of beneficiaries should be clearly specified.

- In education and health programmes especially, the poorest geographical regions, districts or villages should be selected more often.
- More attention should be given to 'demand generation' or 'awareness creation' as well as 'supply-led' approaches.
- There should be greater support of locally initiated and locally owned projects and programmes.
- Innovative approaches to poverty reduction should be supported for potential replication or scaling-up but greater care should be taken to ensure that the initial pilot design is appropriate for local financial and management conditions.
- In order to improve the prospects of poverty-focused projects being sustainable, agencies may need to focus more on the livelihoods of the poor and not just on their access to social services, as well as entering into a long-term commitment with the partner government.
- Sector-wide approaches should be pursued which can potentially have a wider and more cost-effective impact on the poor, but they should be carefully monitored as there is no clear evidence as yet that these approaches will necessarily reach the poor effectively.
- More specific suggestions for improved project design and implementation for benefiting poor people in India are set out in Annex 2. These suggestions may well have relevance for other countries.

Annex 1
Poverty: A Multi-dimensional Concept

(This review was prepared by Tony Killick and
Roli Asthana)

1. **Poverty is multi-dimensional**. *Material deprivation* is at the core
of poverty. This includes low income and consumption levels, leading to poor food and poor nutritional status; inadequate clothing
and housing; and substandard access to health and schooling. It
also includes low command over productive assets, material (land,
equipment and other inputs) and human (education, training,
health). *Vulnerability* and resultant *insecurity* are further characteristics, aggravated by inability to make provision against emergencies:
vulnerability to droughts, floods and other natural disasters; to
human disasters such as the death or illness of a bread-winner, as
well as to war and civil disturbance; and to economic phenomena
such as inflation or market collapses.

Poverty has important less material aspects too. Among the most
important of these is *dependency*, for example arising from unequal
relationships between landlord and tenant, creditor and debtor,
employer and worker, man and woman. A further relational dimension is labelled as *social exclusion*, referring to inferior access to government services and other collective provisions; inferior access to
the labour market, resulting in low mobility, low security of employment and particularly high incidence of unemployment; inferior
opportunities for participation in social life and collective decision-
making; lack of decision-making power. Hopelessness, alienation and
passivity are thus common among those living in poverty. Finally,
we should record the *socially relative* nature of poverty. People can be
said to be poor when they are unable to attain the level of well-being
regarded by society as constituting a reasonable minimum. Poverty

thus relates to an individual's (or family's) standing in society and to her/his self-esteem. 'Absolute' measures of poverty are thus seen as inadequate because they ignore this societal context.

2. **Different conceptualizations yield differing inferences.** While there is no serious disagreement anywhere that poverty is a multifaceted state of deprivation nor that it cannot be wholly divorced from its social context, there remain considerable disagreements about where the balance should be struck, particularly as between income- and consumption-based measurements and other indicators, and between absolute (or objective) and relative (or subjective) conceptualizations, with substantially differing policy conclusions being drawn by the protagonists. Questions of definition and measurement cannot be divorced from issues of policy. Advocates of income-based approaches, for example, place more reliance on the indirect benefits of policies for accelerating economic growth, while those stressing basic needs often favour more direct pro-poor interventions. Different approaches are varyingly sensitive to successful PR policy interventions. Thus, it is complained about income- or consumption-based 'head-count' measures of poverty (which record the proportion of a population living below a poverty line) that they are not very useful for identifying specific groups to target for policy purposes, and that agencies given the task of reducing head-count poverty may be tempted to neglect the particularly difficult plight of the very poor.

Similarly, those identified as poor differ appreciably according to the definition used. One study of data from Côte d'Ivoire (Glewwe and van der Gaag, 1990) applied varying definitions, *confined to material and other objective indicators*, to the same set of data and found that they did not choose the same people, even although all definitions were set so that 30 per cent of the people were classified as poor. There must be a strong presumption that the disparities would have been even greater had the range of definitions employed included more subjective indicators of dependency, insecurity and social exclusion. This presumption is strengthened by what is known in the literature as 'Jodha's paradox', derived from a study of two Indian villages between 1964 and 1984 (Jodha, 1989). Objective measures showed that real incomes had declined during these 20 years but when villagers whose incomes had declined were asked about their well-being they reported their situation as having improved, citing decreased dependence on low-paid jobs and on patrons and landlords, improved mobility, and better consumption patterns.

However, one should not exaggerate the extent of the differences. Although they did identify materially different poverty groups, Glewwe and van der Gaag's definitions were mostly quite strongly correlated with each other. More generally, the subjectively based participatory approaches to poverty identification produce results consistent with those of household expenditure surveys, with the poor stressing the importance of access to jobs and assets such as land and education – all income-related. Similarly, there is broad correlation between the cross-country results of income-based poverty line measures and the Human Poverty Index developed by the UNDP which excludes income variables, particularly for Southern Asia and sub-Saharan Africa, although there are important differences too (UNDP, 1997: 22–3).

3. **The poor are heterogeneous.** It is almost always misleading to talk of 'the poor' as a single category of people. Poverty affects various socio-economic groups and policy measures are likely to affect these groups differentially. A major distinction is between *urban* and *rural* poverty. Most of the poor of developing countries live in rural communities but the share of urban poverty is rising and an urbanization of poverty is occurring. Among the urban poor, it is often useful to distinguish between the *working poor* and the *unemployed*. Within the rural population, we can similarly differentiate between those who have land and the *landless*; and, among the former, between those who participate in the production of *cash crops* and food farmers; and, among the latter, between those who produce a surplus for sale and those who are net *food importers*.

There are two other important differentials:

a) Between *temporary* and *permanent* poverty. There is evidence (mainly based on income-based measurements) of substantial movements in and out of poverty. A study of Pakistan found very few households remained poor (or non-poor) throughout the three-year period studied (Alderman and Garcia, 1993); a study of Côte d'Ivoire found comparably high rates of mobility in and out of poverty (Grootaert and Kanbur, 1995). It seems that the incidence of permanent poverty is much lower than that of total poverty, although this result is doubtless sensitive to the measure of poverty used.

b) Between *poverty* and *destitution*, or between the poor and the very poor. This is probably related to the temporary–permanent distinction. This distinction turns on whether an individual or household has sufficient resources and capacity to function in a sustainable way, albeit at a sub-standard level. There are few exceptions to the rule that it is harder to reach and assist the destitute than the less disadvantaged poor.

4. **But there are regularly recurring causes of poverty** despite the above heterogeneity. These can be organized under three headings: (a) low incomes and productivities, (b) social-political factors; and (c) inequalities. As regards *incomes and productivities*, since the growth of average incomes is the dominant influence on trends in poverty, it follows that poverty is substantially a function of the inadequacy of incomes (and therefore productivities), particularly in agriculture and other rural activities, and in the urban informal sector. The poor have inadequate access to educational and other economic and social services, leaving them with few modern skills. Largely as a result of this, the assets of the poor have low productivities, partly reflecting weak ability to participate in modern production processes and little access to formal sector credit.

Under the heading of *socio-political factors*, economic dependency is a factor perpetuating poverty, that is, a concentration of the un- and under-employed in poverty households, and exceptionally large family sizes, resulting in heavy child dependence. Political fragmentation and civil strife are other potent forces. There is also the issue of power. The poor have little market power and this, in combination with often undemocratic political structures and limited governmental accountability, feeds into weak political power, resulting in pro-urban policy biases and low priorities for anti-poverty measures. In addition, political traditions are often centrist, and top-down, excluding participation of the poor in programmes intended to assist them.

As regards the influence of *inequalities*, the basic point is obvious: for a given total national income, the amount of poverty will be a rising function of the degree of inequality. Measures of inequality typically show high levels in many African and Latin American countries, with a much more mixed picture in Asia. Tendencies towards capital-intensive growth paths, with a corresponding weak growth in the volume of formal-sector employment, further tends to perpetuate poverty. Access to employment is of enormous importance to the poor, both as a direct source of income and as the basis of the urban-to-rural remittances upon which so many (often female-headed) poor rural households rely to augment their incomes.

Inequalities *within households* are a further aspect. These particularly disadvantage women, who frequently have fewer rights to productive resources and household income, are expected to shoulder a disproportionate share of household work, have lower consumption standards, suffer from greater insecurity and dependency, and have often weak participation in household decision-making. In consequence, the gender dimension of poverty is now universally accepted as requiring special attention.

Annex 2
Recommendations and Suggestions from Project Case Studies in India

In India specific recommendations were made for improving the effectiveness and impact of the interventions on poor people in different sectors. Although these reflect the particular socio-economic, political and institutional context of India, the suggestions for improving effectiveness may well have relevance in other developing country situations.

Watershed sector

- Although it is logical to implement watershed development projects strictly on a watershed (and sub- and micro-watershed) basis, this may create tensions where parts of the villages are being left out. As far as possible the projects should include whole villages, even where this is in conflict with watershed boundaries.
- Participatory approaches are clearly necessary but watershed and village committees tend to be dominated by better-off (male) farmers, usually from the dominant caste. In order to reach the poor it is necessary to take participation one step further and support the organization of more homogeneous groups of poor people (self-help groups).
- It will take a long time to make the watershed and village committees effective partners in decision-making. Most of the monitoring in the projects deals with physical outputs.
- Those who can afford it should contribute to sharing the costs. Provision of inputs free of cost contributes to the 'dependency syndrome' and undermines replicability. However, it is of vital importance that a differentiated system of cost-sharing is developed, which may require that the poorest are exempted from payment.
- There needs to be more donor coordination – or learning from each other. Two out of three projects planned in the same Karnataka region have involved no attempts at coordination so far.
- There should be more monitoring of process and poverty reach and not just physical outputs as at present. Participatory monitoring and

evaluation should be built in and there need to be some benchmark surveys and indicators.

Education sector

- Decentralization of planning down to village level is recommended to increase the say of villagers *vis-à-vis* district level authorities. This is likely to bolster participation and sustainability.
- Making villagers responsible for the administration and use of even quite small sums (for example as in DPEP) helps sustain community participation and engender local ownership.
- Mobilizing more than token community contributions to school construction increases local ownership, with the positive 'knock-on' effect of reducing teacher absenteeism and improving prospects for maintenance. However, there must be differential cost-sharing to ensure that the poor are not excluded.
- Greater efforts should be made to realize the potential synergy between women's mobilization and primary education activities, since the attitudes and level of empowerment of women are important factors in determining whether children, and girls in particular, are sent to school.
- Donors should overcome their reluctance to implement their formal commitment to ownership. They need greater determination to capitalize on the potential benefits as well as the risks of a more 'hands-off' approach.

Forestry

- Donors should play a greater (innovative) role in the early stages of projects which originate in Forest Departments and NGOs, to help increase the understanding of the nature of poverty and the constraints facing the poor.
- There should be an attempt to involve both Forestry Departments and NGOs in a coordinated approach to poverty-oriented forestry, since NGOs on their own are not likely to be cost-effective while the forestry departments tend to be bureaucratic, rent-seeking and male-dominated.
- There should be some application of conditionalities by external agencies to help ensure that the forestry departments make PR a priority and devolve power downwards.
- There is a need for better monitoring to ensure prompt action is taken if projects go off the rails during implementation, for instance, when the landless get excluded.

Urban poverty projects

- Urban poverty-focused projects must take account of the nature of the urban economy. Approaches which promote conventional housing should be avoided. They tend to displace the poorest from central city locations by requiring clear titles and building according to pre-determined housing plans which puts them at a disadvantage. Yet these locations provide a multitude of employment opportunities which resettlement cannot do.

- An effective approach was revealed in the Urban Community Development (UCD) programme in Visakapatnam, supported by the UK, which eeks to upgrade poor groups in their existing locations where they have access to multiple employment opportunities. The focus needs to be on health, education and the provision of basic infrastructure and civic amenities, irrespective of tenure conditions. It needs to be a city-wide programme to include slums.
- The local population should be directly involved. Programmes should incorporate existing representative organizations involving the poor and not aim to create parallel organizations. The prospects for sustainability are enhanced if elected local politicians can be incorporated into the project.

Health sector

- External agencies should increase their funding for health, especially given the traditional underfunding (by donors and government) of the social sectors in general and the primary level in particular.
- Genuine commitment and ownership by the State government is essential for effective sustainability and replicability. The government–donor partnership must seek the earliest appropriate opportunity to internalize project innovations.
- Promoting health sector reform requires opportunism, whereby bureaucrats and donors move with the political grain. It is important when setting the reform agenda to trace the links between interventions at different levels of the system and the potential benefits for primary stakeholders.
- Donor conditionality can help officials to push through changes unpalatable to other parts of the bureaucracy. Many officials at central and State level have welcomed strong conditionality as a means to ensure that extra (donor) resources are truly additional. Ideally this influence should be pro-poor.
- Time should be invested in seeking the views of beneficiaries to avoid ill-sited health facilities which limit access and attractiveness to users and health workers.
- Donors and governments need to pay more attention to the quality and appropriateness of services and not just to improving physical accessibility. They should try to ensure that projects provide what people want. More emphasis on simple curative services as well as preventive care could increase utilization and impact.
- More priority should be given to an effective Information, Education and Communication (IEC) strategy for which much knowledge exists. Specific measures that are needed include: giving IEC priority at the project planning stage and involving local people; strengthening the interpersonal (especially listening) skills of project staff; greater use of the mass communication media and local initiatives (for example, traditional media); and provision for preventive maintenance of IEC equipment.

- Greater community participation should be sought to achieve higher levels of utilization and help remedy appalling maintenance problems.
- Project training programmes need to be better integrated into existing State and district training bodies and not provided *ad hoc*.
- More thought needs to be given to the use of control groups and baseline surveys to ensure that the lessons for effective PR are learnt.

Women's training projects

- Women's training projects can be highly relevant in a PR context when they address women's practical and strategic needs (for example, introduction to new methods in agriculture, animal husbandry, sericulture, as well as general awareness and mobilization against discrimination).
- The training centre model (used in the pioneering Women and Youth Training and Extension Project) tends to favour the better-off women and young, unmarried girls and does not benefit enough poor women. The poor, landless agricultural labourers have been bypassed by the project. It is preferable to focus on training in the villages to reach the target group of small and marginal women farmers more effectively (as in Training and Extension for Women in Agriculture Project).
- Since both approaches have largely bypassed landless women, ways should be sought to include landless agricultural labourers in the target group for training.
- The relevance of all the projects to PR could be increased if this objective was clearly stated as one of the primary objectives.
- There should be more monitoring of process and poverty reach and not just physical and financial inputs and outputs. There should be more benchmark surveys and indicators.

Annex 3
The Key to Judgements on the Performance of Specific Interventions with PR Objectives

PR as objective of the project

-    not really applicable. Would be if some projects had an anti-poverty objective
- 0   PR not an objective
- +   PR a secondary objective
- ++ PR primary objective
- ?   Unclear/uncertain

Approach

direct: interventions intended to address the problems of the poor directly and seek to target the majority of the benefits on them

indirect: interventions which are plausibly intended to bring substantial benefits to the poor (though others may benefit)

other: interventions with no clear or short-term link to PR but which may bring benefits to poor – no more nor less than others

Targeting

Design

-    mechanisms targeted to non-poor (designed to exclude the poor)
- 0   no targeting mechanisms
- +   weak targeting mechanisms
- ++ strong targeting mechanisms

Implementation

-   non-poor benefit in reality
0   poor and non-poor benefit alike
+   poor benefit more, but significant targeting errors
++ poor benefit more, no targeting errors

Participation

Design

-   participation of the poor discouraged at design stage
0   no participation planned
+   low participation planned
++ high participation planned from identification onwards

Implementation

-   project discriminates against the poor
0   no participation
+   no participation at identification but some participation introduced during implementation
++ highly participatory throughout

Gender Sensitive

Design

-   poor women discriminated against at design stage
0   poor women not targeted
+   low focus on poor women
++ highly focused on poor women

Implementation

-   project discriminates against women
0   no special focus on women
+   some focus on women
++ highly focused on women

Outputs

-   not applicable
0   no output
+   low outputs
++ high outputs

Overall impact

- — negative impact on PR
- 0 no (or negligible) impact on poor
- + low or moderate impact on poor
- ++ high (substantially positive) impact on poor

NB: It is possible for outputs from interventions to be successful and high but not to have a high impact on the poor.

Replicability

- — very unlikely
- ? uncertain
- + likely, but contingent on other factors
- ++ very likely

Sustainability

[as for Replicability]

Annex 4
Some Effective Specific Interventions for Benefiting the Poor (Supported by the European Agencies)

This Annex aims to give specific insight into individual interventions which have worked reasonably well in relation to the PR objective. They lend some local colour to the otherwise rather aggregated and systematic assessments made of the 90 project or programme cases covered in this research project (see Annex 5). The group of 17 which are extracted and summarized here were effective in their outcomes and impact on the poor to some degree. They encompass 'good practice' approaches to some aspects relating to early identification and focus on poor beneficiaries, targeting mechanisms, participation and gender sensitivity and estimated outputs and impacts on poor people. The cases do not form a random sample of European-supported projects.

	Rating
Country: Tanzania **Sector**: Rural Development **Project**: Rural Integrated Programme Support (RIPS) **Donor(s)**: Finland **Region/district**: Mtwara and Lindi regions, 11 districts; 2 million people **Project-years**: 1988–present	
PR as objective of the project: To assist and support local communities to move towards sustainable livelihoods through interactive communication, democratic processes and human rights as well as access to and development of resources. Strengthen and/or create sustainable rural institutions (e.g. extension, communication, training, financing, securing land rights) that empower the rural poor and create a common ground for participatory and demand-driven development processes.	Direct

(Table continued)

Targeting: 'Client groups': those people whose livelihoods are not reasonably secure, particularly the comparatively poor and disempowered, such as marginal subsistence farmers, particularly the women, youth and children and people in densely populated areas with declining soil fertility.	++ design + implem
Gender-sensitive approach: Women specifically mentioned as a main 'client group'. In most programmes women are the prime focus group, e.g. agriculture, natural resources, credit, education, training, civic education.	++ design ++ implem
Participation: Strong emphasis on participation (PRA and beyond). RIPS only supports efforts and initiatives 'owned' by local people, groups, villages, districts and NGOs. Funding decisions have been integrated into the elected District Councils. The donor, however, runs a parallel administration and retains financial control.	++ design + implem
Monitoring and/or evaluation: Monitoring and evaluation are very difficult because the programme supports more than 100 activities in a vast area with very poor roads and communication facilities. Much effort put into innovating participatory monitoring methods (to serve local needs) and systematic monitoring systems (to serve external monitoring purposes), but the problems of monitoring and evaluation have not been solved yet.	+
Outputs: *Intangible*: New and reformed rural institutions (NGOs and CBOs, credit committees, women's and youth groups, District Councils), changing attitudes ('we can do it'), reformed government bureaucracy ('they – the villagers – can do it'). *Tangible*: Improvements in agricultural extension, goat husbandry; pest and disease control, marine environment protection, forest management, fish farming, soil and water conservation, nutrition status; employment; capital assets; engagement of women in small businesses; credit provision; primary and post-primary education and vocational training, community health education, environmental health; appropriate technology transfer, marketing, zonal and village radio broadcasting.	++
Overall impact on poor: The programme has done much for PR, especially in small livestock and education activities. The area is large, however, (11 districts, 2 mill. people) and very	++

(Table continued)

difficult to serve. Further PR could be achieved by paying
attention to water, health, rural roads, agriculture.

Livelihood: Improved goat husbandry; increased incomes from   + +
cashew, control of plant and animal diseases, vegetable
gardening (women), protection of the livelihoods of
fisherfolk, seaweed farming, community-based forest
management, fish farming, credit schemes in 400 villages,
intermediate transport,marketing support.

Resources: Credit provision, marine resource protection, soil   +
and water conservation, goats as 'banks'.

Knowledge: Environmental health education; training and   + +
re-training of health personnel; training and teacher
training in appropriate technology; increased
knowledge on small stock keeping; extension services;
study trips; increased local participation in school
management, local innovations and influence on national
curricula in work-oriented post-primary education
and teacher-training in girls' vocational education
(catering); local knowledge incorporated in agric. educ.
in primary schools; civic education for women and
for new district councillors; local radio production
and broadcasting. Participatory video-productions.

Rights/Empowerment: Changing attitudes and roles for   + +
government staff; increased sense of ownership and
responsibility among rural communities; training has bred
self-reliance and self-confidence; women's groups and credit
schemes have empowered women. Radio and video give a
voice to the marginalised (e.g. fisherfolk). Elected local
councillors' awareness of their rights and obligations
strengthened.

Sustainability (likely): Institutional and financial sustain-   +
ability of the parallel support structure unlikely due to high
administrative costs and low govt. contributions. Sustainability
of many of the supported activities likely, due to local ownership,
low-cost solutions and increasing local revenue base.

Replicability (likely): The participatory approach and many   + +
of the RIPS innovations are already being replicated in other
projects in Tanzania. The demand-driven, bottom-up approach
is more realistic for the reformed local governments of
Tanzania in the future.

Country: Tanzania Sector: Income-generating Projects Project: PRIDE Tanzania Donor(s): Norway Region/district: Arusha Municipality Project-years: 1993–present	Rating
PR as objective of the project: To provide funding services to micro/small entrepreneurs to increase employment, incomes and stimulate growth through provision of credit and increasing micro-credit networks. Aim to bring substantial benefits to mainly urban poor, although others may also benefit.	Indirect
Targeting: The PRIDE project targets especially micro/ small entrepreneurs in the informal sector who are unable to get alternative credit access (those without formal jobs, often with little or no schooling and households which need to supplement their incomes from agriculture or formal jobs). The self-selecting group guarantee approach enables the majority of low-earners to get access to credit unlike in formal traditional banks. Most agreed that the credit limits and the compulsory weekly hourly sessions are conditions that serve to drive away those that are 'too rich' for the scheme.	+ design + implem
Gender-sensitive approach: Gender not used as an allocation criterion.	0 design 0 implem
Participation: Design based on previous PRIDE experiences in Kenya and the Grameen Bank model from Bangladesh. Implementation relies largely on the activity of the micro-entrepreneurs themselves and their self-selected groups. The project is managed by PRIDE Tanzania, an independent NGO, with financial support from NORAD.	0 design + implem
Monitoring and/or evaluation: Continuous monitoring and self-monitoring is in-built in the step-by-step procedure. Project-level results are not publicly available.	+
Outputs: Venue for savings; access to credit; training; business networks.	++
Overall impact on poor: A 'young' programme, but beneficiaries perceive it as highly relevant and well-targeted for PR. The fact that over 3000 clients are continuing their businesses indicates the positive impact of PRIDE in urban areas.	++
Livelihood: 'Lease of life' for many informal businesses and expansion for some; more incomes; increased employment.	++

(Table continued)

Resources: Increased savings and credit access.	++
Knowledge: Improved knowledge of entrepreneurial planning.	++
Rights/Empowerment: Increased sense of security, self-esteem and self-reliance attitudes in a context where the government is increasingly withdrawing from social security and service provision.	++
Sustainability (likely): Prospects for financial sustainability not yet clear; depends on management, cost-effectiveness and clientele; demand is great, and alternatives are few; institutions enlarged by capacity-building.	+
Replicability (likely):	++

	Rating
Country: Tanzania **Sector:** Rural Development **Project:** Soil and Water Conservation Project (HIMA) **Donor(s):** Denmark **Region/district:** Iringa, 1 district; 150,000 people **Project-years:** 1989–present	
PR as objective of the project: To support broad-based development and PR by improving agricultural productivity and sustainability; natural resource management; catchment protection; soil protection; local institution strengthening. Others may benefit as much as poor; no mechanisms to direct majority of benefits to poor.	Indirect
Targeting: Targeting based on geographical criteria (one catchment at a time) and on willingness of villagers to participate. About 10% of participants belong to the 'poor' category, 5–7% to the 'rich' category, and 80% to the 'intermediate' category. The approach gives very little room for the hard-core poor or destitutes, particularly the disabled.	0 design 0 implem
Gender-sensitive approach: No special focus on women in design but the 'Women's Fund', soft loans and training have helped women to establish small-scale businesses and to increase their incomes; fuel wood planting and milling machines have helped to reduce women's workload. The project has also helped to change attitudes towards women's rights.	0 design ++implem

(*Table continued*)

Participation: The decisions on which villages (catchments) to include are made 'top- down'. Within villages *all villagers who are willing* are welcome to join. Those who join participate in problem identification (PRA). Village government approves the plans which have to be approved by the district. The donor operates through the existing District Council's administrative structure, except that funds have been channelled through the donor's own channels, but also financial integration to districts is being prepared.	0 design + implem
Monitoring and/or evaluation: Monitoring and evaluation easy, because the project concentrates on a small clearly defined area, and only a few activities.	+
Outputs: Improved soil fertility management, increased awareness of the importance of forest conservation and water source protection, improved agricultural productivity (thanks especially to the introduction of composite manure), raised incomes, enhanced planning capabilities, improved housing and clothing, improved accessibility to water, strengthened self-reliance attitudes and reduced workloads for women.	+ +
Overall impact on poor: Project has made contributions to PR; more efforts needed in marketing and rural finance (establishing marketing, saving and credit cooperatives) and improvement of roads.	+
Livelihood: Increased agricultural productivity and incomes; also increased food security for minority poor but not hard core-poor. Women's workload decrease led to greater time for leisure and other activities.	+
Resources: Better housing due to increased incomes; increased forest resources due to forest protection and tree-planting; protection of water resources due to tree-planting.	+ +
Knowledge: Training in environmental conservation and natural resource management.	+
Rights/Empowerment: Increased participation in plan formulation and problem identification has helped change attitudes to women's rights; enhanced capabilities of local communities. Very little room for the hard-core poor or destitutes.	+

(Table continued)

	Rating
Sustainability (likely): Supported activities could be sustained by farmers in the absence of a donor, as the training and participation had already given the villagers the relevant knowledge and capabilities. The support services could not be sustained, as the Central Government, could not pay for transport and allowances of the extension officers. However, increased incomes might enable the District Council to collect more tax revenues and so continue the support services. The use of the existing district council staff and administrative structure is good for capacity building. Environmental sustainability has improved markedly.	+
Replicability (likely): The decision to concentrate on few projects in a clearly defined area was commended. The use of participatory approach and training has strengthened the sense of ownership.	++

	Rating
Country: Tanzania **Sector:** Income-Generating Projects **Project:** Tanga Smallholders Dairy Development Project (TSDDP) **Donor(s):** Netherlands **Region/district:** Tanga region, 5 districts; 1 million people **Project-years:** 1992–present	**Rating**
PR as objective of the project: To provide income and improve the quality of life for project participants through keeping improved dairy cattle. The project does not aim to reach the poorest sections of the society, but there are indirect benefits for them through increased labour opportunities.	Indirect
Targeting: The project has carefully analysed the socio-economic stratification of the population of the area. A deliberate decision has been made to target the 'low' and 'medium' income groups, but not the 'very low' income group, because keeping a dairy cow would be too risky for them.	+ design + implem
Gender-sensitive approach: The goal of the project is that 40% of the newly recruited farmers are female. According to an evaluation in 1996 this goal has almost	++design ++implem

(Table continued)

been reached. The Heifer in Trust scheme (HIT) facilitates
the inclusion of women in the programme. 44% of the
HIT farmers were women. Also zero-grazing approach
facilitates women's participation as cattle are kept near
the house. TSDDP collects gender-disaggregated data on
farmer and cow performance, which shows that female
farmers are less likely to drop out than male. The labour
opportunities created for 'very low' income groups (cutting
grass, transporting milk, etc.) benefit mainly men and
boys, not women, however.

Participation: A fairly technical approach, with little
emphasis on participation. However, cooperative action
promoted. Fairly good cooperation but also some
friction with the government authorities.

0 design
0 implem

Monitoring and/or evaluation: Systematic and frequent
monitoring and evaluations with attention paid to
impacts on the poorer groups and women, too.

0

Outputs: On-farm extension; training; provision of high
quality heifers and veterinary drugs; development of
viable milk marketing and processing strategies.

++

Overall impact on poor: Although project does not have
a PR aim, and does not try to reach the poorest sections,
it does have a PR impact due to the indirectly increased
employment opportunities.

+

Livelihood: For participants: Higher incomes, increased
employment; higher milk consumption; For the poor:
increased job opportunities and incomes.

++

Resources: Dairy infrastructure; better cattle.

+

Knowledge: Dairy husbandry, processing and marketing skills.

++

Rights/Empowerment: Processing and marketing options
empower the participating farmers to seek ways to maximise
the profitability of their efforts.

+

Sustainability (likely): Institutional: training of government
extensionists; financial sustainability after donor withdrawal
doubtful, therefore the TSDDP tries to work through private
enterprises as much as possible, e.g. in provision of veterinary
drugs, and in transporting and processing of milk. There are
plans to privatize the whole project. However, lack of
government support to private sector is seen as a threat.

?

(*Table continued*)

Liberalized imports of milk powder are another threat to the sustainability of fresh milk production; zero-grazing reduces environmental degradation by over-grazing; cow manure contributes to improvement of soil fertility. Poorly managed fodder production has caused some soil fertility problems.	
Replicability (likely): Much effort has been invested in making dairy production viable as a private market operation without government or donor support.	?

	Rating
Country: Bolivia **Sector**: Basic needs **Project**: PROANDES **Donor(s)**: Sweden, Programme run by UNICEF (also receives much funds from other sources; mainly, Spanish UNICEF Committee) **Region/district**: Cochabamba/North of Prosti **Project-years**: 1989–2002, (1) 1989–93: establishment of programme/service provision (Sweden is secondary donor), (2) 1993–97: focus on strengthening participation (Sida is main donor).	
PR as objective of the project: Promote and provide basic services for improvement of survival, development and protection of infants and women farmers in order to alleviate poverty in isolated rural zone with extreme climate conditions.	Direct
Targeting: Poor families directly targeted. Beneficiaries are 300,000 farm families living in poverty; in the area where PROANDES functions population are almost all very poor.	++ design ++ implem
Gender-sensitive approach: Overall objective focuses on women and girls; improvement of women's community role a specific goal. Women are active in water committees and literacy promotion.	++ design ++ implem
Participation: Design by UNICEF and Sida with some involvement of municipalities; implementation sub-contracted to NGOs and local organisations; high community participation at this stage.	0 design ++ implem
Monitoring and/or evaluation: Regular monitoring of outputs and periodic evaluations; however, monitoring does not include specific social indicators. Evaluations have been useful in detecting weaknesses, for example in relation to gender and finding the appropriate	

(Table continued)

level of technology to ensure sustainability and analysing cost recovery strategies.	
Outputs: Provision of basic needs like drinking water, health posts, improved schools; toilets; solar heated showers; complete water systems; crop protection.	++
Overall impact on poor: Impact is low mainly because starting conditions were very harsh and main obstacle – generating income – was not a substantive objective of PROANDES; future training should address this.	+
Livelihood: Improvement particularly through water projects and silos to protect crops but not a major objective.	+
Resources: Schools, health posts, water, sanitation, improved infrastructure, solar energy.	++
Knowledge: Literacy is key component of PROANDES; health awareness, agricultural knowledge and training.	++
Rights/Empowerment: High participation of poor population in implementation and maintenance; communities pay part of costs; strong emphasis on gender.	+
Sustainability (likely): Some doubts. Most outputs unlikely to last if UNICEF pulled out; possibly that would lead trained specialists to leave the zone in search of employment elsewhere. Technology is relatively appropriate, but still costly to maintain; no ready source of materials is available.	?
Replicability (likely): Yes. UNICEF replicates PROANDES already throughout Andean countries and has 'exported' technological and organisational lessons to other areas of the world through its network.	+

	Rating
Country: Bolivia **Sector**: Rural development **Project**: PRODIZAVAT **Donor(s)**: EU. Counterpart: Department of Tarija (in first year CODETAR of Ministry of Planning, then abolished) **Region/district**: Department of Tarija **Project-years**: 1994–1998. (1) 1994 (Oct)–1995 (July) Feasibility studies on technical assistance and establishment of programme but delays till 1996 (July). (2) 1996 (Aug)– 1998: focus on participatory programme and technical assistance and on bio-technologies to improve crop yields and road construction and irrigation infrastructure Introduction of the logical framework procedures.	
PR as objective of the project: Main objective is to improve the quality of life of the rural population, through	Direct

(*Table continued*)

the increase of production and agricultural productivity. This area is characterized by scattered population and emigration. Most of population (32,000 people) live in poverty and the programme is aimed at enabling them to reach food self-sufficiency and prevent emigration to Argentina and the coca-producing areas. Creation of infrastructure to support agricultural production and marketing, introduction of new varieties; seed production; improving productivity; increasing area under irrigation, improving road system and rural electrification.

Targeting: Beneficiaries of the programme are 5,000 families corresponding to two sub-groups: a smaller group of farmers (not very poor) living in the valley region, and numerous very poor peasants living in the arid zone. For the first group, the focus is on diversifying agricultural production (from traditional to cash crops), and to promote access to financial services. For the second group, a main focus is on technical assistance and improved infrastructure.

++ design
++ implem

Gender-sensitive approach: The programme lacks a gender-sensitive approach, but the emigration of many men actually results in most of the programme beneficiaries being women.

0 design
+ implem

Participation: Since 1996, in the context of the Popular Participation Law, the participatory approach has been introduced in the programme (externally more than from local endogenous dynamics.) Led to complete decentralization of the programme.

+ design
+ implem

Monitoring and/or evaluation: Regular monitoring of outputs and periodic evaluations. Excellent monitoring of the farmers' programme, in particular the measurement of agricultural productivity and of social indicators.

++

Outputs: Increased agricultural production and marketing, improved roads and irrigation systems.

++

Overall impact on poor: Impact is high (and visible) through the farmers' programme. In the arid zone the impact is still low.

++

Livelihood: Improvement of the family dairy diet through the identification and production of alternative foods, promoting the participation of the entire nuclear family.

++

Resources: Roads, water electrification, health posts.

++

(Table continued)

Knowledge: Agricultural knowledge and marketing training, know-how on post-harvest techniques, financial services knowledge.	++
Rights/Empowerment: Communities pay part of costs (4% in 1997), participation of poor people in implementation, promotion of community associations.	+
Sustainability (likely): The programme is well implemented and managed. Technology is appropriate and the Department of Tarija's participation is high. Especially important for future sustainability will be the Tomayapo river's flow regulation and the building of dams.	++
Replicability (likely): The EC replicates this kind of programme in other Latin American countries. The technological and organizational approach seems very appropriate for the poor who have the opportunity to became small-scale farmers.	++

Country: Bolivia **Sector**: Food security **Project**: PROSANA **Donor(s)**: GTZ **Region/district**: Department of Cochabamba (3 provinces) **Project-years**: 1991–2001. (1) 91–94: orientation. (2) 94–97: implementation and dissemination. (3) 97–2001: consolidation and follow-up	**Rating**
PR as objective of the project: Improve nutritional conditions; food security; primary health, social organization. Food security strategy targets majority of benefits to poor since area suffers from extreme poverty situation.	Direct
Targeting: Identified very poor area. Design considers multiple facets of food insecurity.	+ design ++implem
Gender-sensitive approach: No particular focus on gender. In implementation, women selected for dissemination of health and nutrition components.	0 design 0 implem
Participation: Identification by regional development corporation; designed with technical assistance from GTZ; farmer organizations participated in planning; regional and local institutions (municipalities mainly) should implement, but PROSANA does most directly.	+design 0 implem

(Table continued)

Not much participation during implementation.

Monitoring and/or evaluation: Evaluation of phase 1 carried   +
out in 1994 of entire project: found planning too ambitious,
lack of focus on women farmers and unclear approach
(research-action). Second evaluation in 1997, with focus on
institutional aspects: recommended extension of project for
3 more years; generally positive.

Outputs: Mostly in terms of institutional capacity   +
and improved social services.

Overall impact on poor: Institutional strengthening,   +
but unclear as to impact on poverty.

Livelihood: No clear benefits identified.   0

Resources: Social services improved.   +

Knowledge: Informal education on practical issues.   +

Rights/Empowerment: Increased awareness by farmers'   + +
associations of their rights and how to participate in
municipal governance.

Sustainability (likely): The integration of project in   ?
Popular Participation (PP) process (i.e., strengthening
local/municipal capacity) is positive sign, as is shift by
project management from direct implementation to
advising and accompaniment of local institutions. But,
once the project terminates, many municipalities may
not be capable of preparing strong proposals for financing,
or carrying them out adequately.

Replicability (likely): Has been replicated; replicability   + +
depends on municipality's absorption capacity.

Country: Bolivia   **Sector**: Capacity building   **Rating**
Project: API. Support to Indigenous Peoples
Programmes   **Donor(s)**: DANIDA. Counterpart:
Undersecretary for Ethnic Affairs   **Region/district**:
Various, 64 municipalities in 7 departments
Project-years: 1996–2002. (1) 1996–97. (2) 1998–2002

PR as objective of the project: Support Popular   Direct
Participation (PP) process, specifically aimed at

(Table continued)

indigenous populations which have been traditionally
marginalized economically, socially and politically.
Main objective is to strengthen capacity of these groups
in order to get access to social services and political
system. Legal assistance to native peoples; especially
to obtain formal recognition of traditional community
structures and land use rights; training of leaders;
support to intercultural education and natural
resources management.

Targeting: Focus of identification and design on indigenous peoples, most of which are very poor. In implementation, it is not clear, but seems that poor benefit most.	++ design + implem
Gender-sensitive approach: Not a particularly strong focus, although there is some attention to training and capacity building of women's associations.	+ design + implem
Participation: Low participation in design, but native peoples' groups are very involved in implementation.	0 design + implem
Monitoring and/or evaluation: Regular monitoring by project team, with continuous feedback workshops involving beneficiaries.	+
Outputs: Outputs are mostly intangible: i.e., increased number of indigenous council members in municipalities and organisations officially registered.	+
Overall impact on poor: In the short term, API does not affect poverty situation very much, but it may contribute over medium term and in indirect manner.	+
Livelihood: Not intended to improve directly.	0
Resources: Assists communities to gain access to social services heretofore denied them.	+
Knowledge: Expansion in community mobilization skills and project design and management.	+
Rights/Empowerment: Legalization of grassroots organizations; promotion of right of participation in community decision-making; especially as indigenous groups traditionally marginalized.	++
Sustainability (likely): In various communities, strong native organizations created and can become	+

(Table continued)

easily independent, but in many others it will be
difficult: political obstacles (i.e., anti-Indian
sentiments) remain strong at regional and national levels.

Replicability (likely): API is extending to an increasing   +
number of municipalities. Spain is funding (1997–)
extension of API to department of Tarija.

Country: Nepal **Sector**: Rural development **Project**: Gorkha Development Project (GDP) **Donor(s)**: GTZ	**Rating**

PR as objective of the project: Poverty-focused;   Direct
to improve living conditions of poor agricultural
households facing acute unemployment. Intended
beneficiaries the poor, with majority of benefits
directed to them.

Targeting: Poor households concentrated in Gorkha   ++ design
community identified and targeted through   ++ implem
organization into self-help groups.

Gender-sensitive approach: Unclear whether   ? design
women targeted in project design. Women   + implem
mobilized during implementation; all-women
groups formed and helped.

Participation: Design is participatory inasmuch as   + design
it learns from previous rural development   ++ implem
programmes; beneficiaries involved at
grassroots level in implementation.

Monitoring and/or evaluation: NA   ?

Outputs: Internal resource mobilization, provision of   ++
inputs, credit, production support, technical support,
road construction, skill enhancement.

Overall impact on poor: Contributed substantially to   +
stabilize the economic condition of rural poor households
by checking deterioration of economic condition and
mass impoverishment.

Livelihood: Livelihoods enhanced through income-   ++
generating activities, provision of credit,

(Table continued)

skill-enhancement, increased productivity, employment generation and labour-intensive technology.	
Resources: Physical infrastructure such as feeder roads improved.	++
Knowledge: Awareness of new technologies and inputs, skill enhancement, managerial capability creation.	+
Rights/Empowerment: Social mobilization through organization into self-help groups.	+
Sustainability (likely): Not known	?
Replicability (likely): Not known	?

Country: Zambia **Sector**: Urban poverty **Project**: Care (Zambia) Project Urban Self- Help (PUSH) **Donor(s)**: ODA **Region/district**: Lusaka and Livingstone **Project-years**: 1991–94, 1994–present	**Rating**
PR as objective of the project: Overall: (a) to reduce urban poverty in four compounds of Lusaka and Livingstone; (b) to establish a replicable model of an urban project which used food-for-work to achieve long-term development objectives of livelihood improvement; participatory appraisal and (c) needs assessment. Immediate: (a) community development; (b) support to city council; (c) gender and development. Directed at poor beneficiaries; with mechanisms to target majority of benefits to them.	Direct
Targeting: The goals of the project are explicit with regard to PR. The targeting is also specific; firstly by location, and, to an extent, by group (women). There have been three stages of project design. The second stage among these was targeting poor locations within districts, based on existing observable characteristics which underline the prevalence of poverty. With the help of city councils, the targeted areas turned out to be four compounds (three in	++ design ++ implem

(Table continued)

Lusaka and one in Livingstone) where low-income
residents reside. The participants in PUSH-II
proved to be mainly women.

Gender-sensitive approach: Women were identified   ++ design
from the first as a specific target group. The Food   ++ implem
For Work (FFW) programmes run under PUSH-II
appear to be appropriate as they tend to be
skewed towards meeting the interests of women.
First, they demand only half the amount of time
that characterizes formal work. In this way, women's
time constraint is alleviated and they are able to
participate. Second, from a gender perspective,
food is generally prepared and handled by women.
Women are the main direct beneficiaries in the
FFW programmes. They constitute at least 90%
of the beneficiaries, and this is a reflection that
the target group was well conceived during the
preparation of the programme.

Participation: PUSH-II benefited a lot not only from   ++ design
PUSH-I and CARE's experiences in other parts of the   ++ implem
world, but also from consultations with previous and
future beneficiaries. Many participatory methods are
used, including: (a) meetings with beneficiaries; (b) use
of the Participatory Appraisal and Needs Assessment
(PANA) which is an iterative process which involves
assessment of priority needs, appraisal, reassessment
and incorporation of these into the programme;
(c) personal empowerment training; (d) establishment
of groups engaged in income generation;
(e) collaboration with local city councils; and
(f) active incorporation of gender issues after
consultations with women.

Monitoring and/or evaluation: Regular monitoring is a   ++
feature of the programme. The monitoring process
involves both participatory and traditional methods.
Livelihood Monitoring Surveys are conducted among
beneficiaries. Further, questionnaire-based surveys are
also carried out from time to time. There has
also been a Personal Empowerment Impact Study.

Outputs: Increased incomes; infrastructure creation;   ++
health, literacy.

(Table continued)

Overall impact on poor: Very successful project both in terms of PR and its other objectives. Well planned. Learned from past experience. Participatory approach. Well targeted.	++
Livelihood: 90% of the beneficiaries have reported increased incomes. 75% of the total work force have formed savings groups. 22% of the total work force graduates received loans. Loan repayments were up 100%. The impact on livelihoods has been very positive.	++
Resources: Both physical and social infrastructure has been built up as a result of PUSH-II. This has had a very positive impact on the beneficiaries.	++
Knowledge: Literacy classes, literacy manuals, increased awareness through health awareness and general education, legal literacy.	++
Rights/Empowerment: High participation at all levels. Empowerment a goal of the project through group formation, legal literacy and other means. Personal empowerment study conducted to test for this.	++
Sustainability (likely): Fungibility addressed from the beginning. Income generation and economic sustainability encouraged.	++
Replicability (likely): Already replication of earlier programme. Could also be replicated among other urban poverty centres.	++

	Rating
Country: Zambia **Sector:** Food security **Project:** Luapula Livelihood and Food Security Programme **Donor(s):** FINNIDA **Region/district:** Luapala **Project-years:** 1994–1998	
PR as objective of the project: Overall: to enhance rural livelihoods and food security in Luapula Province of Zambia. Immediate: (a) sustainable use of natural resource base; (b) improved household food security and nutritional security access; (c) livestock development to improve diversification; (d) improved rural capacity through credit access and income-earning	Indirect

(Table continued)

opportunities; (e) increased farmer participation in extension services; and (f) intensified consideration to gender. Majority of funds and benefits directed at medium ranking in terms of wealth, although the poor also targeted.	
Targeting: Four categories of farmers identified: 1–resource-poor (poor); 2–small-scale (medium); 3–small-scale emergent (rich); 4–emergent and commercial (very rich). Main beneficiaries with greatest potential for improvement seen as in category 2. Other categories also benefited in some ways; category 1 through informal distribution of planting materials to mitigate their food insecurity.	+ design + implem
Gender-sensitive approach: Women one of the focus areas of project. Although not specifically targeted, women's groups have been actively involved but belong mostly to the medium group in wealth ranking.	+ design + implem
Participation: High rate of participation in programme design; PRA exercises carried out at design stage; participation by poor unclear; considerable degree of participation in implementation; role of poor not discussed.	+ design + implem
Monitoring and/or evaluation: Extensive impact assessments built into project design; however, not very effective because no initial data, so no benchmark to compare results with.	+
Outputs: Participatory extension and research; soil fertility improvement; seed multiplication; improved knowledge of animal husbandry; setting up of development fund to provide cheaper credit.	+
Overall impact on poor: PR impact limited because poor not main target group despite good identification exercise. Medium group targeted but even for them livelihood impact difficult to assess as baseline data insufficient.	+
Livelihood: Generally improved probably as farmers have access to seeds and credit; however, impact on poor farmers not known.	?

(Table continued)

	Rating
Resources: Agricultural infrastructure improved; however, medium farmers benefit more.	+
Knowledge: Improved extension services so farmers are more knowledgeable about farming.	++
Rights/Empowerment: Unclear.	?
Sustainability (likely): Sustainability embedded in programme design.	+
Replicability (likely): Not known.	?

	Rating
Country: Zimbabwe **Sector**: Land reform **Project**: Land Resettlement Programme (LRP) **Donor(s)**: ODA **Project-years**: Initiated in 1980; ODA involvement began 1981	**Rating**
PR as objective of the project: To facilitate land transfer from European owners to returning refugees; to alleviate social stress; to produce a more equitable land distribution; to promote political and social stability in rural areas; to maximize use of Zimbabwe's land resources; to relieve pressure on resources in communal areas; to improve the base for productive agriculture. PR effect through asset redistribution to poor.	Direct
Targeting: Attempt made to identify the poorest among the small and landless farmers and to give them priority in the land resettlement programme; followed for the first few years of the programme; subsequently, greater attention was paid to the amount of experience that the farmer had.	++ design + implem
Gender-sensitive approach: No gender component in this phase, though one planned for the next phase.	0 design 0 implem
Participation: Identification and design top-down; same seems to hold for implementation as well.	0 design 0 implem

(*Table continued*)

Monitoring and/or evaluation: ODA established a   ++
monitoring and evaluation unit; Annual Joint Reviews of
the Programme by representatives of both governments;
the results were a series of recommendations and
monitoring their implementation.

Outputs: The LRP as a whole, including parts undertaken   ++
without the help of UK assistance, had up to 1988
involved the resettlement of 40,000 households,
involving at least 250,000 people and 2.2 million
hectares of land. As of September 1996, a total
of 71,000 households had been resettled and a
further 20,000 had benefited from access
to increased grazing.

Overall impact on poor: The PR impact of the project has   ++
been substantial, the direct transfer of land, the major rural
asset, and the government's commitment to the programme
stemming from the political support for it.

Livelihood: Very significant impact; majority of families   ++
benefited through increased opportunities for income
generation and access to health and education services;
majority of the settler families were previously communal
area farmers with limited access to land, among the
poorest members of the population.

Resources: Access to land and other resources like   ++
health and education services.

Knowledge: No direct impact.   0

Rights/Empowerment: No direct impact.   0

Sustainability (likely): There is a concern about   ?
the sustainability of the project, which requires
(a) the continued financing of resettlement areas,
particularly maintenance and administration, which
cost about five times as much as in communal
areas, with settlers making no contribution to the
cost of the scheme, and (b) the issue of representation
of settlers, which prompted the government,
in 1993, to allow the settlers to have elected
representatives.

Replicability (likely): Not known.   ?

Country: India Sector: Primary Education Project: District Primary Education Project (DPEP) Donor(s): ODA/DFID Region/district: Andhra Pradesh Project-years: 1996–2002	Rating
PR as objective of the project: Improving access to and quality of education provision; no explicit focus on potential contributions to PR, either in terms of bolstering rights, or strengthening capabilities and improving livelihoods. Link between project and PR not thought out; however, contributes to PR both due to link between illiteracy and income poverty and because of the targeting mechanisms used – hence 'direct' PR classification.	Direct
Targeting: Educationally backward districts targeted; educational backwardness highly correlated with economic backwardness, tribals and women special focus groups; school-mapping used as targeting tool.	+ + design + + implem
Gender-sensitive approach: Female literacy used as indicator of educational backwardness of district; measures designed to increase enrolment of girls; commitment to increasing female teachers; centres have helped reduce gender bias in education.	+ + design + + implem
Participation: Mechanisms designed and well-implemented; highly successful in social mobilization; high levels of contribution by villagers; decentralized implementation, with villagers deciding themselves how to ensure contributions do not overburden the poor.	+ + design + + implem
Monitoring and/or evaluation: Mainly qualitative information; ODA has supported research to identify means for monitoring and evaluation. Regular joint monitoring missions by government and donors.	+ +
Outputs: Early stages, but considerable achievements in terms of developing district and village level plans, training of administrators and teachers, building of schools.	+
Overall impact on poor: Emphasis and success at targeting resources at least literate should result in positive impact.	+ +

(Table continued)

Livelihood: Extra cash or subsistence income or employment, improved productivity or yields.	0
Resources: Targeting of low literacy areas improves access of those hitherto desired education. Substantial buildings (schools/classrooms) improvement *and* trained teachers.	+ +
Knowledge: Improved literacy, and participation and knowledge through village education committees. Systems being developed to assess learner achievement.	+ +
Rights/Empowerment: Decentralized approach empowers villagers through participation in village-level education plans. Local control over some school resources. Attempts to reduce gender inequalities. Participation evident from substantial contributions, often on a sliding scale dependent on wealth.	+
Sustainability (likely): The 'programme mode' has greater capacity to respond to national concern; also forms integral part of the government's educational machinery; building institutional capacities at all levels is key; seen as riskier by donors used to hands-on approach but less risky in the longer term through sustainability.	+ +
Replicability (likely): DPEP concept founded on replicability; strong potential for 'mainstreaming' the lessons of experience; DPEP is source of pride at central, state and district government level, surest guarantee of replicability and sustainability. Some concerns at over-rapid scaling-up, due to large injection of funding from World Bank.	+ +

	Rating
Country: India **Sector**: Women's training projects **Project**: Mahila Samakhya (MS) **Donor(s)**: DGIS **Region/district**: Uttar Pradesh **Project-years**: 1988–93, 1993–97	
PR as objective of the project: To provide educational opportunities for women in rural areas in a way which contributes to their development and empowerment; poverty well-conceptualized. Poor women directly targeted; majority of benefits directed at them.	Direct

(Table continued)

Targeting: MS takes care to reach the most disadvantaged women, both in terms of caste, class and ethnic group; among the most vulnerable groups identified are landless, illiterates, destitutes, widows, women-headed households and scheduled castes and tribes.	++ design ++ implem
Gender-sensitive approach: Project focused on poor women; both strategic and practical needs met, former through empowerment and prevention of discrimination; latter through literacy courses, child care centres and discussions on a range of topics.	++ design ++implem
Participation: Genuinely participatory; orientation towards process rather than outputs; self-expression and political growth encouraged through group discussions and other means.	++ design ++ implem
Monitoring and/or evaluation: Monitoring primarily in terms of quantitative outputs; difficult to monitor social processes; one evaluation.	+
Outputs: Better access to government programmes like hand pumps; health facilities, school enrolment, scholarships; some savings groups; reduction in wage rate inequality; day-care centres for children; increased knowledge and awareness on health and legal issues.	++
Overall impact on poor: Overall impact very positive especially in terms of knowledge and empowerment; however, increased skill-training and focus on income-generation could increase PR impact greatly.	++
Livelihood: Some, but limited; only through raising wage rates.	+
Resources: Increased access to existing government infrastructure and resources.	++
Knowledge: Increased knowledge about health, legal issues and other topics, increased access to schooling and scholarships, increased enrolment.	++
Rights/Empowerment: Empowerment, bargaining power, rights awareness, advocacy.	++
Sustainability (likely): Uncertain without donor funding.	+
Replicability (likely): Exists in a number of states.	++

	Rating
Country: India **Sector**: Watershed development **Project**: Karnataka Watershed Development Project (KWDP) **Donor(s)**: DANIDA **Region/district**: Karnataka **Project-years**: 1990–97 (Phase I), 1997–2004 (Phase II)	
PR as objective of the project: Sustainable watershed development; improved agriculture. Soil and water conservation; effort to direct benefits to small and marginal farmers.	Indirect
Targeting: Special effort made to ensure small and marginal farmers get their share of benefits; second phase targets entire population although part of the funds for non-land based activities helping landless and women.	+ design 0 implem
Gender-sensitive approach: Special effort to mobilize women, although 25% quota not reached; women tend to have token presence; however, many report rise in self-confidence and empowerment.	++ design + implem
Participation: Top-down to begin with; more participatory in implementation; next phase elaborately participatory in design.	++ design 0 implem
Monitoring and/or evaluation: No formal evaluation yet, although Phase I complete; monitoring of physical outputs, not poverty reach; these lacunae to be addressed in Phase II.	0
Outputs: Soil conservation; agricultural improvement; watershed development.	+
Overall impact on poor: Limited PR impact; favoured areas chosen for implementation (this aspect corrected in Phase II); better-off farmers have cornered majority of benefits; most activities carried out on privately owned lands.	0
Livelihood: Majority of benefits cornered by big farmers outside the target group; 65% of population (poor farmers) get 20–30% of benefits.	0
Resources: Some benefit to poor in terms of physical infrastructure created; but majority cornered by rich farmers.	+

(Table continued)

Knowledge: No direct impact.	0
Rights/Empowerment: Some women report a rise in self-confidence and empowerment, even though committees dominated by men.	0
Sustainability (likely): Expensive physical infrastructure created; some broke down; cost recovery has been difficult; Phase II addresses some of these concerns.	+
Replicability (likely): Good potential to be integrated into government extension system.	+

	Rating
Country: India **Sector**: Health and family welfare **Project**: Integrated Child Development Services Scheme (ICDS) **Donor(s)**: Sida **Region/district**: Tamil Nadu **Project-years**: 1989–93, 1993–95, 1995–98	**Rating**
PR as objective of the project: Innovative approaches to implement nutrition and pre-school components of ICDS. Child health and nutrition at village level would benefit poor substantially, although others benefit as well; however, poverty not well-conceptualized, nor the link between project and PR.	Other
Targeting: Entire population targeted; poor not identified; target groups not specified explicitly.	0 design 0 implem
Gender-sensitive approach: No specific account taken of disadvantaged position of women except in 'adolescent girls scheme'; even here effects marginal, with training not sufficiently oriented towards improving income-earning potential.	+ design 0 implem
Participation: Participatory measures badly designed and implemented, though less so than in other two health projects; lack of ownership.	0 design + implem

(Table continued)

Monitoring and/or evaluation: Limited information, although Sida reports are mentioned.	0
Outputs: Improved health status of mothers and children, reduced malnutrition.	+
Overall impact on poor: ICDS centres positively viewed by beneficiaries, vast majority of whom are poor.	+
Livelihood: Unclear.	?
Resources: ICDS centres a positive resource.	+
Knowledge: Health awareness.	+
Rights/Empowerment: Unclear.	+
Sustainability (likely): Innovative and low cost approaches.	+ +
Replicability (likely): Parts of it can be replicated; however, undermining of participation may hinder that.	+ +

Country: India **Sector**: Slums Development **Project**: Visakhapatnam Slum Improvement Project **Donor(s)**: ODA/DFID **Region/district**: Andhra Pradesh **Project-years**: 1988–96	**Rating**
PR as objective of the project: Emphasis on city-wide upgrading, including the provision of basic amenities and related health, education and community development inputs, and housing. The Urban Community Development (UCD) approaches are the most comprehensive in dealing with poverty; directed at PR through focus on those issues seen as important by the poor themselves; comprehensive and multi-dimensional conceptualization of poverty.	Direct
Targeting: Target population of 200,000 covering 170 slums. Each community group, called Neighbourhood Committees, incorporates a women's group and a youth wing.	+ + design + implem

(Table continued)

Gender-sensitive approach: The Neighbourhood Committees are supposed to have half their members as women addressing gender issues.	++ design ? implem
Participation: The community is organized into local groups which can manage the facilities created and be responsible for cost recovery, through the Neighbourhood Committees. Institutionally there is also a UCD wing in the municipality and Project Steering Committee. But the local population is not directly involved and project agencies see participation in terms of consultation or focus on non-critical issues, thereby eroding credibility.	++ design + implem
Monitoring and/or evaluation: Ownership within the project is very much with ODA/DFID which has played a strong interventionist and directive role. Indirectly, the programme is also influenced by the State and Central government since the administration wings of the local government play a key role.	++
Outputs: Housing is less important than a concentration on basic services and civil improvements, such as upgrading canal system to reduce flooding, roads, sewerage, drainage.	++
Overall impact on poor: Effective in addressing the immediate needs of poor groups particularly when there is a focus on health, education and provisions of basic infrastructure and civic amenities irrespective of tenure conditions. Also successful because it was a city-wide programme pushing policy to include slums in all categories of tenure.	++
Livelihood: Upgrades poor groups in their existing locations, providing access to multiple economic opportunities in urban context.	++
Resources: Increased employment opportunities.	++
Knowledge: Not known.	?
Rights/Empowerment: Involvement through the NCs; responsible for cost recovery and facilities management.	++

(Table continued)

Sustainability (likely): Dependent upon the relationship with local political agents. In the past they have had little role. The UCD approach holds the potential to be sustainable after donor funding is withdrawn especially if they manage to incorporate local politicians in the project.	+
Replicability (likely): The UCD approaches are highly comprehensive in dealing with poverty, and may therefore form a model for future approaches.	+

Annex 5
Complete List of Countries, Projects and Donors Reviewed

Donor Country	India		Bolivia		Nepal	
Denmark	rural dev	1	other	1	education	2
	forest	1				
	drinking water	1				
	health	1				
	women	2				
	NGOs	4				
Denmark/ Sweden						
EC	rural dev	2	rural dev	2		
	education	1				
Finland					rural dev	1
					rural dev	1
France					rural dev	1
					(jointly with EC)	
Germany GTZ	NGOs	2	other	1	credit	1
			health	1	rural dev	1
Germany KFW	rural dev	2				
	urban pov	2				
Ireland						
Netherlands	rural dev	1	other	1	rural dev	1
	drinking water	3				
	women	1				
	urban pov	1				
Norway						
Spain			rural dev	1		
Sweden	forest	1	rural dev	1		
	health	1				
	education	1				
Switzerland					other	1
UK	rural dev	1			rural dev	1
	forest	1				
	health	1				
	education	1				
	urban pov	2				
Country Total		34		8		10

Tanzania		Zambia		Zimbabwe		Burkina Faso		Donor Total
rural dev	1	health	1			rural dev	2	19
education	1	credit	1					
				infrastru	1			1
rural dev	1	credit	2	health	1			9
rural dev	1	other	1					5
forest	1							
						education	1	4
						rural dev	1	
						water & sani	1	
rural dev	1	forest	1			rural dev	1	11
health	1	fish	1					
								4
rural dev	1							2
education	1							
rural dev	2			health	1			12
				NGOs	1			
credit	1							1
								1
education	1	rural dev	1	rural dev	1			8
				education	1			
health	1							2
health	1	NGOs	1	rural dev	2			11
	15		9		8		6	90

Notes

Chapter 2   Poverty Reduction Goals and Strategies of the European Development Cooperation Agencies

1   The World Social Summit 1996 involved a donor commitment to agree mutually with developing country partners to allocate an average 20 per cent of aid budgets to match 20 per cent of national budgets for priority human social programmes, defined as basic education, basic health, water and sanitation, nutrition and reproductive health and population. Although somewhat controversial because of its rather rigid figures which may not always be appropriate in every specific country or donor situation, the commitment is nevertheless likely to represent a shift in aid spending intentions to the potential benefit of poor people who can gain easier access to these types of resources. Information on how far donors are actually financing the appropriate social expenditures is not yet available.

2   The 1999 Cologne Summit initiative linking debt reduction for the heavily indebted poor countries to poverty reduction objectives represents a further major commitment by the European governments *inter alia*. Key issues will be the way the link with poverty reduction is forged and the extent to which debt relief will be additional to normal concessional aid flows of the individual agencies.

3   This section draws on two recent and important critiques of the 'donor consensus' of so-called pro-poor growth, namely, Michael Lipton (1997) and Hanmer *et al.* (1997).

   The World Bank has recently emphasized that most of sub-Saharan Africa and many other developing countries will not achieve the levels of growth needed to halve the proportion of poor by 2015, and that complementary measures are essential. The Bank is currently reviewing its PR strategy and will produce a *World Development Report* on the theme of poverty in 2001.

4   This is a slightly edited version of Professor Sobhan's comments recorded at a workshop in London on 8 April 1998 on the UK White Paper on Eliminating World Poverty.

Chapter 3   Role and modes of Intervention of the Development Cooperation Agencies for Poverty Reduction

1   There are wider international roles that donors can play to contribute to a better understanding of the nature of poverty and exchange of ideas on

how it can be tackled, for example within the Special Programme of Assistance for Africa (SPA) network. They can also help form an international consensus and undertake specific commitments.

Chapter 4   The Approach to Poverty Reduction in the Country Programmes

1   Much analytical work has been done on the nature of pro-poor macroeconomic and sectoral strategies relevant to the poor, especially by the World Bank. A recent manual sponsored by the UNDP is *Poverty Analysis Manual, 1998*, published by the Université Nationale du Benin and the Université Laval. See below.
2   In the case of Germany, the division of labour between the BMZ, GTZ and KfW makes their involvement in dialogue different from the other European agencies. While the GTZ has a mandate to engage in directly targeted self-help support for the poor, it has no mandate to engage in policy dialogue which remains the responsibility of the BMZ/Ministry of Foreign Affairs. Internal harmony between these agencies is sometimes lacking.

Chapter 7   Options for Reaching the Poor More Effectively: Some New Thinking

1   SPA = Special Programme of Assistance for Africa is a joint discussion, learning and coordination forum of 17 bilateral donors, the World Bank and the African Development Bank. It has a working group on poverty, social policy and gender.
2   Lomé Conventions I and II involved contractual relations between EC and ACP countries but this gave the Commission no mandate to engage in dialogue or question the choice of projects of its partners. However, this has changed in subsequent protocols and only an aura of contractuality remains.
3   The EC evaluations recommended greater participation and leadership in dialogue by the Commission, greater improvement in administrative and accounting practices and procedures for planning and monitoring and evaluation of these programmes, and finally more effective targeting mechanisms through direct budget support.
4   A recent analytical and technical guide to poverty is the UNDP's 1998 *Poverty Analysis Manual*. This not only covers issues of measurement and conceptualization of poverty and poverty information systems but also provides a reference framework for developing and implementing a poverty alleviation strategy and policies, together with illustrative applications to Benin by Gilbert Aho, Sylvain Lariviere and Frederick Martin from Université Laval and Université Nationale du Benin, chapters 7 and 9.

Chapter 8   Poverty Reduction: Organization and Management of the European agencies

1   Since this study was completed there has been a major review of all OECD development cooperation agencies, commissioned by the OECD/DAC Informal Network on Poverty Reduction (Cox, 1999). Work is now in progress to prepare DAC Guidelines for donors in this area.

2   The World Bank is different in providing many directives and considerable best practice guidance to its programme managers.

3.   It is interesting that the World Bank has now made its country directors accountable for an effective (PR) strategy to a central PR review group as well as to the Board for performance of Country Assistance Strategies. The European agencies might well monitor how well this works and consider a similar system for themselves. From the evidence available, World Bank/IDA Country Assistance Strategies seem more focused on poverty reduction than those of the European agencies in the later 1990s.

References

Alderman, H. and M. Garcia (1993) 'Poverty, Household Food Security and Nutrition in Rural Pakistan'. IFPRI Research Report No. 96. Washington, DC.

Bourguignon, F. and C. Morrisson (1992) *Adjustment and Equity in Developing Countries: A New Approach*. Paris: OECD Development Centre.

Bruno, M., M. Ravallion and L. Squire (1998) *Equity and Growth in Developing Countries*. World Bank Policy Research Working Paper 1563. Washington, DC: World Bank.

Caputo, E. (1997) 'The Case of the European Union' in *Evaluating Programme Aid*, Vol. 1. The Hague: Institute of Social Studies.

Carlsson, Jerker (1998) *Swedish Aid for Poverty Reduction*. ODI/NAI Working Paper 107. London: Overseas Development Institute.

Cassels, Andrew (1997) *A Guide to Sector-wide Approaches for Health and Development*. Geneva and London: WHO.

Council of Ministers of the European Union (1993) *Resolution on the Fight Against Poverty*. Brussels: European Commission.

Council of Ministers of the European Union (1996) *Resolution on Human and Social Development and European Union Development Policy*. Brussels: European Commission.

COWI (1996) *Evaluation of Poverty Reduction in Danish Development Assistance at Policy, Sector and Country Levels*. Copenhagen: Ministry of Foreign Affairs.

Cox, Aidan (2000) *UK Aid Policy and Management for Poverty Reduction*. ODI Working Paper. London: Overseas Development Institute. (Forthcoming).

Cox, A. (ed.) (1999), *DAC Scoping Study of Donor Poverty Reduction Policies and Practices*. Synthesis Report, Paris: OECD, March.

Cox, Aidan, John Healey and Antonique Koning (1997) *How European Aid Works: A Comparison of Management Systems and Effectiveness*. London: Overseas Development Institute.

Cox, Aidan, Steen Folke, Lau Schulpen and Neil Webster (2000) *Do the Poor Matter? A Comparative Study of European Aid for Poverty Reduction in India*. ODI/CDR Working Paper. London, Overseas Development Institute. (Forthcoming).

Cromwell, Elizabeth (1995) 'Zambia: A Wind of Change in Expenditure Management?', in John Healey and William Tordoff (eds), *Votes and Budgets: Comparative Studies in Accountable Governance in the South*. London: Macmillan/St Martins Press/Overseas Development Institute.

de Boisdeffre, Lionel (1998a) 'Burkina Faso: The Political, Institutional and Economic Background'. Paris: DIAL, (mimeo).

de Boisdeffre, Lionel (1998b) 'L'aide française à la réduction de la pauvreté au Burkina Faso: étude comparative des approches européennes de l'aide à la réduction de la pauvreté au Burkina Faso'. Paris: DIAL, (mimeo).

de Boisdeffre, Lionel (1997) *French Aid Policies for Poverty Reduction*. ODI/DIAL Working Paper 103. London: Overseas Development Institute.

Demery, L., F.C. Leal, J. Dayton and K. Mehra (1998) *Public Social Spending in Africa: Do the Poor Benefit?* Washington, DC: World Bank.

DFID (1997) *Eliminating World Poverty*. Cm. 3789. London: HMSO.

European Commission (1994a) *Communication of the Commission to the Council and Parliament on Co-ordination between the Community and Member States on Education and Training Schemes in Developing Countries*. Com (1994) 399 Final. Brussels.

European Commission (1994b) *Communication on the Community and Member States Policy on Cooperating with the Developing Countries in the Field of Health*. Com (1994) 77 Final. Brussels.

Federal Ministry of Economic Co-operation (Germany) (1996) 'Conclusions from a Serial Evaluation: Reducing Poverty and Reaching Target Groups in Development Cooperation Projects'. Berlin, February (mimeo).

Foster, Mick, John Healey, Matthew Martin and Howard White (1999), 'Linking HIPC II Debt Relief with Poverty Reduction and Wider Aid Issues: Reflections and Suggestions'. London, Overseas Development Institute (mimeo).

Freres, Christian and José Luis Rhi-Sausi with S. Donoso (2000) *European Donors and Poverty Reduction in Bolivia*. ODI Working Paper. London: Overseas Development Institute (forthcoming).

Freres, Christian and Jesús Corral (1997) *Spanish Aid Policies for Poverty Reduction*. ODI/AIETI Working Paper 104. London: Overseas Development Institute.

Glewwe, P. and J. Van der Gaag (1990) 'Identifying the Poor in Developing Countries: Do Different Definitions Matter?' *World Development*, 18(6), June; pp. 803–14.

Grootaert, C. and R. Kanbur (1995) 'The Lucky Few Amidst Economic Decline: Distributional Change in Cote d'Ivoire as seen through Panel Data Sets, 1985–88'. *Journal of Development Studies*, 31(4), pp. 603–19.

Gsaenger, Hans and Timo Voipio (1999) *European Aid for Poverty Reduction in Nepal*. ODI/GDI/IDS Working Paper. London: Overseas Development Institute.

Haggard, S. and R. Kaufman (eds) (1992) *The Politics of Economic Adjustment*. Princeton: Princeton University Press.

Hanmer, L., G. Pyatt and H. White (1997) *Poverty in Sub-Saharan Africa*. The Hague: Institute of Social Studies.

Healey, John and J. Rand (1994) *The Effectiveness of EDF Development Aid to ACP Countries in the 1980s*. London: Overseas Development Institute.

Hoebink, Paul and Lau Schulpen (1998) *Aid Policy and Management of Netherlands Aid Programme*. ODI Working Paper. London: Overseas Development Institute.

IMF (1997) *IMF and the Poor*. Document 8 presented at the OECD Forum on Key Elements for Poverty Reduction, 4–5 December. Washington, DC: IMF Expenditure Policy Division, Fiscal Affairs Department.

Jodha, N.S. (1989) 'Social Science Research on Rural Change: Some Gaps', in P. Bardhan (ed.), *Conversations between Economists and Anthropologists:*

Methodological Issues in Measuring Economic Change in Rural India, Delhi: Oxford University Press, Chapter 7, pp. 174–99.

Kayizzi-Mugerwa, S. (1998) 'Africa and the Donor Community: From Conditionality to Partnership', *Journal of International Development*, 10, pp. 219–25.

Killick, Tony (1998) *Aid and the Political Economy of Policy Change*. London: Routledge.

Killick, Tony, Jerker Carlsson and A. Kierkegaard (1998) *European Aid and the Reduction of Poverty in Zimbabwe*. ODI/NAI Working Paper 109. London: Overseas Development Institute.

Lipton, Michael (1997) 'Poverty – Are There Holes in the Consensus?', *World Development*, 25(7), pp. 1003–7.

Loquai, Christiana and Kathleen Van Hove (1997) 'Preliminary Findings on EU Donor Approaches Towards Poverty Reduction in Burkina Faso'. Maastricht: ECDPM (mimeo).

Loquai, Christiana, Jean Bossuyt and Kathleen Van Hove (1998) *European Community's Approach to Poverty in Development Cooperation*. ODI/ECDPM Working Paper 111. London: Overseas Development Institute.

Maxwell, Simon and Roger Riddell (1998) 'Conditionality or Contract: Perspectives on Partnership for Development', *Journal of International Development*, 10, pp. 257–68.

Ministry of Foreign Affairs (Netherlands) (1996) *Netherlands Aid Review*. The Hague: Policy and Operations Department, Ministry of Foreign Affairs.

Nelson, Joan (1992) 'Poverty, Ethics and Politics of Adjustment' in Haggard and Kaufman.

OECD (1998) *DAC Guidelines for Gender Equality and Women's Empowerment in Development Co-operations*. Paris: OECD.

OECD (1992) *DAC Principles of Effective Aid*. Paris: OECD.

Raftopoulos, Brian and Niki Jazdowska (1997) 'The Political and Institutional Environment for Poverty Reducing Aid to Zimbabwe'. Report for ODI. Harare Institute of Development Studies, University of Zimbabwe. (mimeo).

Rhi-Sausi, José Luis and Marco Zupi (1997) *Italian Aid Policies for Poverty Reduction*. ODI/CeSPI Working Paper 102. London: Overseas Development Institute.

Riddell, R. (1997) *Synthesis of the Impact of NGO Evaluation*. Report prepared for the OECD Aid Evaluation Group. Paris: OECD/DAC.

Saasa, O.J., Jerker Carlsson and P. Chibbamulilo (1998) 'Poverty Reduction in Zambia: Context, Policies, Strategies and Experiences with Aid from Members of the European Union'. London: Overseas Development Institute (mimeo).

Sahn, D.E. (ed.) (1996) *Economic Reform and the Poor in Africa*. Oxford: Clarendon Press.

Sawadogo, K. (1997) *La Pauvreté au Burkina Faso; une analyse critique des politiques et des stratégies d'intervention locales*. ECDPM Working Paper 51. Maastricht: ECDPM.

Secrétariat d'Etat à la Coopération (France) (1997) 'La Reduction de la Pauvreté; Reflexions et Orientations de Aide Française'. Paper presented at the OECD Forum on Key Elements for Poverty Reduction, 2–4 December. Paris: Ministère des Affaires Etrangères.

Swedish Government (1996–7) *The Rights of the Poor – Our Common Responsibility. Poverty Reduction in Swedish Development Cooperation.* Stockholm: Ministry of Foreign Affairs.

Tripp, A.M. (1992) 'Local Organisations, Participation and the State in Urban Tanzania' in Hyden G. and M. Bratton (eds), *Governance and Policies in Africa.* Boulder, CO: Lynne Rienner.

Udsholt, Lars (1997) *Danish Aid Policies for Poverty Reduction.* ODI Working Paper 100. London: Overseas Development Institute/Centre for Development Research.

UNDP (1997) *Human Development Report.* New York and Oxford: Oxford University Press for UNDP.

UNDP (1998) *Poverty Analysis Manual: with Applications in Bénin.* Under the direction of Gilbert Aho, Sylvain Larivière and Frédéric Martin, Université Nationale der Bénin and Université Laval.

Vaidyanathan, A. (1996) 'Poverty Alleviation Programmes: Some Lessons of Indian Experience'. Report to the Swedish International Development Agency. (mimeo).

Voipio, Timo (1998) *Finnish Aid Policies for Poverty.* ODI/IDS Working Paper 108. London: Overseas Development Institute.

Voipio, Timo and Paul Hoebink (1999) *European Aid for Poverty Reduction in Tanzania.* IDS/ODI Working Paper 116. Helsinki and London: IDS/ODI.

Von Gleich, A. (1997) 'The Experience of Bolivia'. Paper presented at the OECD Forum on Key Elements for Poverty Reduction, 4–5 December. Paris: Development Centre, DAC/OECD.

Wangwe, S.M. (1997) 'Macroeconomic Policies and Poverty Reduction in Tanzania'. New York: UNDP, Social Development and Poverty Elimination Division, Bureau of Development Policy (mimeo).

Weidnitzer, Eva (1997) *German Aid Policies for Poverty Reduction.* ODI/DIE Working Paper 101. London: Overseas Development Institute.

World Bank (1990) *World Development Report.* New York: Oxford University Press.

World Bank (1995) *India: Public Expenditure Review. Annex V. Anti Poverty Programmes.* Washington, DC: World Bank, India Dept.

World Bank (1997) *World Development Indicators.* Washington, DC: World Bank.

Index